VOLUME 588

JULY 2003

THE ANNALS

of The American Academy of Political
and Social Science

ROBERT W. PEARSON, *Executive Editor*
ALAN W. HESTON, *Editor*

Islam: Enduring Myths and Changing Realities

Special Editor of this Volume

ASLAM SYED
Quaid-i-Azam University

SAGE Publications Ⓢ Thousand Oaks · London · New Delhi

The American Academy of Political and Social Science

3814 Walnut Street, Fels Institute of Government, University of Pennsylvania,
Philadelphia, PA 19104-6197; (215) 746-6500; (215) 898-1202 (fax); www.aapss.org

Origin and Purpose. The Academy was organized December 14, 1889, to promote the progress of political and social science, especially through publications and meetings. The Academy does not take sides in controverted questions, but seeks to gather and present reliable information to assist the public in forming an intelligent and accurate judgment.

Meetings. The Academy occasionally holds a meeting in the spring extending over two days.

Publications. THE ANNALS of The American Academy of Political and Social Science is the bimonthly publication of the Academy. Each issue contains articles on some prominent social or political problem, written at the invitation of the editors. Also, monographs are published from time to time, numbers of which are distributed to pertinent professional organizations. These volumes constitute important reference works on the topics with which they deal, and they are extensively cited by authorities throughout the United States and abroad. The papers presented at the meetings of the Academy are included in THE ANNALS.

Membership. Each member of the Academy receives THE ANNALS and may attend the meetings of the Academy. Membership is open only to individuals. Annual dues: $71.00 for the regular paperbound edition (clothbound, $108.00). For members outside the U.S.A., add $24.00 for shipping of your subscription. Members may also purchase single issues of THE ANNALS for $21.00 each (clothbound, $29.00). Student memberships are available for $49.00.

Subscriptions. THE ANNALS of The American Academy of Political and Social Science (ISSN 0002-7162) (J295) is published six times annually—in January, March, May, July, September, and November— by Sage Publications, 2455 Teller Road, Thousand Oaks, CA 91320. Telephone: (800) 818-SAGE (7243) and (805) 499-9774; FAX/Order line: (805) 499-0871. Copyright © 2003 by The American Academy of Political and Social Science. Institutions may subscribe to THE ANNALS at the annual rate: $454.00 (clothbound, $513.00). Add $24.00 per year for subscriptions outside the U.S.A. Institutional rates for single issues: $88.00 each (clothbound, $98.00).

Periodicals postage paid at Thousand Oaks, California, and at additional mailing offices.

Single issues of THE ANNALS may be obtained by individuals who are not members of the Academy for $33.00 each (clothbound, $46.00). Single issues of THE ANNALS have proven to be excellent supplementary texts for classroom use. Direct inquiries regarding adoptions to THE ANNALS c/o Sage Publications (address below).

All correspondence concerning membership in the Academy, dues renewals, inquiries about membership status, and/or purchase of single issues of THE ANNALS should be sent to THE ANNALS c/o Sage Publications, 2455 Teller Road, Thousand Oaks, CA 91320. Telephone: (800) 818-SAGE (7243) and (805) 499-9774; FAX/Order line: (805) 499-0871. *Please note that orders under $30 must be prepaid.* Sage affiliates in London and India will assist institutional subscribers abroad with regard to orders, claims, and inquiries for both subscriptions and single issues.

Printed on recycled, acid-free paper

THE ANNALS

© 2003 by The American Academy of Political and Social Science

Editorial Office: 3814 Walnut Street, Fels Institute for Government, University of Pennsylvania, Philadelphia, PA 19104-6197.

For information about membership° (individuals only) and subscriptions (institutions), address:

Sage Publications
2455 Teller Road
Thousand Oaks, CA 91320

Sage Production Staff: Scott Locklear, Matthew Adams, and Paul Doebler

From India and South Asia, write to:
SAGE PUBLICATIONS INDIA Pvt Ltd
B-42 Panchsheel Enclave, P.O. Box 4109
New Delhi 110 017
INDIA

From Europe, the Middle East, and Africa, write to:
SAGE PUBLICATIONS LTD
6 Bonhill Street
London EC2A 4PU
UNITED KINGDOM

°Please note that members of the Academy receive THE ANNALS with their membership.
International Standard Serial Number ISSN 0002-7162
International Standard Book Number ISBN 0-7619-2856-1 (Vol. 588, 2003 paper)
International Standard Book Number ISBN 0-7619-2855-3 (Vol. 588, 2003 cloth)
Manufactured in the United States of America. First printing, July 2003.

The articles appearing in *The Annals* are abstracted or indexed in Academic Abstracts, Academic Search, America: History and Life, Asia Pacific Database, Book Review Index, CAB Abstracts Database, Central Asia: Abstracts & Index, Communication Abstracts, Corporate ResourceNET, Criminal Justice Abstracts, Current Citations Express, Current Contents: Social & Behavioral Sciences, e-JEL, EconLit, Expanded Academic Index, Guide to Social Science & Religion in Periodical Literature, Health Business FullTEXT, HealthSTAR FullTEXT, Historical Abstracts, International Bibliography of the Social Sciences, International Political Science Abstracts, ISI Basic Social Sciences Index, Journal of Economic Literature on CD, LEXIS-NEXIS, MasterFILE FullTEXT, Middle East: Abstracts & Index, North Africa: Abstracts & Index, PAIS International, Periodical Abstracts, Political Science Abstracts, Psychological Abstracts, PsycINFO, Sage Public Administration Abstracts, Social Science Source, Social Sciences Citation Index, Social Sciences Index Full Text, Social Services Abstracts, Social Work Abstracts, Sociological Abstracts, Southeast Asia: Abstracts & Index, Standard Periodical Directory (SPD), TOPICsearch, Wilson OmniFile V, and Wilson Social Sciences Index/Abstracts, and are available on microfilm from University Microfilms, Ann Arbor, Michigan.

Information about membership rates, institutional subscriptions, and back issue prices may be found on the facing page.

Advertising. Current rates and specifications may be obtained by writing to *The Annals* Advertising and Promotion Manager at the Thousand Oaks office (address above).

Claims. Claims for undelivered copies must be made no later than six months following month of publication. The publisher will supply missing copies when losses have been sustained in transit and when the reserve stock will permit.

Change of Address. Six weeks' advance notice must be given when notifying of change of address to ensure proper identification. Please specify name of journal. POSTMASTER: Send address changes to: *The Annals* of The American Academy of Political and Social Science, c/o Sage Publications, 2455 Teller Road, Thousand Oaks, CA 91320.

THE ANNALS

OF THE AMERICAN ACADEMY OF POLITICAL AND SOCIAL SCIENCE

Volume 588   July 2003

IN THIS ISSUE:

Islam: Enduring Myths and Changing Realities

Special Editor: ASLAM SYED

FORTHCOMING

*Misleading Evidence and Evidence-Led Policy:
Making Social Science More Experimental*
Special Editor: LAWRENCE SHERMAN
Volume 589, September 2003

Rethinking Sustainable Development
Special Editor: JUDE FERNANDO
Volume 590, November 2003

Abstinence as Social Policy
Special Editor: REBECCA MAYNARD
Volume 591, January 2004

Preface

The unhappy prejudices of the Christian world against the professors of Mahomet's creed, which had been instilled into my mind, led me to fear a thousand dangers where none existed. . . . When the seaman approaches that part of Asia inhabited by the Turks, he may with safety burn all alarm, and rest satisfied, that although he is not near a Christian country, still he will find among the inhabitants, all the virtues possessed by Christians, with but few of their vices.

—Samuel Elliot (1819, as quoted in Finnie 1967, 21)

For here [on the Tripoli beachhead,] bribery, treachery, rapine, murder, and all the hedious [*sic*] offspring of accursed tyranny, have often drenched the streets in blood, and dealt, to the enslaved inhabitants, famine, dungeons, ruin and destruction. On yonder noddling tower, once waved the banners of the all-conquering Rome, when these fruitful regions were styled the Eden of that empire, now Gothic ruins, and barbarous inhabitants curse the half-tilled soil.

—William Ray (1808, as quoted in Baepler 1999, 36)

While these two statements reflect the experiences of their respective authors, they also manifest a dichotomous American experience with Islam: positive impressions are confined to the exceptional interludes of optimists who earn the wrath and ridicule of those who do not approve of such views,[1] while disparaging statements remain alive, reactivated with each new foreign venture.

The history of American encounters with the Muslim states is almost as old as the American independence. The first decade of the nineteenth century, for example, witnessed American involvement with the North African states over the question of American captives, leading to what is known in U.S. history as the Barbary

DOI: 10.1177/0002716203255390

Wars. This issue could have been resolved through diplomacy, but Jefferson needed a navy and "respect" from the European countries that he hoped would result from a display of military prowess. Arabs actually helped the Americans and some Europeans in this venture, but the subsequent chronicles of glory neither mention their help nor emphasize the true nature of the conflict. Instead, multiple narratives preached hatred against Islam and Muslims, even as the United States devoted itself during the rest of the nineteenth century to missionary and commercial activities with Turkey, Egypt, Syria, and India.

During the cold war, Islam was discovered to be an effective weapon against an atheistic Soviet Union and was frequently used not only against Moscow but also against secular and socialist Muslim societies like Egypt, Indonesia, Algeria, and Syria, culminating in the Afghan Jihad against the Red army.

The present volume reflects how negative images of Islam have long endured in the United States in the face of the complex and changing realities of the religion and the regions of the world in which it is observed.

After the end of the cold war, Europe was liberated and the "menace" of Communism became a part of history, although the question of Israel's "security" was not resolved. This issue has shaped U.S. policy both during and beyond the cold war, especially as it relates to American policy in the Middle East. Because Muslim countries surround Israel, Islam became the new enemy. The "clash of civilizations" was crafted, and the New American Century Project was launched to remove the remaining obstacle to a secure Middle East. The explosions at the World Trade Center in 1993, the bombing of the American embassies in Africa in 1998, and, finally, the events of 9/11 substantiated the theory of a new enemy on the horizon. But again we are confronted with a puzzle: from the Afghan Jihad to the war against terrorism, the United States has received help, active cooperation, and even manpower from Muslim countries of different kinds of religiosity like Saudi Arabia and Turkey. Yet Islam continues to be demonized and disparaged. Why? I think it is time for Americans and Muslims to find answers to this question.

The present volume reflects how negative images of Islam have long endured in the United States in the face of the complex and changing realities of the religion and the regions of the world in which it is observed. I was asked to edit this volume in the post-9/11 period of anguish and anxiety that still continues to shape global politics and perceptions of the "us" and the "other." What will be lost and what will be gained in these political and psychological processes is difficult to gauge at this moment. However, it can be stated without any fear of contradiction that the truth is always at risk of being sacrificed on the altars of imperial ambition and fundamentalist fervor. Professor Bulliet's article in this volume amply demonstrates this trend. Reflective and autobiographical, it shows how connections between Islam and terrorism were invented. It also points out the dangers inherent in such an exercise: the rise of a new anti-Semitism against Muslims, which is already visible not only in the corridors of the American establishment but also on the streets of New York.

Mohammed Arkoun's piece invites social scientists to develop an epistemological project to study Muslim societies and to liberate studies of Islam from the paradigms of politically crafted theories. Ali Asani invites his fellow Americans to see Islam in the spirit of the American constitution and civic values, which are emphasized in the Holy Book of Islam. Extensively quoting from the Quran, he demonstrates that Islam stands for cultural pluralism, something that both Muslim clerics and anti-Islam ideologues choose to ignore.

Susan Douglass and Ross Dunn's article reveals the hidden and visible biases against Islam in the classrooms of American schools. Situating Islam outside the mainstream of world history and isolating it from its Judeo-Christian traditions has been the main concern of U.S. textbook writers since the seventies, when the Israeli-Arab war brought Islam to the miniscreen of American homes. Fawaz Gerges traces the factors that shape American policy toward Muslims in "Islam and Muslims in the Mind of America." Domestic politics and Israel's perception of the Arabs have been identified as the predominant forces in shaping the American perceptions of Islam. Paul Baepler takes us to the early images of Islam and the Arabs emanating from popular stories written by the American captives in the Maghreb. Allan Heston traces the economic origins of the two themes, Crusades and Jihad, that have dominated the discourse on Islam and Christianity.

Barbara Metcalf looks at Jihad from the perspective of the Tablighi Jamaʻat, a global organization dedicated to reconverting nominal Muslims into pious and observing believers. Here Jihad is seen as inner struggle through the lenses of Tassawuf. Vincent Houben's article demolishes many myths about Southeast Asian Islam perpetuated by scholars like Clifford Geertz. Unlike most scholars of Islam, he does not see Southeast Asian Islam on the peripheries of the Muslim World but as a phenomenon that is worth studying in its own right. And last but not least, Jack Shaheen brings to light a very important but hitherto ignored field in educating Americans about Arabs in the cool recesses of American movie theaters. Hollywood's role in the character assassination of Arabs leaves a durable—and largely negative—impression in the minds of cinema-goers across the United States.

This volume would not have been possible without the help of our contributors and publishers; thanks are due to them. I gratefully acknowledge the help that was graciously extended by the staff of *The Annals*. Robert Pearson has been patient and extremely helpful in sorting out the details about copyrights, editing, and pulling out the highlights of these articles. I am indeed thankful to him. Alan Heston's contribution not only as a writer but also as a source of inspiration in planning this volume has been greater than he knows. I am indebted to him. I only hope that these essays generate questions aimed at self-analysis and reflection because any transcultural inquiry invariably leads to self-discovery and acts as a mirror in which we see our true images. If that image is distorted and not reassuring, the fault lies not in the mirror; as Arthur Schopenhauer put it, "If a donkey looks into the mirror, the man will not look out of it."

ASLAM SYED

Note

1. Because of his admiration of Islam and adoption of Muslim dress, Samuel Elliot was called "the renegade" by none other than the president of the United States.

References

Baepler, Paul, ed. 1999. *White slaves, African masters: An anthology of American Barbary captivity narratives*. Chicago: University of Chicago Press. (Quoting William Ray, *Horrors of Slavery, or the American Wars in Tripoli*, Troy, NY: Oliver Lyon, 1808)

Finnie, David H. 1967. *Pioneers east: The early American experience in the Middle East*. Cambridge, MA: Harvard University Press.

Rhetoric, Discourse, and the Future of Hope

By
RICHARD W. BULLIET

Misperceptions, farfetched stories about Islam, and invented connections between Muslims and terrorism have been the guiding factors in shaping the attitudes of the American establishment toward the Muslim world. This article sheds light on the post-1993 bombing of the World Trade Center when journalists and evangelicals looked for sensational and inflammatory statements about the so-called Islamic militancy toward the United States. In this process, the preachers of hatred against Islam attempted to portray the Muslim faith as monolithic, unchanging, and viciously directed against Americans. What they did not choose to highlight was the enormous diversity among Muslim cultures or the focus within many Muslim groups on building community. The article anticipates that such enduring myths about Islam could lead to the rise of a new anti-Semitism in the United States: not against Jews, but against Muslims.

Keywords: fundamentalism; stereotypes; media hype; coded language; rhetoric; Orientalism; the future of Islam

O n a recent trip with a group of Columbia professors and graduate students to Uzbekistan, Kazakhstan, and Kyrgyzstan, I fell into conversation with a fundamentalist. This was a gentleman of around sixty, very charming

Richard W. Bulliet is a professor of history at Columbia University. His work specializes in Middle Eastern history, the social and institutional history of Islamic countries, and the history of technology. He received his B.A. from Harvard in 1962 and his Ph.D. from Harvard in 1967. He is the author of The Patricians of Nishapur: A Study in Medieval Islamic History *(1972),* The Camel and the Wheel *(1975),* Conversion to Islam in the Medieval Period: An Essay in Quantitative History *(1979), and* Islam: The View from the Edge *(1994). He edited* Under Siege: Islam and Democracy *(1994) and* The Columbia History of the Twentieth Century *(1998), coedited* The Encyclopedia of the Modern Middle East *(1996), and coauthored* The Earth and Its Peoples: A Global History *(1997).*

NOTE: "Rhetoric, Discourse, and the Future of Hope" by Richard W. Bulliet was originally published in *Under Siege: Islam and Democracy* (New York: Columbia University, The Middle East Institute Occasional Papers 1, 1994). Reprinted with permission.

DOI: 10.1177/0002716203255395

and formal in manner, who talked forcefully about the confrontation between
Islam and the West. He described how it was going to be played out in Central Asia
in almost Armageddon-like terms. He described how Iranian religious activists are
spreading the word through Central Asia, not through official organs of religion
and state, but through the coffeehouses. He spoke ominously of Iran's ultimate
acquisition of nuclear weapons.

Now this fundamentalist was from Fort Lauderdale, Florida. He was a diligent
Protestant working for an organization called "Evangelical Explosion." His job was
to supervise Protestant missionaries in the Central Asian republics. Though this
conversation took place in a Moscow airport, we had heard about such movements
from the Deputy Qadi of Kyrgyzstan. He had told us he hoped that we had not met
with insulting or rude behavior on the part of people in his mosque or elsewhere in
Kyrgyzstan; but if we had, we should understand that Americans were not very well
liked because some of them were Protestant fundamentalist activists who were
causing great disruption in the community.

*I asked her whether as a newsperson she
thought it was appropriate to ask me to invent
connections for which no evidence existed.*

The only Muslim activists that we encountered during our trip were in
Samarqand. They belonged to Dar al-Arkan, a quietist, separatist movement based
in Kuala Lumpur, Malaysia. Quite distinctive in their gray gowns and turbans, they
were in Uzbekistan for educational and medical purposes, not for politics.

Reflecting on the incendiary militancy of the gentleman from Fort Lauderdale
and the quiet daʿwa of the Muslims from Malaysia raises questions of how we perceive religious activism in the world today. I know of no one who characterizes the
United States, in general, as a fundamentalist country and an exporter of inflammatory preachers. But Muslim states are frequently so judged. How in situations like
these do we interpret reality?

The man from Fort Lauderdale will surely confirm the worst fears of everyone
in his congregation back home with his tales of confrontation between Islam and
Christianity on the Central Asian frontier. He will undoubtedly repeat for them
what he told us: that Central Asian Muslims, once they receive the truth of Christianity, will be on the side of righteousness when the great war comes, and that Iran
has already purchased three nuclear weapons, information he claimed from no less
an authority than the captain of the Soviet submarine that had shadowed *Red October*. No matter how far-fetched his story, it will surely be credited by some of the

pious folks of Fort Lauderdale, just as some of the conscientious Muslims of Kyrgyzstan seem convinced that the United States is directing a stream of Christian fundamentalists against them.

Networks of information that exist about Islam's relation with the West, or with democracy, or with Christianity vary greatly. Scholars at a university conference meet in an atmosphere of cordiality and mutual respect and indulge in subtlety, nuance, and irony in their presentations in full knowledge that they will be understood as constructive contributors to an educated discourse. But there are other levels of discourse in our society and in Muslim society. How do we perceive those other levels? How can we address and inform them? After the World Trade Center bombing in 1993, faculty of Columbia's Middle East Institute gave about forty news interviews. They focused on every possible aspect of that tragic criminal act.

One exchange with a reporter sticks in my memory. She asked whether it was true that terrorist organizations in the Islamic world funded the World Trade Center bombing. I replied that I did not know but that none of the information then published indicated such to be the case. Then she asked, "Well, if the bombing was funded by an international Islamic terrorist ring, which do you think would have done it?" I asked her whether as a newsperson she thought it was appropriate to ask me to invent connections for which no evidence existed. She was somewhat miffed by this, but she indicated that the desire of her news director to gather vivid material was uppermost in her thinking.

Along similar lines was a conversation with a newsman who interviewed me about a news release from the Republican staff of a congressional committee. It reported that a decision had been taken at the highest level in Tehran to launch terrorist attacks on American targets around the world on a certain day in March. I told him, "This is really stupid." He said, "Yeah, I think it is too, but the news director doesn't think it is." He went on to say that he did not like reporting such inflammatory speculations as news, but editors and news directors were eager for hot copy.

In 1894, Alfred Dreyfus was convicted of treason by a French military court. The press debate surrounding that gross miscarriage of justice was the catalyst for the rediscovery of profound anti-Semitic feelings in Europe. It was a sort of world-remaking event. In 1994, exactly one century later, some Muslims from the New York area are going to be tried for seditious conspiracy to commit criminal acts, including the blowing up of tunnels under the Hudson River. A guilty verdict will send a chill of fear throughout America. A not-guilty verdict will raise the specter of irresponsible indictment on the part of the Department of Justice.

While Dreyfus was unjustly charged and the soundness of the indictments against the Muslim conspirators may be proven in court, French anti-Semitism surfaced before the truth was known. The question is whether the United States is going to witness a new anti-Semitism, based not on Judaism or theories of Semitic race but on Islam. Given the propensities of the nonelite news media to overpublicize, hype, and sell hostility to Islam, we at some point are going to reach a threshold, and it seems not far away, where people no longer need evidence to believe in a generic terrorist threat from religious Muslim fanatics.

Clinton administration Middle East specialist Martin Indyk delivered a speech in the spring of 1993 in which he described the administration's new dual-containment policy. I'll leave it to others to discuss the policy and concern myself here only with the rhetoric of its presentation by Mr. Indyk. He remarks, "Decades of neglect and dashed hopes for political participation and social justice have nurtured some violent movements cloaked in religious garb that have begun to challenge governments across the Arab world with potential of destabilizing the region." Note here the "movements cloaked in religious garb." Further on he says, "We must not oversimplify a complex challenge with differing regional and national wellsprings, and we must not dismiss all religious reformers as extremists. Neither, however, can we afford to ignore that in their resort to violence, some religious extremists have found succor from fundamentalist regimes in Iran and Sudan. . . . The Middle East is finely balanced with two alternative futures: One in which extremists cloaked in religious or nationalist garb would hold sway across the

The tainting of an entire religion and all of its adherents seems perilously close at hand.

region, wielding weapons of mass destruction loaded onto ballistic missiles." Later he comments, "Our success in both realms will affect our ability to help friendly governments create a better life for their people than that offered by the proponents of violence." Now isn't that an interesting idea? You have a government, on the one hand, and then, on the other, you have some people who are violent. They wake up in the morning and say, perhaps, "I feel violent and extreme. I feel extremely violent. I'm going to go out and preach violence. I'm going to go out and stir up violence. I'm going to go out and terrorize somebody." What Mr. Indyk suggests is that our success in the Middle East will be measured by our ability to help governments give a better life to their people than do these purported proponents of violence. His unexpressed thought in this would seem to be that these proponents of violence are actually saying something in addition to "let's be extremely violent." But he does not say what it is. Instead, he portrays these people as if their whole being is defined by violence, as if they have no agenda, no goals, as if they respond to no need, react to no oppression. All they do is propound violence and carry out extremist acts. Yet he cannot get away from the fact that they are offering something to the people and that our policies must work to counteract. Yet this term in the equation that expresses what it is that the "friendly governments" are really competing against in striving to better the lot of their citizens is entirely missing.

A speech like this must be viewed as a carefully constructed discourse in which the actual state of affairs is tacitly recognized, but in which the author tries to construct it in such a way as to lead an audience to the notion that there is a penchant for violence among certain Muslims that adequately defines their political stance. Islam in this construction is completely secondary. If this kind of rhetoric could be confined to describing a small segment of the world of politically active Muslims, maybe we could live with it. But you can't contain rhetoric like that very easily when our national psyche is in the process of shifting from identifying this person or that group as extremists to beginning to identify Islam as a whole with the subset of violent activists so luridly described in the rhetoric of the press, and in the rhetoric of the government. The tainting of an entire religion and all of its adherents seems perilously close at hand.

Samuel Huntington's recent "Clash of Civilizations" article in *Foreign Affairs* is a case in point. Future conflicts will not be Left against Right, Communist versus Capitalist; they will be between Civilizations, particularly between the West and a putative Islamic-Confucian conspiracy. The confluence of Islamic terrorism and the Yellow Peril in Mr. Huntington's mind should not be casually dismissed. It is simply a scaling up to macrocosmic level of the fear of violent movements cloaked in religious garb and proponents of violence adduced by Mr. Indyk to buttress his defense of a policy of economically isolating Iran.

The area that I am most interested in is education. Against the simple scare tactics of the press and the government stand a variety of other attitudes toward Islam. Most often, Islam is reified as a readily understandable entity, a set of principles, a way of life, a system of law. Others argue that Islam must be deconstructed into a welter of more complex and nuanced phenomena subject to a broad spectrum of interpretations. In either case, Islam is usually portrayed as doing something: Islam remakes itself, Islam awakens, Islam resurges. Edward Said has argued that this reification of Islam originated as part of the malevolent agenda of the European Orientalists of the nineteenth and twentieth centuries, extending down to the Middle East Studies establishment of today. Mr. Said's argument is generally very persuasive, but to my mind he credits the Orientalists with more originality and more purposeful intent than they had. They did not invent their notion of Islam; they read it. Books by Muslim ulama frequently describe Islam in just this absolute and reified way. The Orientalists read such books, translated them, wrote English or French précis of them, and taught their contents to their students.

There has been throughout Islamic history a tension between a centripetal force in Islam—people trying to understand Islam whole, people trying to codify it, trying to say, "This is the Sunna, this the Sharia; and we brook no deviation"—and a centrifugal force exerted by Muslims in different times and places who say, "We're living this way in our community. You can come and you can preach and you can say what you want about our practice. But what you say isn't necessarily going to affect the way we live." When you look around the Islamic world, you find enormous variety. Muslims individually make disposition of their religious faith. They decide who they are; they decide what, as Muslims, they do. Throughout history, the hallmark of Islam has not been leader and follower. It has been Muslims building their local communities and choosing among options or inventing their own options.

I think that we need a reorientation in how we talk about Islam, how we teach about Islam. I think the notion of starting with Muhammad, the Quran, and the five pillars, is valid. But that is not necessarily how Islam has been lived. The idea that the Sharia has always been there, that the ulama has always been there, that Islam has always been the same and united, isn't so. There has to be a recognition of this because the diversity and effervescence of Islam in its early and middle centuries is with us again today. Adapting to change and confronting conflicting elements inherited from tradition has been a continuous process. Islam is a vital religion, a religion of change and diversity; yet it also is subject to a centripetal that formulates and reformulates a self-proclaimed normative core. Through its continual local development and gradual modification of a normative core, Islam has changed in the past and is doing so now.

I think it is difficult sometimes to remember how we in the West arrived at our current conceptions of society and government. Notions like human rights, equality, and civil liberties did not come from documents. They came from struggles.

What, then, of the future? Historians are the only people fully qualified to predict the future. This is not because the future is born from the past, because we all know that history is also valued in that sense, but because historians claim the professional qualification to study things that happened when neither they nor anyone else alive was present. Historians invent understandings of things that may have happened before living memory and are honored for the feeling their writings convey that things must have happened just as they say. The future of twenty-five to fifty years from now being a place we have never been, and probably will not live to see, is, therefore, appropriate territory for a historian to try to map. I would like to hazard six guesses about that unknown land.

First, the current perception of an Arab-Persian-Turkish hegemony in the Islamic world is going to erode. We have been teaching about Islam as if it were a Middle Eastern phenomenon for so long that even when we caution students to remember that most of the world's Muslims live east of Kabul, we neglect to remember them ourselves. Teachers and policy makers in the future will discover that the familiar generalizations about Islam derived from study of the faith in its Middle Eastern manifestations is necessarily going to become more complex, more diverse. This is a trend we should welcome without complaining that we may have to learn two or three more languages.

Second, I would suggest that there is going to develop a substantial conflict within the growing community of Muslims who strongly identify with their religion and feel that their understandings of Islamic values should provide the underpinnings for social and political life. The current idea that the primary significant dichotomy is that between Muslims with secular outlooks and Muslims with religious outlooks will have to make room, as the Islamic daiwa or tajdid progresses, for deep conflicts of interpretation as to how Islam should be articulated as a social and political system in a modern world. While it would be lovely to think that a harmonious umma will evolve over the coming years, that seems to me improbable.

Third, I would predict that the Islamic movement, or variegated movements proclaiming themselves to be Islam, will steadily grow. It should increase enormously in influence and very possibly become over the next twenty-five to fifty years the primary orientation of government in much of the world that is populated predominantly by Muslims.

Fourth, I think there will be internal evolution on social issues.

I think it is difficult sometimes to remember how we in the West arrived at our current conceptions of society and government. Notions like human rights, equality, and civil liberties did not come from documents. They came from struggles. Anyone who is aware of the feminist movement in this country can see such a struggle taking place, a struggle that has yet to succeed but that probably will in time. Struggles cannot be fought from the outside; they must occur internally. What struggles will take place within the community of Muslims I would not hazard to say. Nor would I venture an opinion as to whether the Muslims of the twenty-first century will follow the direction of the West in their controversies over political and social norms, or whether they will find unique resolutions to unavoidable contradictions. Either way, conflict, diversity, and evolutionary change seem inevitable despite the powerful appeal of a traditional core of norms and values.

Fifth, although I deeply abhor the likelihood, I fear we are going to find the growth of a new kind of anti-Semitism defined by Islam. What I mean by anti-Semitism is a willingness on the part of substantial portions of the American population to vilify others, both in this country and abroad, because of the accident of their birth into a Muslim family or their choice of the Muslim religion. It is a hateful prospect, but it is one that seems certain to occur unless it is actively counteracted by the media, the government, and our educational institutions.

Finally, I would say that any lights that we see in the tunnel do not come from the end. Many people who think about Islam look to a Sayyid Qutb, an Au Shariati, or a Maududi for a final, authoritative understanding of what Islam should be in the world of today. It is natural to search for the right voice so we can see where everything is going. But wishing for something does not mean that it is there to be found.

I believe that the ideas that will be taken as the most authoritative synthesis of Islam and modern conditions fifty years from now have not yet been thought and are not on the current agenda. People living now will be looked back to as guides to the path that leads to an answer, or as deviants from that path; but where the path will eventually lead is no more perceivable than the course of democratic, egalitarian government was in the midst of the French Revolution.

In looking with hope to the eventual emergence of a new synthesis of Islam, I must confess a personal bias. I am inclined to believe that intellectuals are and always have been on the trailing edge of important changes in world history, not on the cutting edge. All they do is enshrine those changes in print for later historians to study. What we really should be looking at is what is happening in residential neighborhoods in Tashkent and Bishkek and Samarqand where you see bricks stacked up and a mosque being built in the aftermath of two generations of Soviet rule. When you talk to the Imam Khatib of the mosque, he says, "Well, this is for the neighborhood. People in the neighborhood are giving the money. We want to rebuild Islam here." He does not say that he also wants to destroy the United States. And that to me is the hope of all this—people constructing in their own communities lives of religious worth and aspiration without regard to foreign policy objectives or conflicts. In this hope, we should do our best in the educational arena, or whatever arena we work in, to try to make people see that the discourse on Islam currently presented to us, with all of its confrontational, hostile, and potentially disastrous rhetoric, is counteracted, softened, and turned into something that will lead ultimately to a modus vivendi between our future and the future of the Islamic world.

Rethinking Islam Today

By
MOHAMMED ARKOUN

Islamic revivalism and the activities of those who are its real or perceived proponents have monopolized the discourse on Islam. This article explores how this focus has totally ignored an overwhelming majority of Muslims. Social scientists have failed to liberate Islamic studies from pro- and anti-Orientalism clichés. Islam is still imagined as inferior (to Jewish and Christian traditions), unchanging, and militant by the West; and superior, dynamic, and peace loving by Muslims. The article outlines a need to study Islam as an epistemological project. It argues for a new *ijtihād* for Muslim as well as non-Muslim scholars to initiate a process of new thinking on Islam with tools such as history of thought rather than political events or fixed parameters; to make unthinkable notions—a historical rather than a religious postulate—thinkable; and to relate secularism, religion, and culture to contemporary challenges rather than substituting one for the other.

Keywords: Orientalism; rationalism; epistemology; historicity; deconstruction

Islam holds historical significance for all of us, but at the same time, our understanding of this phenomenon is sadly inadequate. There is a need to encourage and initiate audacious, free,

Mohammed Arkoun is currently an emeritus professor at La Sorbonne as well as a senior research fellow and member of the Board of Governors of the Institute of Ismaili Studies. A native of Great Kabylia, Algeria, he studied at the Faculty of Literature of the University of Algiers and at the Sorbonne in Paris. He established his scholarly reputation with his early studies (1969, 1970) of the historian and philosopher Miskawayh. A former editor of Arabica, *he has played a significant role in shaping Western-language scholarship on Islam. He is the author of numerous books in French, English, and Arabic, including* Rethinking Islam *(Boulder, CO, 1994),* L'immigration: défis et richesses *(Paris, 1998), and* The Unthought in Contemporary Islamic Thought *(London, 2002). His shorter studies have appeared in many academic journals and his works have been translated into several languages.*

NOTE: "Rethinking Islam Today" by Mohammed Arkoun was originally published as an occasional paper (Washington, DC: Georgetown University, Center for Contemporary Arab Studies, 1987). Reprinted with permission.

DOI: 10.1177/0002716203255396

productive thinking on Islam today. The so-called Islamic revivalism has monopolized the discourse on Islam; the social scientists, moreover, do not pay attention to
what I call the "silent Islam"—the Islam of true believers who attach more importance to the religious relationship with the absolute of God than to the vehement
demonstrations of political movements. I refer to the Islam of thinkers and intellectuals who are having great difficulties inserting their critical approach into a
social and cultural space that is, at present, totally dominated by militant
ideologies.

. . . [T]he main intellectual endeavor represented by thinking Islam or any religion today is to evaluate, with a new epistemological perspective, the characteristics and intricacy of systems of knowledge—both the historical and the mythical. I
would even say that both are still interacting and interrelated in our modern
thought after at least three hundred years of rationalism and historicism. There is
no need to insist on the idea that *thinking* Islam today is a task much more urgent
and significant than all the scholastic discussions of Orientalism; the ultimate goal
of the project is to develop—through the example set by Islam as a religion and a
social-historical space—a new epistemological strategy for the comparative study
of cultures. All the polemics recently directed against Orientalism show clearly that
so-called modern scholarship remains far from any epistemological project that
would free Islam from the essentialist, substantialist postulates of classical metaphysics. Islam, in these discussions, is assumed to be a specific, essential,
unchangeable system of thought, beliefs, and non-beliefs, one which is superior or
inferior (according to Muslims or non-Muslims) to the Western (or Christian) system. It is time to stop this irrelevant confrontation between two dogmatic attitudes—the theological claims of believers and the ideological postulates of positivist rationalism. The study of religions, in particular, is handicapped by the rigid
definitions and methods inherited from theology and classical metaphysics. The
history of religion has collected facts and descriptions of various religions, but religion as a universal dimension of human existence is not approached from the relevant epistemological perspective. This weakness in modern thought is even more
clearly illustrated by the poor, conformist, and sometimes polemical literature on
the religions of the Book, as we shall see.

. . . Thus presented, the enterprise of thinking Islam today can only be
achieved—if ever—by dynamic teams of thinkers, writers, artists, scholars, politicians, and economic producers. I am aware that long and deeply rooted traditions
of thinking cannot be changed or even revised through a few essays or suggestions
made by individuals. But I believe that thoughts have their own force and life.
Some, at least, could survive and break through the wall of uncontrolled beliefs and
dominating ideologies.

. . . Many other problems must be raised and solved because Islam has regulated every aspect of individual and collective life; but my wish here is to indicate a
general direction of thinking and the main conditions necessary to practice an
ijtihād [—my intellectual effort to find adequate answers—] recognized equally by
Muslims and modern scholars.

I. Tools for New Thinking

Periodization of the history of thought and literature has been dictated by political events. We speak currently of the Umayyad, Abbasid, and Ottoman periods. However, there are more enlightening criteria that we can use to distinguish periods of change in the history of thought. We must consider the discontinuities affecting the conceptual framework used in a given cultural space. The concepts of reason and science (*'ilm*) used in the Qur'ān, for example, are not the same as those developed later by the *falāsifa* according to the Platonic and the Aristotelian schools. However, the concepts elaborated in Qur'ānic discourse are still used more or less accurately today because the *épistème* introduced by the Qur'ān has not been intellectually reconsidered.

Épistème is a better criterion for the study of thought because it concerns the structure of the discourse—the implicit postulates which command the syntactic construction of the discourse. To control the epistemological validity of any discourse, it is necessary to discover and analyze the implicit postulates. This work has never been done for any discourse in Islamic thought (I refer to my essay "Logocentrisme et verité religieuse selon Abu al-Hasan al-'Amiri," in *Essais sur la pensée islamique*, Maisonneuve-Larose, third edition, 1984). This is why I must insist here on the new épistème implicit in the web of concepts used in human and social sciences since the late sixties.

It is not possible, for example, to use in Arabic the expression "problem of God," associating Allah and *mushkil* (problem); Allah cannot be considered as problematic. He is well-known, well-presented in the Qur'ān; man has only to meditate, internalize, and worship what Allah revealed of Himself in His own words. The classical discussion of the attributes has not been accepted by all schools; and finally the attributes are recited as the most beautiful names of Allah (*asma' Allah al-ḥusna*) but are neglected as subjects of intellectual inquiry.

This means that all the cultures and systems of thought related to pagan, polytheistic, *jāhili* (pre-Islamic), or modern secularized societies are maintained in the domain of the *unthinkable* and, consequently, remain *unthought* in the domain of "orthodox" Islamic thought or the thinkable. In European societies since the sixteenth century, the historical role that the study of classical antiquity played in initiating the modern ideas of free thinking and free examination of reality is significant; based on this link we can understand the intellectual gap between Muslim orthodoxy and Western secularized thought (cf. Marc Augé, *Le Génie du paganisme*, Gallimard, 1982).

Tradition, orthodoxy, myth, authority, and historicity do not yet have relevant conceptualizations in Arabic. Myth is translated as *ustura*, which is totally misleading because the Qur'ān uses the word for the false tales and images related in "the fables of the ancient people," and these *asatir* are opposed to the truthful stories (*qaṣaṣ ḥaqq* or *ahsan al-qaṣaṣ* told by God in the Qur'ān. The concept of myth as it is used in contemporary anthropology is related more to *qaṣaṣ* than to *ustūra*, but even anthropology has not yet clarified the difference between myth and mythology, mystification and mythologization, as well as the semantic relationship between myth and symbol and the role of the metaphor in mythical and symbolic discourse.

We still approach these concepts and use them with a rationalist positivist system of definitions, as the Qur'ān did with *asāṭīr al-awwalīn* (pre-Islamic mythology of the ancient people). However, the Qur'ān created a symbolic alternative to the competing mythical and symbolic constructions of the ancient cultures in the Middle East. Our positivist rationalism criticizes symbols and myths and proposes, as an alternative, scientific conceptualism. We have neither a theory of symbol nor a clear conception of the metaphor to read, with a totalizing perspective, the religious texts. Religious tradition is one of the major problems we should *rethink* today. First, religions are mythical, symbolic, ritualistic ways of being, thinking, and knowing. They were conceived in and addressed to societies still dominated by *oral* and not written cultures. Scriptural religions based on a revealed Book contributed to a decisive change with far-reaching effects on the nature and functions of religion itself. Christianity and Islam (more than Judaism, until the creation of the Israeli state) became official ideologies used by a centralizing state which created written historiography and archives.

There is no possibility today of *rethinking* any religious tradition without making a careful distinction between the mythical dimension linked to oral cultures and the official ideological functions of the religion. We shall come back to this point because it is a permanent way of thinking that religion revealed and that social, cultural, and political activity maintained.

Tradition and *orthodoxy* are also unthought, unelaborated concepts in Islamic traditional thought. Tradition is reduced to a collection of "authentic" texts recognized in each community: Shī'i, Sunni, and Khāriji. If we add to the Qur'ān and Hadith, the methodology used to derive the Sharī'a and the *Corpus juris* in the various schools, we have other subdivisions of the three axes of Islamic tradition. I tried to introduce the concept of an *exhaustive tradition* worked up by a critical, modern confrontation of all the collections used by the communities, regardless of the "orthodox" limits traced by the classical authorities (Bukhari and Muslim for the Sunnis; Kul'i, Ibn Bābūyē, Abu Ja'far al-Tūsi for the Imāmis; Ibn 'Ibād and others for the Khārijis). This concept is used by the Islamic revolution in Iran, but more as an ideological tool to accomplish the political unity of the *umma*. The historical confrontation of the corpuses, and the theoretical elaboration of a new, coherent science of *Uṣūl al-fiqh* and *Uṣūl al-din*, are still unexplored and necessary tasks.

Beyond the concept of an *exhaustive tradition* based on a new definition of the *Uṣūl*, there is the concept of tradition as it is used in anthropology today—the sum of customs, laws, institutions, beliefs, rituals, and cultural values which constitute the identity of each ethno-linguistic group. This level of tradition has been partially integrated by the Shari'a under the name of *'urf* or *'amal* (like al *'amal al-fāsi* in Fās), but it is covered and legitimized by the *uṣūli* methodology of the jurists. This aspect of tradition can be expressed in Arabic by *taqālīd*, but the concept of exhaustive tradition can be expressed by the word *sunna* only if it is re-elaborated in the perspective I mentioned.

Likewise, *orthodoxy* refers to two values. For the believers, it is the authentic expression of the religion as it has been taught by the pious ancestors (*al-salaf al-ṣāliḥ); the "orthodox" literature describes opposing groups as "sects" (firaq).* For the historian, orthodoxy refers to the ideological use of religion by the competing groups in the same political space, like the Sunnis who supported the caliphate—legitimized afterwards by the jurists—and who called themselves "the followers of the tradition and the united community" (*ahl al-sunna wa-al-jamāʿa*). All the other groups were given polemical, disqualifying names like *rawāfiḍ, khawārij,* and *bāṭinīyya*. The Imamis called themselves "the followers of infallibility and justice" (*ahl al ʿiṣma wa-al-ʿadāla*), referring to an orthodoxy opposed to that of the Sunnis.

There has been no effort (*ijtihād*) to separate orthodoxy as a militant ideological endeavor, a tool of legitimation for the state and the "values" enforced by this state, from religion as a way proposed to man to discover the Absolute. This is another task for our modern project of *rethinking* Islam, and other religions.

II. Modes of Thinking

I would like to clarify and differentiate between the two modes of thinking that Muslim thinkers adopted at the inception of intellectual modernity in their societies (not only in thought), that is, since the beginning of the *Nahḍa* in the nineteenth century. I do not need to emphasize the well-known trend of *salafi* reformist thought initiated by Jamāl al-Dīn al-Afghāni and Muḥammad ʿAbduh. It is what I call the *iṣlāḥi* way of thinking which has characterized Islamic thought since the death of the Prophet. The principle common to all Muslim thinkers, the *ʿulamāʾ mujtahidūn,* as well as to historians who adopted the theological framework imposed by the division of time into two parts—before/after the Hijra (like before/after Christ)—is that all the transcendent divine Truth has been delivered to mankind by the Revelation and concretely realized by the Prophet through historical initiatives in Medina. There is, then, a definite model of perfect historical action for mankind, not only for Muslims. All groups at any time and in any social and cultural environment are bound to *go back* to this model in order to achieve the spirit and the perfection shown by the Prophet, his companions, and the first generation of Muslims called the pious ancestors (*al-salaf al-ṣāliḥ*).

This vision has been faithfully adopted and assumed by the program of the International Institute of Islamic Thought (founded in 1981 in Washington, D.C., "for the reform and progress of Islamic thought"). The publication of the Institute's International Conference in the Islamicization of Knowledge notes that the "human mind by itself with its limitations cannot comprehend the totality of the matter." This means that there is an "Islamic framework" constantly valid, transcendent, authentic, and universal in which all human activities and initiatives ought to be controlled and correctly integrated. Since the Islamic framework is part of the "Islamic legacy," one must always *look back* to the time when the Truth was formulated and implemented either in the model set in Medina by the Prophet and the Revelation or by recognized *'ulama' mujtahidun* who correctly derived the Sharica using the rules of valid *ijtihad*.

This is at the same time a methodology, an epistemology, and a theory of history. It is certainly an operative intellectual framework used and perpetuated by generations of Muslims since the debate on authority and power started inside the community according to patterns of thinking and representing the world specific to the *islahi* movement.

. . . To *rethink* Islam one must comprehend the socio-cultural genesis of *iṣlāḥi* thinking and its impact on the historical destiny of the societies where this thinking has been or is actually dominant. To assess the epistemological validity of *iṣlāḥi* thinking, one has to start from the radical and initial problems concerning the generative process, the structure and the ideological use of knowledge. By this, I mean any kind and level of knowledge produced by man living, acting, and thinking in a given social-historical situation. Radical thinking refers to the biological, historical, linguistic, semiotic condition shared by people as natural beings. From this perspective, the Revelation of Islam is only one attempt, among many others, to emancipate human beings from the natural limitations of their biological, historical, and linguistic condition. That is why, today, "Islamicizing knowledge" must be preceded by a radical epistemological critique of knowledge at the deepest level of its construction as an operative system used by a group in a given social- historical space. We need to differentiate *ideological* discourses produced by groups for assessing their own identity, power, and protection, from *ideational* discourses, which are controlled along the socio-historical process of their elaboration in terms of the new critical epistemology.

. . . The difference between the new emerging rationality and all inherited rationalities—including Islamic reason—is that the implicit postulates are made explicit and used not as undemonstrated certitudes revealed by God or formed by a transcendental intellect, but as modest, heuristic trends for research. In this spirit, here are six fundamental heuristic lines of thinking to recapitulate Islamic knowledge and to confront it with contemporary knowledge in the process of elaboration.

1. Human beings emerge as such *in* societies through various changing uses. Each use in the society is converted into a *sign* of this use, which means that realities are expressed through languages as systems of *signs*. Signs are the radical issue for a critical, controlled knowledge. This issue occurs *prior* to any attempt to interpret Revelation. Holy scripture itself is communicated through natural languages used as systems of signs, and we know that each *sign* is a locus of convergent operations (perception, expression, interpretation, translation, communication) engaging all of the relations between language and thought.

Remark 1.1: This line of research is directly opposed to a set of postulates developed and shared by Islamic thought on the privilege of the Arabic language elected by God to "teach Adam all the names." The ultimate teaching is the Qur'ān as revealed in the Arabic language. These postulates command the whole construction of *Uṣūl al-dīn* and *Uṣūl al-fiqh* as a correct methodology with which to derive from the holy texts the divine laws. The core of Islamic thought is thus represented as a linguistic and semantic issue. (This is true for all religious traditions based on written texts.)

Remark 1.2: This same line is equally opposed to the philological, historicist, positivist postulates imposed by Western thinking since the sixteenth century. That is why we have made a clear distinction between the modernity (or rationality) of the Classical Age and the heuristic trends of the present rationality (Prefigurative Age). (I refer to my book, *L'Islam hier, demain,* Buchet-Chastel, second edition, 1982.)

It is time to stop this irrelevant confrontation between two dogmatic attitudes—the theological claims of believers and the ideological postulates of positivist rationalism.

---

2. All semiotic productions of a human being in the process of his social and cultural emergence are subject to historical change which I call historicity. As a semiotic articulation of meaning for social and cultural uses, the Qur'ān is subject to historicity. This means that *there is no access to the absolute* outside the phenomenal world of our terrestrial, historical existence. The various expressions given to the ontology, the first being the truth and the transcendence by theological and metaphysical reason, have neglected historicity as a dimension of the truth. Changing tools, concepts, definitions, and postulates are used to shape the truth.

Remark 2.1: This line is opposed to all medieval thinking based on stable essences and substances. The concept of Revelation should be reworked in the light of semiotic systems subjected to historicity. The Muʿtazili theory of God's created speech deserves special consideration along this new line.

Remark 2.2: The Aristotelian definition of formal logic and abstract categories also needs to be revised in the context of the semiotic theory of meaning and the historicity of reason.

3. There are many levels and forms of reason interacting with levels and forms of imagination as is shown in the tension between *logos* and *muthos*, or symbol and concept, metaphor and reality, or proper meaning, *ẓāhir* and *bāṭin* in Islam.

Recent anthropology has opened up the field of collective social *imaginaire*[1] not considered by traditional historiography and classical theology. Imagination and social *imaginaire* are reconsidered as dynamic faculties of knowledge and action. All the mobilizing ideologies, expressed in a religious or a secular framework, are produced, received, and used by social *imaginaire*, which also is related to imagination. The concept of social *imaginaire* needs more elaboration through many societies and historical examples. In Muslim societies, its role today is as decisive as in the Middle Ages because rationalist culture has less impact and presence there than in Western societies, which, nevertheless, also have their own *imaginaire* competing with various levels and forms of rationality.

4. Discourse as an ideological articulation of realities as they are perceived and used by different competing groups occurs *prior* to the faith. Faith is shaped, expressed, and actualized in and through discourse. Conversely, faith, after it has taken shape and roots through religious, political, or scientific discourse, imposes its own direction and postulates to subsequent discourses and behaviors (individual and collective).

Remark 4.1: The concept or notion of faith given by God and the classical theories of free will, grace, and predestination need to be re-elaborated within the concrete context of discourses through which any system of beliefs is expressed and assimilated. Faith is the crystallization of images, representations, and ideas commonly shared by each group engaged in the same historical experience. It is more than the personal relation to religious beliefs; but it claims a spiritual or a metaphysical dimension to give a transcendental significance to the political, social, ethical and aesthetic values to which refers each individual inside each unified social group, or community.

5. The traditional system of legitimization, represented by *Uṣūl al-dīn* and *Uṣūl al-fiqh*, no longer has epistemological relevance. The new system is not yet established in a unanimously approved form inside the *umma*. But is it possible today, given the principles of critical epistemology, to propose a system of knowledge or science *particular* to Islamic thought? What are the theoretical conditions of a modern theology not only for political institutions, but also for universal knowledge, in the three revealed religions? We are in a crisis of legitimacy; that is why we can speak only of heuristic ways of thinking.

Remark 5.1: This line is opposed to the dogmatic assurance of theology based on the *unquestionable* legitimacy of the Sharīʿa derived from Revelation or the classical ontology of the first Being, the neo-Platonic One, the Origin from which the Intellect derives and to which it desires to return. That is why the problem of the state and civil society is crucial today. Why should an individual obey the state? How is the legitimacy of power monopolized by a group over all other established groups?

6. The search for ultimate meaning depends on the radical question concerning the relevance and existence of an ultimate meaning. We have no right to reject the possibility of its existence. What is questionable is how to base all our thoughts on the postulate of its existence. Again, we encounter the true responsibility of the critical reason: To reach a better understanding of the relationship between meaning and reality, we must, first, improve our intellectual equipment—vocabulary, methods, strategies, procedures, definitions, and horizons of inquiry.

To illustrate all these theoretical perspectives, let us give an example from classical Islamic thought. Ghazali (d. 505/1111) and Ibn Rushd (d. 595/1198) developed an interesting attempt to *think* Islam in their historical context. . . . The most relevant to our project is to be found in *Faysal al-tafriqa bayn al-islām wa-al-zandaqa* by Ghazali and *Fasl al-maqāl* written as an answer by Ibn Rushd. Ghazāli declared the *falāsifa* infidels on three bases: They deny the resurrection of the body; they deny the knowledge of particulars (*juz'iyyāt*) by God; and they claim that God is anterior ontologically, not chronologically, to the world. These three theses are matters of belief, not demonstrative knowledge. The *falāsifa* have been wrong in trying to transfer to demonstrative knowledge matters which, in fact, depend on belief. Ibn Rushd used the methodology of *Uṣūl al-fiqh* to solve a philosophical question; even the formulation of the problem, at the beginning of the *Faṣl*, is typically juridical.

This does not mean that Ghazali chose the right way to tackle the question. Actually, the most significant teaching for us is to identify, through the discussion, the epistemic limits and the epistemological obstacles of Islamic thought as it has been used by its two illustrious representatives. The new task here is not to describe the arguments (cf. G. H. Hourani, ed. trans. of *Faṣl*), but to *think* the consequences of the epistemic and epistemological discontinuities between classical Islamic thought (all included in medieval thought) and modern thought (Classical Age, from the fifteenth to the twentieth century, up to the 1950s; Prefigurative Age of a new thought, since the 1950s). Before we move ahead in the search for an unfettered way of *thinking* Islam today, it is worth noting some theories on the medieval system of intelligibility as it is shown in Ghazāli and Ibn Rushd's discussion.

1. Both thinkers accept the cognitive priority of revealed truth in the Qur'ān. Reason has to be submitted totally to this clearly formulated truth (Ghazāli) or to be elaborated as a coherent articulation of the truth established through demonstrative knowledge (in the conceptual and logical framework of Aristotelian methodology and philosophy) and the revealed truth. This last contention is served by intermingling or interweaving juridical and philosophical methodologies.

2. Both mix at different degrees but with a common psychology commanded by beliefs between religious convictions and legal norms on one side (*ahkām*, explicated by the science of *Uṣūl al-dīn* and *Uṣūl al-fiqh*) and philosophical methodology and representations on the other side. Left to themselves, the milk-sisters (*Sharʿ* and *Hikma*) are "companions by nature and friends by essence and instinct"(*Faṣl* 26).

3. Both ignore the decisive dimension of historicity to which even the revealed message is subjected. Historicity is the unthinkable and the unthought in medieval thought. It will be the conquest—not yet everywhere complete—of intellectual modernity.[2]

4. Historiography (*ta'rīkh*) has been practiced in Islamic thought as a collection of information, events, biographies (*tarājim, siyar*), geneologies (*nasab*), knowledge on countries (*buldān*), and various other subjects. This collection of facts is

related to a chronology representing time as *stable*, without a dynamic movement of change and progress. No link is established between time as a historical dynamic process (historicity) and the elements of knowledge collected by historiography. Ibn Khaldun can be cited as the exception who introduced the concept of society as an object of knowledge and thought,[3] but even he could not think of religion, society, history, or philosophy as related levels and ways to achieve an improved intelligibility. On the contrary, he contributed to eliminating philosophy and to isolating the Ash'ari vision of Islam from history as a global evolution of societies influenced by various theological expressions of Islam.

Muslims do not feel concerned by the secularized culture and thought produced since the sixteenth century.

---

5. In the case of Islamic thought, the triumph of two major official orthodoxies with the Sunnis (since the fifth century Hijra) and the Shi'a (first with the Fatimids and second with the Safavids in Iran) imposed a mode of thinking narrower than those illustrated in the classical period (first to fifth century Hijra). Contemporary Islamic thought is under the influence of categories, themes, beliefs, and procedures of reasoning developed during the scholastic age (seventh to eighth century Hijra) more than it is open to the pluralism which characterized classical thought.

6. The historical evolution and intellectual structure of Islamic thought create the necessity of starting with a critique of Islamic reason (theological, legal, historiographical) as well as of philosophical reason as it has been understood and used through Aristotelian, Platonic, and Plotinist traditions (or legacies).

We shall not do this here.[4] We have to think more clearly about new conditions and ways to *think* Islam today.

Intellectual modernity started with Renaissance and Reform movements in sixteenth-century Europe. The study of pagan antiquity and the demand for freedom to read the Bible without the mediation of priests (or "managers of the sacred," as they are sometimes called) changed the conditions of intellectual activities. Later, scientific discoveries, political revolutions, secularized knowledge, and historically criticized knowledge (historicism practiced as philosophies of history) changed more radically the whole intellectual structure of thought for the generations involved in the Industrial Revolution with its continuous consequences.

This evolution was achieved in Europe without any participation of Islamic thought or Muslim societies dominated, on the contrary, by a rigid, narrow conservatism. This is why Muslims do not feel concerned by the secularized culture and thought produced since the sixteenth century. It is legitimate, in this historical process leading to intellectual modernity, to differentiate between the ideological aspects limited to the conjunctural situations of Western societies and the anthropological structures of knowledge discovered through scientific research. Islamic thought has to reject or criticize the former and to apply the latter in its own contexts.

We cannot, for example, accept the concept of secularization or *laïcité* as it has been historically elaborated and used in Western societies. There is a political and social dimension of this concept represented by the struggle for power and the tools of legitimization between the church and the bourgeoisie. The intellectual implications of the issue concern the possibility—political and cultural—of separating education, learning, and research from any control by the state as well as by the church. This possibility remains problematical everywhere.

Similarly, we cannot interpret religion merely as positivist historicism and secularism did in the nineteenth century. Religion is addressed not only to miserable, uncultivated, primitive people who have not yet received the light of rational knowledge; human and social sciences, since 1950–60, have changed the ways of thinking and knowing by introducing a pluralist changing concept of rationality, according to which religion is interpreted in a wider perspective of knowledge and existence.

The project of *thinking* Islam is basically a response to two major needs: 1) the particular need of Muslim societies to think, for the first time, about their own problems which had been made unthinkable by the triumph of orthodox scholastic thought; and 2) the need of contemporary thought in general to open new fields and discover new horizons of knowledge, through a systematic cross cultural approach to the fundamental problems of human existence. These problems are raised and answered in their own ways by the traditional religions.

III. From the Unthinkable to the Thinkable

Islam is presented and lived as a definite system of beliefs and non-beliefs which cannot be submitted to any critical inquiry. Thus, it divides the space of thinking into two parts: the unthinkable and the thinkable. Both concepts are historical and not, at first, philosophical. The respective domain of each of them changes through history and varies from one social group to another. Before the systemization by Shafi'i of the concept of *sunna* and the *uṣūli* use of it, many aspects of Islamic thought were still thinkable. They became unthinkable after the triumph of Shafi'i's theory and also the elaboration of authentic "collections," as mentioned earlier. Similarly, the problems related to the historical process of collecting the Qur'ān in an official *muṣḥaf* became more and more unthinkable under the official pressure of the caliphate because the Qur'ān has been used since the beginning of the Islamic state to legitimize political power and to unify the *umma*. The last official decision closing any discussion of the readings of the received orthodox *muṣḥaf* was made by the *qāḍi* Ibn Mujahid after the trial of Ibn Shunbūdh (fourth/tenth century).

We can add a third significant example to show how a thinkable is transformed into an unthinkable by the ideological decision of the leading politico-religious group. The Muʿtazila endeavored by their *ijtihad* to make thinkable the decisive question of God's created speech, but in the fifth century the caliph al-Qadir made this question unthinkable by imposing, in his famous *ʿAqīda*, the dogma of the uncreated Qurʾān as the "orthodox" belief (cf. G. Makdisi, *Ibn ʿAqīl et la resurgence de l'Islam traditionaliste au Xiᵉ siècle*, Damascus, 1963).

As we have said, the unthinkable or the not yet thought (*l'impensé*) in Islamic thought has been enlarged since intellectual modernity was elaborated in the West. All the theories developed by sociology and anthropology on religion are still unknown, or rejected as irrelevant, by contemporary Islamic thought without any intellectual argument or scientific consideration.

It is true that traditional religions play decisive roles in our secularized, modernized societies. We even see secular religions emerging in industrialized societies, like fascism in Germany and Italy, Stalinism and Maoism in the communist world, and many new sects in liberal democracies. If we look at the revealed religions through the parameters set by recent secular religions, we are obliged to introduce new criteria to define religion as a universal phenomenon. To the traditional view of religion as totally revealed, created, and given by God, we cannot simply substitute the sociological theory of religion generated by a socio-historical process according to the cultural values and representations available in each group, community, or society. We must rethink the whole question of the nature and the functions of religion through the traditional theory of divine origin and the modern secular explanation of religion as a social historical production.

This means, in the case of Islam, rewriting the whole history of Islam as a revealed religion and as an active factor, among others, in the historical evolution of societies where it has been or still is received as a religion. Orientalist scholars have already started this study, inquiring even into the social and cultural conditions of the *jāhiliyya* period in which Islam emerged; but I do not know any Orientalist who has raised the epistemological problems implicit in this historicist approach. No single intellectual effort is devoted to considering the consequences of historicist presentations of the origins and functions of a religion *given* and *received* as being *revealed*.[5]

We need to create an intellectual and cultural framework in which all historical, sociological, anthropological, and psychological presentations of revealed religions could be integrated into a system of thought and evolving knowledge. We cannot abandon the problem of revelation as irrelevant to human and social studies and let it be monopolized by theological speculation. One has to ask, then, why sociology and anthropology have been interested in the question of the sacred and in ritual, but not in revelation. Why, conversely, has theology considered revelation, but not so much the sacred and the secular, until it has been influenced by anthropology and social sciences.

IV. The Societies of the Book

. . . I call Societies of the Book those that have been shaped since the Middle Ages by the Book as a religious and a cultural phenomenon. The Book has two meanings in this perspective. The Heavenly Book preserved by God and containing the entire word of God is called *Umm al-kitāb* in the Qur'ān. Geo Widengren has demonstrated the very ancient origin of this conception in Near East religious history (cf. his *Muhammad, The Apostle of God and the Heavenly Book*, Upsala, 1955). The importance of this belief for our purpose is that it refers to the verticality which has constituted the religious *imaginaire* in the Near East. Truth is located in Heaven with God, who reveals it in time and through the medium He chooses: the prophets, Himself incarnated in the "Son" who lived among people, the Book transmitted by the messenger Muhammad. There are different *modalities* for the delivery of parts (not the whole) of the Heavenly Book, but the Word of God as God Himself is the same from the point of view of the anthropological structures of religious *imaginaire*.

The modalities for the delivery of parts of the Heavenly Book have been interpreted by each community, raised and guided by a prophet, as the absolute expression of God Himself. The cultural, linguistic, and social aspects of these modalities were unthinkable in the mythical framework of knowledge particular to people who received the "revelations." When theologians came to systematize in conceptual, demonstrative ways the relations between the Word of God (*Umm al-kitāb*) and its manifested forms in Hebrew, Aramaic, and Arabic, they used either literalist exegesis of the scripture itself or rational categories and procedures influenced by Greek philosophy. Grammar and logic have been used as two different ways to reach and to deliver the meaning of the manifested revelation in relation to the grammatical and logical "reading," but they did not lead to a radical critique of the postulates used in the different exegeses developed in the Middle Ages. This issue needs to be rethought today in light of the new knowledge of language, mind, logic, and history, which means that all the ancient exegesis has to be reworked, too. We are obliged today to consider differently the second meaning of the concept of Book in our expression "Societies of the Book." The Mu'tazila touched on this point in their theory of God's created speech. The *Mushaf* as well as the Bible, are the manifested, *incarnated* word of God in human languages, transmitted orally by human voices, or fixed in written material. One has to answer here to a Christian objection on the specificity of Christian revelation made through Jesus as the incarnated God, not through human mediators. As I said, this is a difference in modality, not in the relation between the Heavenly Book and its terrestrial manifestations through religious *imaginaire*. Theological theorizations transformed into substantial transcendental truths revealed by God what, in fact, had been historical, social, and cultural events and manifestations. The delivery of the Word of God by Jesus in a given society and period of history, using the Aramaic language, is a historical event just like the delivery of the Qur'ān by Muhammad. That Jesus is presented as the "Son of God" and the Qur'ān a speech worded by God Himself are theological definitions used in systems of beliefs and non-beliefs particular to Christian and Islamic dogma. These definitions do not change the linguistic and historical fact that the messages of Jesus and Muḥammad (and, of course, the prophets of Israel) are transmitted in human languages and collected in an "orthodox" closed corpus (Bible, Gospels, and Qur'ān) in concrete historical conditions. Then, the Heavenly Book is accessible to the believers only through the written version of the books or scriptures adopted by the three communities. This second aspect of the Book is then submitted to all the constraints of arbitrary historicity. The books or scriptures are read and interpreted by the historical communities in concrete, changing, social, political, and cultural situations.

The societies where the Book—or Holy Scriptures—is used as the revelation of the divine will developed a global vision of the world, history, meaning, and human destiny by the use of hermeneutic procedures. All juridical, ethical, political, and intellectual norms had to be derived from the textual forms of the revelation. The Torah, Canon Law, and the Sharīʿa have been elaborated on the basis of the same vision of revealed Truth and "rational" procedures from which norms have been derived. There is a common conception of human destiny commanded by the eschatological perspective (the search for salvation by obedience to God's will) and guided in this world by the norms of the law.

The new dimension which I aim to explain by the concept of the Societies of the Book is the process of *historicization* of a divine category: Revelation. The believers in the three religions claim, even in the context of our secularized culture, that divine law derived from Revelation is not subject to historicity. It cannot be changed by any human legislation and it is a totally *rationalized* law. Scientific knowledge cannot demonstrate that this belief is based on a wrong assumption, but it can explain how it is possible psychologically to maintain the affirmation of a revealed law in the form presented in the Torah, Canon Law, and the Sharīʿa, against the evidence of its historicity.

Traditional theological thought has not used the concept of social *imaginaire* and the related notions of myth, symbol, sign, or metaphor in the new meanings already mentioned. It refers constantly to *reason* as the faculty of true knowledge, differentiated from knowledge based on the representations of the imagination. The methodology elaborated and used by jurists-theologians shares with the Aristotelian tradition the same postulate of rationality as founding the true knowledge and excluding the constructions of the imagination. In fact, an analysis of the discourse produced by both trends of thinking—the theological and the philosophical—reveals a simultaneous use of reason and imagination. Beliefs and convictions are often used as "arguments" to "demonstrate" propositions of knowledge. In this stage of thinking, metaphor is understood and used as a rhetorical device to add an aesthetic emotion to the *real* content of the words; it was not perceived in its creative force as a semantic innovation or in its power to shift the discourse to a global metaphorical organization requiring the full participation of a coherent imagination. The philosophers, however, recognized the power that imagination as a faculty of privileged knowledge bestowed on the prophet especially. Ibn Sīna and Ibn Ṭufayl used this faculty in each of their accounts of *Ḥayy ibn yaqẓān*, but this did not create a trend comparable to the logocentrism of the jurists, the theologians, and the *falāsifa* who favored Aristotelianism.

This lack of attention to the imagination did not prevent the general activity of social *imaginaire*—the collective representations of the realities according to the system of beliefs and non-beliefs introduced by revelation in the Societies of the Book. The social imaginaire is partially elaborated and controlled by the *'ulamā'* with their 'Aqā'id (like the one written by Ibn Batta, French translation by H. Laoust, *La profession de foi d'Ibn Baṭṭa*, Damascus, 1958); but it is structured as well by beliefs and representations taken from the cultures preceding Islam. In all Islamic societies, there are two levels of traditions—the deepest archaic level going back to the *jāhilīyya* of each society and the more recent level represented by Islamic beliefs, norms, and practices as they have been developed since the foundation of the Muslim state. The revealed Book assumed a great importance

---

All the theories developed by sociology and anthropology on religion are still unknown, or rejected as irrelevant, by contemporary Islamic thought . . .

---

because it provided a strategy of integration for all norms, beliefs, and practices proper to each social group. This means that the social *imaginaire* is generated by the interacting layers of traditions, so that it is not correct from an anthropological point of view to describe the Societies of the Book as if they were produced exclusively by the Book used as their constitution. The revealed Book had an influence on all cultural activities and political institutions to some extent. It generated a civilization of written culture opposed to, or differentiated from, the oral civilization.

The key to the Societies of the Book is thus the intensive dialectic developed everywhere between two strongly competitive forces: On the one hand, there is the state using the phenomenon of the Book in its two dimensions—the transcendent, divine, ontological message and the written literature and culture derived from it. This comprises the official culture produced and used under the ideological supervision of the state, that is the orthodox religion defined and enforced by doctors of law (jurists-theologians). On the other hand, there are the non-integrated, resisting groups using oral, non-official culture and keeping alive non-orthodox beliefs (called heresies and condemned by the official *'ulamā'*). The struggle between the reformed church and the Catholic church in the sixteenth century is a typical example of this competition. In Islam, we have many examples in history from the first century to the contemporary revivalist movements. The segmentary groups per-petuating oral cultures and traditions and adhering to archaic beliefs under the name of Islam, have resisted to their integration into the Muslim state. This is why the *'ulamā'* and contemporary—regularly condemned the "superstitions" and "heresies" of these groups, as long as they resisted the norms of the Societies of the Book.

. . . Religions are superior to any scientific theory because they give imaginative solutions to permanent issues in human life, and they mobilize the social *imaginaire* with beliefs, mythical explanations, and rites. (For more explanations, see my *Lectures du Coran*, op. cit.)

V. Strategies for Deconstruction

. . . Thinking about our new historical situation is a positive enterprise. We are not aiming for a negative critique of the previous attempts at the emancipation of human existence as much as we wish to propose relevant answers to pending and pressing questions. This is why we prefer to speak about a strategy for deconstruc-tion. We need to deconstruct the social *imaginaire* structured over centuries by the phenomenon of the Book as well as the secularizing forces of the material civilization[6] since the seventeenth century.

We speak of one social *imaginaire* because secularization has not totally elimi-nated from any society all the elements, principles, and postulates organizing the social *imaginaire* in the Societies of the Book.

This is, I know, a controversial point among historians. Karl Lowith (*Meaning in History*, 1968) has shown that so-called modern ideas are just the secularized reshaping and re-expressing of medieval Christian ideas. More recently, Regis Debray (*Critique de la raison politique*, Gallimard, 1981) underlined the Christian origins of the present socialist utopia.

Hans Blumenberg tried to refute these positions in his dissertation on *The Legitimacy of the Modern Age* (MIT Press, 1983). He showed how modernity is an alternative to Christian medieval conceptions. According to him, the modern idea of progress is the product of an imminent process of development rather than a messianic one. Long-term scientific progress guided by pluralist method and experimentation, continuity of *problems* rather than *solutions*, and history as a pos-itive whole process cut from the transcendent God, are characteristics of the mod-ern age. Should one, then, accept the definition of secularization as a long-term process through which religious ties, attitudes toward transcendence, the expecta-tion of an afterlife, ritual performances, firmly established forms of speech, a typi-cal structure of the individual *imaginaire*, specific articulation and use of reason and imagination, become a private concern separated from public life? One could add the triumph of *pragmatism*, which gives priority to action over contemplation, verification over truth, method over system, logic over rhetoric, future over past, and becoming over being.

Along this line of thinking, secularization is usually presented as one of the following: a decaying of the former capacity for receiving divine inspiration and guidance; a cultural and political program of emancipation from theological thinking and ecclesiastical dominance; the domination of nature to increase the powers of man; or the substitution of a public system of education for the private one. This is known in France as *laïcité*, which often has been expressed as a militant attitude against the religious vision of the world, as we saw during 1982-83 when the socialist government wanted to "unify" the national educational system (cf. Guy Gautier, *La laïcité en miroir*, Grasset, Paris, 1985).

Whatever the relevance of these observations to the long-term process of change undertaken first in Western societies and extended more and more to the rest of the world, two remarks are in order. First, references to traditional religions—especially the three revealed religions—are frequent and even dominating everywhere. Second, secular "religions," like fascism, Stalinism, and Maoism, are produced by contemporary societies and govern the social *imaginaire* with their so-called values, norms, aims, beliefs, and representations. Secularism appears, then, as a change of methods, styles, procedures, and forms of expression in human existence; but it does not affect the ultimate force structuring and generating the human condition through the existential and historical process.

How can we obtain a clear vision of this force and describe it? Religions have mobilized it, shaped it, and formulated it by using various cultural systems, myths, rites, beliefs, and institutions. Modern ideologies do the same by using secularized languages and collective organizations. What is the common unifying reality of all these religious and ideological constructions? To answer this question we must avoid the usual opposition between the "true" religious teaching and the "false" secularist conceptions. We will be better able to discover the reality if we deconstruct methodically all the manifested cultural constructions in the various societies. Returning to the Societies of the Book, we can show a deep, common mechanism described by Marcel Gauchet (*Le désenchantement du monde*, Gallimard, 1985) as "the debt of meaning."

All known societies are built on an *order*, a hierarchy of values and powers maintained and enforced by a political power. On what conditions is a political power accepted and obeyed by the members of the society? How is it legitimized? There is no possible legitimation of any exercised power without an authority spontaneously internalized by each individual as an ultimate reference to the absolute truth. In traditional societies, authority is the privilege of a charismatic leader able to mediate the meaning located in an extra- or super-worldliness, meaning possessed by a god (or gods), and this leader delivers it in various ways to human beings. Thus, this process creates a recognition of *debt* in each individual consciousness and, consequently, an adherence to all the commandments of the leader.

The example of Islam gives a clear illustration of this general mechanism, one which is at the same time psychological, social, political, and cultural. A very small group of believers followed Muḥammad, a charismatic leader related to the known paradigm of prophets and messengers of God in the history of salvation common to the "People of the Book." Muḥammad, supported and inspired by God, had the ability to create a new relationship to the divine through two simultaneous and interacting initiatives as all charismatic leaders do with different levels of success and innovation. He announced the absolute truth in an unusual Arabic form of expression, and he engaged the group in successive, concrete experiences of social, political, and institutional change. The Revelation translated into a sublime, symbolic, and transcendental language the daily public life of the group whose identity and *imaginaire* were separated from the hostile, non-converted groups (called infidels, hypocrites, enemies of God, errants, and bedouins). We can follow in the Qur'ān the growth of a new collective social-cultural *imaginaire* nourished by new systems of connotation whose semantic substance was not primarily an abstract vision of an idealistic dreaming mind but the historic crystallization of events shared at the time by all the members of the group.

The "debt of meaning" incurred in such conditions is the most constraining for the individuals who are the actors of their own destiny. The relation to the source of authority is not separated from obedience to the political power exercised in the name of this authority. But already, in this first stage of setting up and internalizing the debt of meaning, we must pay special attention to a structural process not yet deconstructed by historians and anthropologists.

When we write the history of these twenty years (612-632) during which Muḥammad created a new community, we mention the principal events in a narrative style. We neglect to point out the use made of these events by later generations of believers. In other words, how does the "debt of meaning" historically operate on the collective *imaginaire* to produce the concrete destiny of each group in each society? There is, in fact, a double line to follow in writing the history of societies commanded by an initial "debt of meaning" incurred in the Inaugural Age. The first is to index, describe, and articulate all the significant events and facts that occurred in each period; the second is to analyze the mental representations of these events, facts, and actions shaping the collective *imaginaire* which becomes the moving force of history. This study of psychological discussions of history is more explanatory than the positivist narration of "objective" history. It shows the powerful capacity of imagination to create symbolic figures and paradigms of meaning from very ordinary events and persons, at the first stage, then the transformation of these symbols into collective representations structuring the social *imaginaire*.

Thus, the idealized figures of Muḥammad, 'Ali, Ḥusayn, and other imams have been constructed to enlighten and legitimize the historical development of the community. The biographies (*sīra*) of Muḥammad and 'Ali, as they have been fixed in the Sunni and Shi'i traditions, are the typical production of the same social *imaginaire* influenced by a highly elaborated mythical vision provided by the Qur'ān. The whole Qur'ānic discourse is already a perfect sublimation of the concrete history produced by the small group of "believers" in Mecca and Medina.

. . . [H]istorians of Islam, so far, have not considered the question of the *imaginaire* as an important historical field. I have mentioned this concept several times because it is unavoidable when we want to relate political, social, and cultural events to their psychological origins and impacts. The narrative history suggests that all the events are understandable according to a "rational" system of knowledge. No one historian raises the question, How does one rationalize, for example, the history of Salvation as it is proposed by the Holy Scriptures—Bible, Gospels, and Qur'ān—and as it is received, integrated, and used by the individual and the collective *imaginaire?* There is no possibility to interpret the whole literature derived from those Scriptures without taking into account the representations of Salvation perpetuated in the behaviors and the thinking activity of all believers, so that all history produced in the Societies of the Book is legitimized and assimilated by the *imaginaire* of Salvation, not by any "rational" construction. The theological and juridical systems elaborated by so-called "reason" are also related to the *imaginaire* of Salvation.

The writing and the understanding of the so-called "Islamic" history would change totally if we accept to open the field of research on social *imaginaire*, and the anthropological structures of this *imaginaire* as we can describe it, for example, through *Ihyā' 'ulūm al-dīn* of Ghazali, the literature of Qur'ān exegesis, the present discourse of Islamist movements (I refer to my essay, "L'Islam dans l'histoire," in *Maghreb-Mashreq* 1985, no. 102).

VI. Revelation and History

The strategy of deconstruction leads to the ultimate decisive confrontation in the Societies of the Book. When we discover the function of social *imaginaire* as producing the history of the group, we cannot maintain the theory of revelation as it has been elaborated previously, that is, as images produced by the complex phenomenon of prophetic intervention.

The Qur'ān insists on the necessity of man to listen, to be aware, to reflect, to penetrate, to understand, and to meditate. All these verbs refer to intellectual activities leading to a kind of rationalization based on existential paradigms revealed with the history of salvation. Medieval thought derived from this an essentialist, substantialist, and unchangeable concept of rationality guaranteed by a divine intellect. Modern knowledge, on the contrary, is based on the concept of social-historical space continuously constructed and deconstructed by the activities of the social actors. Each group fights to impose its hegemony over the others not only through political power (control of the state) but also through a cultural system presented as the universal one. Seen from this perspective, the Qur'ān is the expression of the historical process which led the small group of believers to power. This process is social, political, cultural, and psychological. Through it, the Qur'ān, presented as the revelation and received as such by the individual and the collective memory, is continuously reproduced, rewritten, reread, and reexpressed in a changing social-historical space.

History is the actual incarnation of the revelation as it is interpreted by the *'ulamā'* and preserved in the collective memory. Revelation maintains the possibility of giving a "transcendent" legitimization to the social order and the historical process accepted by the group. But this possibility can be maintained only as long as the cognitive system, based on social *imaginaire*, is not replaced by a new, more plausible rationality linked to a different organization of the social-historical space. . . .

The struggle between the inherited thinkable and the not yet thought has become more intense in Muslim societies since the violent introduction of intellectual modernity; but, as we have seen, the same struggle between the paradigms of knowledge and action started in Western societies in the sixteenth century. The result has been the inversion of the priorities fixed by the revelation. Economic life and thought had been submitted to ethical-religious principles until the triumph of the capitalist system of production and exchange, which replaced the symbolic exchanges practiced in traditional societies with the rule of profit.

The nostalgia for a unified vision
[of human destiny] explains the
re-emergence of religion.

Within this new value system, ethical thinking has less relevance than the technical regulations of the market and the efficient control of productive forces. Democracy limits the source of authority to the acquiescence expressed in different circumstances of various professional or political groups. There is no longer any reference to the transcendental origin of authority. The question of revelation is thus eliminated; it is neither solved intellectually nor maintained as a plausible truth according to the pragmatic reason prevailing in so-called modern thought. All relations are based on the respective power of nations, groups, and individuals; ethical principles, founded on metaphysical or religious visions, lose their appeal. I do not mean that we have to go back to the "revealed" truth according to *iṣḥāḥi* thinking. I am stressing a major difficulty of our time: the rupture between ethics and materialism. At the same time, social *imaginaire* is not more controlled or used in a better way by "scientific" knowledge. Rather, it is mobilized more than ever by ideologues who take advantage of the modern mass media to disseminate slogans taken from religious (in Muslim societies) or secular ideologies, or from a mixture of both (in the so-called socialist regimes).

If we sum up the foregoing analysis and observations, we can stress the following propositions:

1) The social-historical space in which religions emerged, exercised their functions, and shaped cultures and collective sensibilities is being replaced by the secular positivist space of scientific knowledge, technological activities, material civilization, individual pragmatic ethics and law.

2) Scientific knowledge is divided into separate, technical, highly specialized disciplines. Religions, on the contrary, have provided global, unified, and unifying systems of beliefs and non-beliefs, knowledge and practice, as well as pragmatic solutions to the fundamental problems of human destiny: life, death, love, justice, hope, truth, eternity, transcendence, and the absolute. The nostalgia for a unified vision explains the re-emergence of religion.

3) Positivist scientific knowledge has discredited or eliminated religious functions in society without providing an adequate alternative to religion as a symbol of human existence and a source of unifying ethical values for the group. This happened in Western societies under the name of secularism (or *laïcisme* in French), liberalism, and socialism.

4) Present thought has not yet recognized the positive aspect of secularism as a cultural and intellectual way to overcome fanatic divisions imposed by the dogmatic, superstitious use of religion. At the same time, the specific role of religion as a source for symbols in human existence also goes unrecognized.

5) Islam is not better prepared than Christianity to face the challenge of secularism, intellectual modernity, and technological civilization. The so-called religious revivalism is a powerful secular movement disguised by religious discourse, rites, and collective behaviors; but it is a secularization without the intellectual support needed to maintain the metaphysical mode of thinking and to search for an ethical coherence in human behavior. Theological and ethical thinking has reappeared in contemporary Islamic thought in the form of the ideology of liberation (political and economic). There is little intellectual concern with genuine religious issues like the consciousness of culpability, the eschatological perspective, or revelation as a springboard for mythical, or symbolic thinking.

6) The concept that the Societies of the Book could help to build a new humanism which would integrate religions as cultures and not as dogmas for confessional groups (or *ṭawā'if*, as in Lebanon or Ireland) is not taken seriously either in theology or in the social scientific study of religions. But there is hope that semiotics and linguistics can create the possibility of reading religious texts in the new way we have mentioned.

7) The study of Islam today suffers particularly from the ideological obstacles created, since the nineteenth century, by the decay of the Muslim intellectual tradition, as it had developed from the first to the fifth century Hijra, and by the economic pressure of the West, the general trend of positivist rationalism and material civilization, the powerful impact of demography since the late fifties and the necessity of building a modern state and unifying the nation.

8) World system economists insist on the opposition between the center and the periphery. Likewise, in intellectual evolution, we should pay attention to the increasing domination of Western patterns of thought which have not been duly criticized, controlled, or mastered in Western societies themselves. Islam, which has a rich cultural tradition, is facing major issues in a generalized climate of semantic disorder; our thinking should be directed to the dangers resulting from this threat.

9) We should not forget that man agrees to obey, to be devoted, and to obligate his life when he feels a "debt of meaning" to a natural or a supernatural being. This may be the ultimate legitimacy of the state understood as the power accepted and obeyed by a group, community, or nation. The crisis of meaning started when each individual claimed himself as the source of all or true meaning; in this case, there is no longer any transcendent authority. Relations of power are substituted for relations of symbolic exchanges of meaning. To whom do we owe a "debt of meaning"?

It is our responsibility to answer this question after man has changed himself by his own initiatives, discoveries, performances, and errors. It seems that the answer will be conjectural and more and more bound to empirical research instead of to divine guidance taught by traditional religions. I learned through the Algerian war of liberation how all revolutionary movements need to be backed by a struggle for meaning, and I discovered how meaning is manipulated by forces devoted to the conquest of power. The conflict between meaning and power has been, is, and will be the permanent condition through which man tries to emerge as a thinking being.

Notes

1. I prefer to use the French word for this important concept because it has no exact correspondent in English. Cf. C. Castoriadis, *L'institution imaginaire de la société*, Seuil, 1977.

2. Cf. my *Ta'rīkhiyyat al-fikr al-ʿarabi al-islāmi*, Dar al-inmā' al-ʿarabi Beirut, 1985.

3. Miskawayh did this before in his philosophical and historiographical works. Cf. my *Humanisme arabe au IV siècle*, 2d ed., Vrin, 1982.

4. Cf. my essays in *Critique de la Raison islamique*, Paris, 1984; and *L'islam: morale et politique*, UNESCO—Desclée De Bronwer, 1986.

5. Given and received are technical terms in linguistic and literary analyses. Islam is given as revealed in the grammatical structure of Qur'ānic discourse, and it is received as such by the psychological consciousness generated by this discourse and the ritual performances prescribed by it. For more thorough elaboration of this approach, I refer to my essay, *The Concept of Revelation: From Ahl al-Kitāb to the Societies of the Book*, Claremont Graduate School, California, 1987.

6. I use this expression according to its historical elaboration by F. Brandel.

"So That You May Know One Another": A Muslim American Reflects on Pluralism and Islam

By
ALI S. ASANI

This article addresses the anguish and concerns raised by the events of 11 September 2001 among Americans—both Muslims and non-Muslims—about mutual hatred and distrust in light of the Quran. The Holy Book of Islam teaches pluralism, yet on both sides of the imagined fence, this message is misunderstood. It is not so much a clash of civilizations, as some American ideologues propagate, but a clash of ignorance that leads to such perilous situations. The complex economic, political, and global issues have been put under the rubric of stereotypes that dehumanize the "other." The Quran reveals the beauty of human diversity, accepts the truth of Jewish and Christian traditions, and promotes the idea of pluralism for cooperation, respect, and understanding among various communities. While both Muslims and non-Muslims frequently misuse the Quranic verses for political purposes, Muslim history, on the whole, demonstrates more tolerance and appreciation of other religious traditions than the histories of other religions do.

Keywords: stereotypes; pluralism; Quran; tolerance; fundamentalism

As a Muslim involved in teaching and scholarship on the Islamic tradition, I have received many invitations in recent months to speak about the role that religion and religious

Ali S. Asani is Professor of the Practice of Indo-Muslim Languages and Culture at Harvard University. His books include The Bujh Niranjan: An Ismaili Mystical Poem; The Harvard Collection of Ismaili Literature in Indic Literatures: A Descriptive Catalog and Finding Aid; Celebrating Muhammad: Images of the Prophet in Muslim Devotional Poetry (coauthor); Al-Ummah: A Handbook for an Identity Development Program for North American Muslim Youth; Aaiye Urdu parheN: Let's Study Urdu (coauthor, forthcoming); and Ecstasy and Enlightenment: The Ismaili Literature of South Asia (London: I.B. Tauris, 2002). He also serves on the advisory board of the Harvard Foundation for Intercultural and Race Relations. Professor Asani recently received the Harvard Foundation medal for promoting intercultural and racial understanding at Harvard and in the nation.

NOTE: The author would like to acknowledge his appreciation to Michael Currier and Wayne Eastman for their comments and suggestions on various drafts of this

DOI: 10.1177/0002716203255392

40

ANNALS, AAPSS, 588, July 2003

ideas may or may not have played in the horrific events of 11 September 2001. Non-Muslim audiences have wanted to know how Islam, a religion whose very name signifies peace to many Muslims, could be used to promote violence and hatred for America and the West. Why, many wonder, are some Muslims and some governments in Muslim nations anti-American, antagonistic to America and the West, and willing to condone or even applaud the loss of innocent American lives? For their part, Muslims I have spoken to have expressed similar concerns. Why, many of them wonder, are some Americans and Europeans and some American and Western policies anti-Islamic, antagonistic to Muslim interests, and heedless of the loss of innocent Muslim lives? Under the circumstances, they ask, is peaceful coexistence and harmony between Muslim and non-Muslim really possible? Is there hope for reconciliation?

Many believe that what we witnessed on 9/11 and in the string of events unfolding in its aftermath is symptomatic of a "clash of civilizations": a battle between two civilizations, Western and Islamic, each espousing a worldview fundamentally antagonistic to the other. According to this perspective, there can be no peace in this world, no resolution of conflicts, until one civilization defeats and dominates the other politically, economically, and culturally. Adherents of this viewpoint hold that the differences between the two are irreconcilable and conflicts and wars are inevitable.

Though this mode of analysis has been popular in some circles, I believe that it is flawed in its formulation, for it oversimplifies many complexities. What we are witnessing is not so much a clash of civilizations as it is a clash of ignorances. In this clash of ignorances, deep-seated stereotypes and prejudices have resulted in the "other," whether the "other" is the West or Islam, being perceived as evil, barbaric, and uncivilized. Moreover, it has led to the dehumanization of each side, the inability to accept the fundamental humanity of the other. Such stereotypical perceptions are the unfortunate result of centuries-old antagonisms originating not merely in religion but in an intricate web of political and economic factors, specifically the competition for hegemony and control, expressed in the rhetoric of conquest and reconquest, crusade and jihad, imperialism and nationalism, occupation and liberation.

Over the past year and a half, as I have been engaged in providing audiences with historical and religious perspectives on the complex factors that have created such deep and profound misunderstandings, I have thought to myself on a number of occasions, Where does the common ground lie? Is there a bond that can serve as a bridge promoting understanding and tolerance? I believe that there is. I have come to the conclusion that the reconciliation and peace that we all long for must begin with the nurturing and fostering of a genuine ethos of pluralism. It seems to me that one of the principal causes underlying many of the seemingly irresolvable wars and conflicts that riddle our world today is the failure to come to terms with the essential pluralism of human societies. Bosnia, Rwanda, Afghanistan, Sri

article. Some sections of this article were previously published by the author in an article titled "Pluralism, Intolerance and the Quran," *American Scholar* 71, no. 1 (winter 2002): 52-60.

Lanka, Ireland, India, Pakistan, and the Ivory Coast are examples of nations that have experienced conflict as a result of one religious, ethnic, or tribal group being unable to respect and value the essential equality and humanity of groups different from itself. As a result, dominant religious, ethnic, or tribal groups seek to control and homogenize society by eradicating or marginalizing those who are different from themselves.

What we are witnessing is not so much a clash of civilizations as it is a clash of ignorances.

My conviction that hope lies in cultivating pluralism stems from the fact that pluralism is an ideal whose value has come to be recognized by many societies. History shows us that there are some societies that have been more successful in promoting this ideal, while for others, this ideal has remained just that and has never been realized in practice. History also shows us that in most societies, pluralism does not occur naturally; it must be deliberately and carefully nourished, for it evolves gradually. It must also be protected and never taken for granted, for we have plenty of examples of societies that were once pluralist becoming exclusivist and antipluralistic. The difficulties in nurturing and maintaining pluralism should not, however, preclude us from promoting it more aggressively as a means to achieve reconciliation.

In the Islamic tradition, the pluralist nature of human societies is well recognized. Contrary to the misinformed comments usually made about it, the Quran, the scripture of Islam, has much to say on respect and tolerance for difference as principles for human coexistence. In this article, I would like to outline some of the core ideas in the Quran regarding pluralism, ideas that form the seeds for a theology of pluralism within Islam. I believe that such a theology of pluralism, based on the teachings of the Quran, can provide an authentic and solid foundation on which we can encourage pluralism within the world's many different Muslim communities and nations.[1]

Let me begin by sharing with you a verse in the Quran that, for me, has come to best represent the pluralist ethos that lies at the heart of this text. When I was nine or ten years old and wondering about racial and religious diversity, I recall asking my father, a devout Muslim, "Why didn't Allah make human beings all the same? Why did Allah make us all different?" In response to my question, he quoted a verse from the Quran:

> O humankind, We [God] have created you male and female, and made you into communities and tribes, so that you may know one another. Surely the noblest amongst you in the sight of God is the most godfearing of you. God is All-knowing and All-Aware. (Quran 49:13)

This verse from the Quran formed the first teaching I received as a child on the subject of pluralism. Now, many years later, as I reflect on it and its meaning, I believe it is clear that from the perspective of the Quran, the divine purpose underlying the creation of human diversity is to foster knowledge and understanding, to promote harmony and cooperation among peoples. God did not create diversity for it to become a source of tensions, divisions, and polarization in society. Indeed, whether humans recognize it or not, human diversity is a sign of divine genius. These sentiments are, in fact, echoed in another Quranic verse in which God addresses humankind and affirms the principle that human plurality is not an accident but, in fact, a result of Divine will: "If Your Lord had willed, He would have made humankind into one nation, but they will not cease to be different . . . and for this God created them [humankind]" (Quran 11:118-19).

An important aspect of the pluralist message of the Quran is its emphasis on the universality of God's message: God has revealed his message to *all* peoples and to *all* cultures; not a single people or nation has been forgotten (Quran 35:24). Although humans may have misinterpreted that message to suit their needs in creating conflicting traditions, all religions, at their core, have sprung from the same divine source and inspiration. The idea that God's message is universal, but its manifestations plural, provides the basic underpinning to the manner in which the Quran relates itself and the faith that it preaches with the religious traditions that preceded it in the Middle East, namely, Judaism and Christianity. Far from denying the validity of these predecessor traditions, the Quran repeatedly affirms their essential truth, acknowledging that their message comes from one and the same God and that the Quran is only the latest of God's revelations to affirm the revelations that preceded it. Characteristic of this affirmative and pluralistic stance is the following command to believers:

> Say: we believe in God and what has been revealed to us and what was revealed to Abraham, Ismail, Isaac, Jacob, and the tribes, and in what was given to Moses, Jesus, and the prophets from their Lord. We make no distinction between one and another among them and to Him [God] do we submit. (Quran 3:84)

Quranic beliefs in the truth of the Judaic and Christian traditions are also encapsulated in another term: the *ahl al-kitab*, or People of the Book. This is the umbrella term in the Quran that refers to communities, or peoples, who have received revelation in the form of scripture. It is commonly used to refer to the Jews, Christians, and Muslims. The pluralistic nature of this term is evident in the use of the noun *book* in the singular rather than in the plural, meant to emphasize that the Jews, Christians, and Muslims follow one and the same book, not various conflicting scriptures. The Old and New Testaments and the Quran are seen as being plural, earthly manifestations of the one heavenly scripture in which God has inscribed the divine word. Significantly, the Quran does not claim that it abrogates the scriptures revealed before it. On the contrary, it affirms their validity. Another verse addressed to the Muslim faithful states,

> And argue not with the People of the Book unless it be in a way that is better, save with such of them as do wrong; and say we believe in that which has been revealed to us and to you; and our God and your God is one and unto Him we submit. (Quran 29:46)

While the concept of the People of the Book was originally coined to refer to the major monotheistic traditions in the Arabian milieu, there were attempts to expand the term theologically to include other groups, such as the Zoroastrians in Iran and Hindus and Buddhists in India, as the Islamic tradition spread beyond the Middle East. For instance, in seventeenth-century India, Dara Shikoh, a prince from the

---

[T]he Quran . . . has much to say on respect and tolerance for difference as principles for human coexistence.

---

ruling Mughal dynasty, who was strongly influenced by the pluralistic teachings within Islamic traditions of mysticism, considered the Hindu scriptures, the Upanishads, to be the "storehouse of monotheism" and claimed that they were the *kitab maknun*, or "hidden scripture," referred to in the Quran (Quran 56:77-80). Hence, he personally translated these Sanskrit texts into Persian and urged that it was the duty of every faithful Muslim to read them. Admittedly, not all Muslims were comfortable with the broadening of the term "People of the Book" to include religious scriptures and traditions not mentioned specifically by name in the Quran, but the fact remains that these types of interpretations were made possible by the pluralistic nature of the Quranic worldview.

With such a universalist perspective, it goes without saying that the Quran does not limit salvation exclusively to Muslims. Salvation, according to the Quran, will be granted to any person who submits to (i.e., is a submitter) to the one God and to Divine Will (the literal meaning of the word *Muslim* in Arabic is "submitter"). Indeed, Islamic scripture regards Abraham, the patriarch, and all the other prophets of the Judeo-Christian tradition, including Moses and Jesus, as being *Muslim* in the true sense of the word. Repeatedly, the Quran declares that on the Day of Judgment all human beings will be judged on their moral performance, irrespective of their formal religious affiliation (see Sachedina 2001, 28).

> Those who believe, those who follow Jewish scriptures, the Christians, the Sabians, and any who believe in God and the Last Day, and do good, all shall have their reward with their Lord and they will not come to fear or grief. (Quran 5:72)

One other aspect of the Quran's teaching on tolerance is worth mentioning here. The Islamic scripture, while acknowledging diversity of belief and interpretation, specifically upholds the right of individuals to hold different opinions by declaring that belief is a matter of choice. God has blessed humans with intellect so that they may apply it to all aspects of life, including faith. Just as they have the ability to choose between good and evil, right and wrong, they have the right to choose when it comes to matters of faith. One of the most often quoted verses of the Quran declares, "Let there be no compulsion in religion" (Quran 2:256), explicitly acknowledging that individuals cannot be forced to profess beliefs contrary to their will. Even if individuals perversely choose disbelief, they nevertheless have the right to make that choice, too. A chapter of the Quran titled, *The Unbelievers*, referring to those who reject the message of monotheism preached by the prophet Muhammad, stresses that belief is a matter of personal conviction and that difference in faith should not be the cause for persecution or abuse.

> Say: O you who disbelieve, I worship not that which you worship, nor will you worship that which I worship, and I will not worship that which you have worshipped, and you will not worship that which I worship, to you is your path [religion] and to me is mine. (Quran 111)

The Quran's endorsement of religiously and culturally plural societies and the recognition of the salvific value of other monotheistic religions greatly affected the treatment of religious minorities in Muslim lands throughout history. From the earliest periods of Muslim history, we have examples of a great deal of respect for the rights of non-Muslims under Muslim rule. Typical of this tolerance was a treaty that the Prophet Muhammad signed with the Christian community of Najran:

> To the Christians of Najran and the neighboring territories the security of God and the pledge of His Prophet are extended for their lives, their religion, and their property—to the present as well as the absent and others besides; there shall be no interference with the practice of their faith, in their observances; nor any change in their rights or privileges; no bishop shall be removed from his office; nor any monk from his monastery, nor any priest from his priesthood, and they shall continue to enjoy everything great and small as heretofore; no image or cross shall be destroyed; they shall not oppress or be oppressed . . . no tithes shall be levied from them, nor shall they be required to furnish provision for troops. (Ali 1946, 273)

Ali ibn Abi Talib (d. 661), one of the early Caliphs to succeed the Prophet Muhammad, instructed his governor in Egypt to show mercy, love, and kindness to all subjects under his rule, including non-Muslims, whom he declared to be "your equals in creation." Such tolerance was later reflected in the policies of the Arab dynasties of Spain, the Fatimids in North Africa, and the Turkish Ottomans in the Middle East, all of which granted maximum individual and group autonomy to those adhering to a religious tradition other than Islam. We can also cite the example of the Mughal Emperor Akbar (d. 1605), who, much to the dismay of the religious right wing of his time, promoted tolerance among the various traditions that compose the Indian religious landscape. While there have been instances when religious minorities were grudgingly tolerated in Muslim societies, rather than being respected in the true spirit of pluralism, the Quranic endorsement of a pluralistic ethos explains why violent forms of anti-Semitism generated by exclusivist Christian theology in medieval and modern Europe, and the associated harsh treatment of Jewish populations culminating eventually in the Holocaust, never occurred in regions under Muslim rule.

Although the Quran, when properly understood, espouses an essentially pluralist worldview, one that promotes peace and harmony among nations and peoples, its message has been perverted over time by those who have sought to interpret it in antipluralist or exclusivist ways. Such exclusivist interpretations of the Quran, premised on the hegemony of Islam over non-Islam, first emerged in the eighth and ninth centuries, when Islam became the religion of the Arab empire. Muslim exegetes, seeking religious legitimation for political hegemony, began reinterpreting Quranic verses to justify essentially political goals. By promoting the idea that Muslims, as followers of the latest of the monotheistic revelations, were superior to Jews, Christians, and all previous religious communities, they were able to forge a social and political solidarity among various Arab tribes and clans. This solidarity became the backbone of the early Arab Muslim empire, providing "an effective basis for aggression against those who did not share this solidarity with the community of believers" (Sachedina 2001, 29). It is within this context that political concepts such as *dar al-islam* (territories under Muslim suzerainty) and *dar al-harb* (territories under non-Muslim control) became prominent, although they have no real basis in the Quran. In the same vein, the notion of *jihad*, a term fraught with definitional ambiguities, was reinterpreted to justify imperial expansion. Under the influence of the political realities of later centuries, which witnessed an expansion of Arab rule, what was clearly a reference in the Quran to a moral struggle, or an armed struggle in the face of provocation and aggression, came to be interpreted as a general military offensive against nonbelievers and as a means of legitimizing political dominion.[2]

To be sure, the religious legitimation of hegemonic interests had to be sought in the Quran, the very text that forbade compulsion in religious matters and contained verses of an ecumenical nature recognizing not only the authenticity of other monotheistic traditions but the essential equality of all prophets sent down by God. For this purpose, as Abdulaziz Sachedina has so ably demonstrated in his book, *The Islamic Roots of Democratic Pluralism* (2001), some Muslim exegetes devised terminological and methodological strategies to mold the exegesis of the sacred text to provide a convincing prop for absolutist ends. The principal means by which the exclusivists were able to promote their view was through the declaration that the many verses calling for pluralism, commanding Muslims to build bridges of understanding with non-Muslims, had been abrogated by other verses that call for fighting the infidel. It is only by decontextualizing the exegesis of such verses, by disregarding their original historical context of revelation and by using them to engage in a large-scale abrogation of contradictory verses, that the exclusivist Muslim exegetes have been able to counteract the pluralist ethos that so thoroughly pervades the Quran.

From a historical perspective, exclusivist interpretations of the Quran have been used to justify political hegemony over not only non-Muslims but also over fellow Muslims whose interpretation and religious practices were perceived as deviating from the norms established by exclusivists. For instance, during the seventeenth and eighteenth centuries, several areas of the Muslim world witnessed the rise of movements that, in response to what was perceived as a general moral laxity and decline, attempted to "purify" Islam. The leaders of these movements targeted a whole range of practices and beliefs among fellow Muslims that, in their eyes, constituted evidence of religious backsliding. In certain instances, the attack took on a military character; that is, a "jihad" was launched against fellow Muslims. Not surprisingly, such exclusivist groups, which were harsh on fellow Muslims, came to consider Jews and Christians to be infidels rather than monotheists.

From a historical perspective, exclusivist interpretations of the Quran have been used to justify political hegemony over not only non-Muslims but also over fellow Muslims . . . .

In recent times, the exclusivist view has been heavily promoted by the so-called fundamentalist groups in the Muslim world. The reasons for the rise of such groups are complex. Broadly speaking, these movements are a reaction against modernity, Westernization, global hegemony by Western powers (particularly the United States), and support of such powers for repressive regimes in predominantly Muslim lands. The failure of borrowed ideologies, such as capitalism, communism, or socialism, to deliver economic and social justice in many Muslim countries has created exclusivist groups looking for a "pure" and "authentic" language in which to criticize the failed modern Muslim state, a state that has marginalized or displaced traditional religious authorities in a bid to maximize political hegemony. The search for a solution to the myriad of political, social, and economic problems confronting Muslims has led exclusivist groups to use Islam as a political ideology for the state: "Islam is the solution." The commitment of such groups to understand

Islam in a "pure" monolithic form, to engage in revisionist history, and to read religious texts in an exclusivist manner that denies any plurality of interpretations has
unleashed a struggle in the Muslim world between the exclusivists and those who
uphold the pluralist teachings of the Quran. An important dimension of the struggle between the exclusivists and the pluralists is the debate over the role and status
of women in Muslim societies, for exclusivists tend to be antiegalitarian in their
interpretations of gender roles. It is worth noting that groups such as the Taliban and
al-Qaida, which attack Western targets, are at the same time attacking a centuries-
old multivocal tradition of pluralism within Islam.

For Muslims to participate in the multireligious and multicultural world of the
twenty-first century, it is essential that they fully embrace Quranic teachings on
"religious and cultural pluralism as divinely ordained principle of co-existence
among human societies" (Sachedina 2001, 13).

The implications of the Quranic sanctioning of diversity and its injunction to
create harmony in diverse societies through the promotion of mutual knowledge
needs to be more seriously explored by Muslim theologians and interpreters of the
Islamic holy scripture.[3] Exclusivist interpretations of the Quran that are premised
on the hegemony of Islam over non-Islam and promote the use of a rhetoric of hate
and violence to attain such goals are outdated in a global society in which relations
between different peoples are best fostered on the basis of equality and mutual
respect—a basic principle underlying the Quranic worldview.

Since, in several key Muslim nations, the exclusivist message has been propagated by *madrasas*, or religious schools, sponsored by exclusivist groups or the state
itself, a key to the outcome of the struggle between pluralism and exclusivism in the
Islamic tradition lies in the reeducation of Muslim peoples concerning the pluralism that lies at the heart of the Quran. Without this pluralist education, they will
continue to rely on the monolithic interpretations of scholars and demagogues to
access the Quran. Alongside promoting religious literacy, it is equally essential to
promote programs to eradicate poverty. As His Highness the Aga Khan, the leader
of the Ismaili Muslim community, correctly pointed out in a recent speech, "Left
alone, poverty will provide a context for special interests to pursue their goals in
aggressive terms."[4] Indeed, recent history is replete with examples of well-
financed exclusivist groups recruiting support for their cause in poverty-stricken
Muslim communities by virtue of being the sole providers of educational and medical services.

As a pluralist Muslim who is American, I am struck by the resonance between
the pluralism espoused in the Quran and that in the constitution and civic culture
of the United States. Contrary to what some may claim, one can be fully American
and Muslim simultaneously. In this regard, I was pleased recently to see a series of
advertisements in major American newspapers that had chosen to stress the com-
patibility between being a Muslim and an American, presenting a Muslim American face of Islam. The underlying message of this campaign is laudable: Muslims
are not the "other." However, even well-intentioned efforts to affirm the compati-
bility of Muslim and American identities may sometimes presuppose an unduly
narrow and exclusionary vision of Islam. For instance, a recent ad in the *New York*

Times, intending to explain the significance of the head covering, showed a Muslim woman in *hijab*. Unfortunately, the ad also implied that all "good" Muslim women cover their heads, not recognizing that there is a great deal of diversity in this practice among Muslim women both here in the United States and in other parts of the world. Not all Muslim women choose to define and express their religious identity through the headscarf. It is a matter of choice.

Muslim Americans are a remarkably diverse group, belonging to more than fifty different ethnicities and nationalities, mirroring, in fact, the diverse face of America itself. They come from many parts of the world and represent many different interpretations of Islam. Indeed, no other country in the world has a Muslim population that is as diverse as that of America. It is, therefore, crucial that this plurality is recognized in our understanding of what it means to be Muslim in America today. We should guard against presupposing unduly narrow and exclusionary visions of Islam as being representative of the whole. The plurality of cultures and interpretations within Islam in America presents a unique set of challenges. As Muslim Americans come to terms with the challenges posed by this internal pluralism, as well as the pluralism of America, I hope they will, God willing, have the unique opportunity to become champions of pluralism in the larger international Muslim world. My call for the enhancement of pluralism within Muslim societies as a means of reconciling Muslim with non-Muslim and Muslim with Muslim, however, must also be coupled with my challenging a phenomenon that threatens the pluralist fabric of my adopted country.

Post-9/11, America has witnessed an alarming rise of Islamophobia—expressions of hatred for Muslims, for Islam and everything Islamic. Islam has been equated with Nazism. The Quran has been compared to Hitler's *Mein Kampf*, with the suggestion that reading it in the current context is an act of treason. Muslims have been likened to creatures who separate "like protozoa into cells from two to infinity." The Prophet Muhammad has been declared to be a terrorist on a prominent national TV show. American Muslims have been declared to be Trojan horses and a danger to the national security and should, therefore, all be deported, while the holy city of Mecca should be nuked to send a message to all Muslims. A magazine with national circulation even printed an article calling for Muslims to be buried in pigskins and lard! Two members of the Washington state legislature walked out of prayers led by a Muslim imam at the beginning of legislative sessions because they considered their participation in the prayers to be un-American and unpatriotic. Such actions and remarks may be too quickly dismissed "as understandable under the circumstances" or as being the rantings, ravings, and uninformed acts of individuals and not representative of national sentiments. Yet these are individuals with national stature, often belonging to the vocal Christian Right. As their opinions are expressed in national media, there is a tendency to manipulate maliciously and exploit the profound ignorance and stereotypes about Islamic matters prevalent in the general American population. As I write, however, and over recent months, it seems that anything can be said about Islam and Muslims, no matter how distasteful and demeaning. Muslims of America, themselves reeling from the impact of 9/11 on their communities and the resulting insecurities, find themselves besieged on almost a daily basis by vicious hate speech emanating from various media targeted at them or their religious beliefs. Hate crimes against Muslims have risen by a dramatic 600 percent. In addition, several mosques have been vandalized, the most recent incident occurring on 12 March 2003, when projectiles were hurled through the windows of one of the largest mosques and schools in America. The FBI predicts that as a result of the war against Iraq, there will be a further rise of violence against Muslims.

[P]luralism, tolerance, freedom to practice one's faith openly without fear of being stigmatized, and respect for difference—these fundamental America values—are all under attack.

Incredibly, many of the public explanations of Islamophobia have been the direct result of certain government policies introduced in recent months in the interests of promoting national security. While it is debatable whether such policies are, in fact, effective in promoting security by apprehending potential terrorists, these policies are clearly Islamophobic in effect if not intent. They have contributed to the escalation of fear in America about Islam and Muslims. As a result, they have also created fear and anxiety among many of America's Muslims, many of whom are afraid to attend mosques lest they be profiled. Some Muslim women are afraid to wear their headscarves in public, and some have even resorted to changing their names so that they cannot be identified as Muslim. A prominent Muslim civil rights advocate has described this situation as a "virtual internment."[5] In the fall of last year, the Canadian government issued a travel advisory for Canadian citizens of Muslim faith travelling to, or through, the United States in response to the discriminatory profiling and violation of fundamental liberties experienced by Muslim Canadians. Ironically, this advisory, from our neighbor and strong ally, was issued at about the same time as the State Department began airing ads in Indonesia and other Muslim countries with the intention of promoting the image that Muslims in America practice their faith freely.

Today, I fear that pluralism, tolerance, freedom to practice one's faith openly without fear of being stigmatized, and respect for difference—these fundamental American values—are all under attack. There has been an ominously deafening silence from leadership at all levels of society concerning the rise of Islamophobia. This silence itself is complicit in creating an atmosphere of fear and anxiety among American Muslims. We can no longer afford to remain silent when we encounter such bigotry; the consequences of silence are too dangerous for our nation and for the world. Certainly, such silence is not very helpful in nurturing much-needed understanding, goodwill, and respect between America and the nations of the Muslim world. We must not surrender the public arena to the forces that seek to promote hatred and polarization amongst the various communities in our nation. Islamophobia must be actively resisted and responded to so that such hate speech becomes totally unacceptable in our national vocabulary and in our national conscience. If unchallenged and unchecked, hate speech can erode and destroy the traditions of pluralism and respect for these differences that have made America the great nation that it is today. Every Islamophobic statement or action, no matter how ridiculous, is a deliberate attack on the pluralist fabric of our society and on our shared values that demand justice, respect, tolerance, and compassion for all who live in our nation. We can best cultivate these values by paying heed to the Quran's call for "knowing one another" and struggling (jihad) against the most dangerous type of ignorance—the ignorance that dehumanizes. I close with a verse from Sadi (d. 1292), one of the great Muslim humanist poets of Iran:

Human beings, created from the same essence, are limbs of one another
When one limb aches, the other limbs are restless, too
O you who are indifferent to the pains of others
You do not deserve to be called human.

Notes

1. My understanding of the theological basis for pluralism within Islam has been greatly influenced by Abdulaziz Sachedina's (2001) pioneering study. I am also indebted to my colleague Roy Mottahedeh, whose 1992 article, "Towards an Islamic Theology of Toleration," I have found helpful.

2. For the theological debates on the term *jihad* in early Islam, see Roy Mottahedeh and Ridwan Al-Sayyid (2001).

3. For a further discussion of this issue, see Khaled Abou El-Fadl (2002, 15-17).

4. His Highness Prince Karim Aga Khan, Keynote Speech Concluding the Prince Claus Fund's Conference on Culture and Development, Amsterdam, 7 September 2002.

5. Salam al-Marayati, Founder and Director, Muslim Public Affairs Council, at the Islam in America 2003 conference held at the Harvard Divinity School on 9 March 2003.

References

Ali, Ameer. 1946. *The Spirit of Islam*. London: Christophers.

El-Fadl, Khaled Abou. 2002. *The place of tolerance in Islam*. Boston: Beacon.

Mottahedeh, Roy. 1992. Towards an Islamic theology of toleration. In *Islamic law reform and human rights*, edited by T. Lindholm and K. Vogt. Oslo: Nordic Human Rights Publications.

Mottahedeh, Roy, and Ridwan Al-Sayyid. 2001. The idea of *jihad* in Islam before the Crusades. In *The Crusades from the perspective of Byzantium and the Muslim world*, edited by A. Laiou and R. Mottahedeh. Washington, DC: Dumbarton Oaks.

Sachedina, Abdulaziz. 2001. *The Islamic roots of democratic pluralism*. Oxford: Oxford University Press.

Interpreting Islam in American Schools

By
SUSAN L. DOUGLASS
and
ROSS E. DUNN

How is Islam taught in American schools? Teaching Islam to young Americans is a relatively recent phenomenon. The Israeli-Arab conflict shaped the contours of the study of Islam with images and stereotypes inherited from the Crusades and Colonialism. Islam has been taught not as an essential ingredient of the World History but through the political conflicts of Israelis and Arabs as well as the American global agenda within which Qaddafi, Hafez al-Asad, and Ayatullah Khomeini emerged as the representatives of Islam. The Muslim population in America grew dramatically in the twentieth century, and curriculum was devised to include Islam without disturbing the unitary narrative of Western Civilization: The textbooks disconnect Islam from the Judeo-Christian tradition even as they emphasize how Islam borrowed from Jewish and Christian scriptures. Textbook writers portrayed Islam in light of the Arab nomadic society and the life of the Prophet of Islam while deliberately downplaying the Abrahamic legacy in Islam.

Keywords: stereotypes; media images; history textbooks; multiculturalism; religion in American schools; American schools in the twentieth century; curriculum reform

Twenty-five years ago it was quite possible for a citizen of the United States to grow up, graduate from a major university, and pursue a career without knowing anything about Islam or the Muslim world. The entire school curriculum made no more than passing reference to Muslims in history, in connection with the Crusades, perhaps, or the fall of Constantinople to the

Susan L. Douglass is principal researcher and writer for the Council on Islamic Education, Fountain Valley, California. Her publications include a seven-part series of elementary teaching units on Muslim history (International Institute of Islamic Thought and Kendall/Hunt, 1994-96), Strategies and Structures for Presenting World History, *with Islam and Muslim History as a Case Study (Amana Publications, 1994), and teaching resources such as* Beyond a Thousand and One Nights: A Sampler of Literature from Muslim Civilization *(Council on Islamic Education, 2000),* Images of the Orient: Nineteenth-Century European Travelers to Muslim Lands *(National Center for History in the Schools, 1998), and (coauthored with Karima D. Alavi)* The Emergence of

DOI: 10.1177/0002716203255397

Turks. A smattering of innovative programs beginning in the 1960s introduced students to Indian, Chinese, or Mesoamerican culture at the secondary level, but Islam was excluded. Until the 1960s, few American universities offered courses on Asian, African, or Middle Eastern history. Consequently, most history and social studies teachers entered the profession possessing no systematic knowledge of these regions to pass on to youngsters, even if they might have been predisposed to do so. World history was defined largely as synonymous with the history of Greece, Rome, medieval Christendom, and modern Europe. Apart from small numbers of university specialists interested in Asia or Africa, the vast majority of Americans acquired what scant information they had on Islam and Muslims from television, films, advertising and print journalism.

Stereotypes and misrepresentations of Islam have been deeply ingrained in American culture. Just as the legacy of slavery has shaped popular images of Africa as a continent of heathen tribes and impenetrable jungles, so the western medieval and colonial heritage of hostility to Islam has underlain modern miseducation about Muslim society and history. In the mass media, cultural bias in coverage of the Muslim world has been so pervasive as to merit academic study (Friedlander 1981; Shaheen 1980, 1984). American public reactions to the Suez Crisis, successive Arab-Israeli conflicts, the Arab oil embargo, the seizure of the US embassy in Tehran, and the political activism of such leaders as Qaddafi, Hafez al-Assad, and Ayatollah Khomeini have shaped journalistic treatment of all Muslim societies. On the whole, teachers have been poorly equipped to examine critically the faulty assumptions and misunderstandings that infect this coverage. Consequently, the popular media's interpretation of Islam and the Muslim world has flowed freely into schoolrooms and then back out again to the wider public without being subjected to much critical analysis and correction.

The cultural and social conditions for learning about Islam and Muslims in American schools slowly began to change in the 1970s. This pattern is most conspicuous in the instructional materials that teachers and students read. To the extent that young Americans are exposed to interpretations of Islam and Muslim history independent of the mass media, they get them from the commercial textbooks that schools adopt, as well as from ancillary print and visual materials selected by teachers. Teachers also receive guidelines for instruction about Islam from national, state and local educational agencies. It is no exaggeration to affirm that commercial textbooks, together with the academic standards documents that

Renaissance: Cultural Interactions between Europeans and Muslims (*Council on Islamic Education, 1999*).

Ross E. Dunn is a professor of history at San Diego State University and director of World History Projects for the National Center for History in the Schools, University of California, Los Angeles. His books include Resistance in the Desert: Moroccan Responses to French Imperialism 1881-1912 *(University of Wisconsin Press, 1977) and* The Adventures of Ibn Battuta, a Muslim Traveler of the 14th Century *(University of California Press, 1990).*

NOTE: "Interpreting Islam in American Schools" by Susan L. Douglass and Ross E. Dunn first appeared in Hastings Donnan, ed., *Interpreting Islam* (London: Sage, 2002). Reprinted with permission.

most states have recently developed, are the intellectual tools with which most young Americans undertake any study of Islam and Muslim societies.

The Context: International Education in American Schools

. . . What and how much students learn about Islam in public (that is, publicly financed) schools depends generally on the commitment of their particular state or school district to what professional educators commonly call "global education." In other words, educational reformers who urge improved instruction about world societies, religions and history have not generally singled out Islam as deserving especially meticulous investigation. Rather, they have implicitly included Islam and Muslim regions in their calls for a more geographically and culturally inclusive curriculum and for world history education that is not limited to the Christian peoples of Western and Central Europe.

In the 1970s, media representations of Islam and Muslims were growing steadily more negative and cliché-ridden, owing to the fourth Arab-Israeli war, the oil embargo and the Iranian revolution. Ironically, it was in this same decade that educators built a persuasive case for improving global history, foreign language training and knowledge of world affairs. A number of developments inspired this campaign. One was recognition that political multipolarism, the proliferation of new nation-states, global economic complexities and the electronic revolution required that young Americans know much more about the world around them than they appeared to know. For global educators of the 1970s, the most compelling symbol of the new international order was the "big blue marble": the earth photographed from the moon. Planetary unity demanded an ecumenized citizenry.

Another factor in curriculum reform was the extraordinary growth of knowledge in history and the social sciences. This phenomenon included new research in American and European social history and an explosion of knowledge about African, Asian and Native American peoples. Internationally minded reformers called for inclusion of this new knowledge in school curricula. Surely, they argued, the American public recognized the importance of this research, because in 1958 it supported the National Defense Education Act, which generously funded scholarship on the history, economy and languages of developing countries. As the corpus of scholarly publication grew, school texts that limited African history to the story of European imperialism, had nothing to say about China before 1840, or took Muslim history seriously only up to the tenth century seemed behind the times.

A third impetus for curriculum reform was the rapidly changing demographic profile of the United States. As new immigration patterns of the 1970s and 1980s dawned in American social and political consciousness, educators called for a multicultural curriculum that would take into account the backgrounds and identities of schoolchildren freshly arrived from Guatemala, Vietnam, Iran and other corners of the world. Insistent demands for multicultural studies came from African American, Latino, Native American Indian and feminist organizations in the wake of the civil rights movement. Advocates argued that affirmation of the social and cultural identities of all groups within the American body politic required inclusion of their ethno-racial ancestors and women of all backgrounds—in the elementary and secondary curriculum alongside the traditional pantheon of white male luminaries.

Multiculturalist strategies for history education, which at first appeared sensible and pragmatic to most Americans, became increasingly controversial in the 1980s. This happened because multiculturalism entailed reconstruction of Americans' collective memory, as well as competition among numerous contending groups. Many educational leaders argued that the United States was religiously and ethnically the most diverse country in the world and should therefore put forth a model of social education that addressed the struggle for "a more perfect union." Recognizing various groups' roles in this common endeavor would encourage toleration and understanding among citizens. By contrast, traditionalists on the political right

Multiculturalists argued that the curriculum should include Islam and other world religions, not because world history does not make sense without them, but because Muslims and others now form significant groups within the American population.

asserted that from the founding of the nation to the 1960s, or, as Congressman Newt Gingrich put it, "from de Tocqueville to Norman Rockwell's paintings," all Americans shared and should appreciate a single consensual vision of the national past. These critics feared that critically analyzing and then rewriting the existing story of one nation, one people would ultimately tear the country apart (Bennett 1992; Gingrich 1995; Gitlin 1995; Nash et al. 1997; Schlesinger 1991). Public debates in the 1980s and early 1990s over proposals for improved international and world history education were less controversial because they touched nerves of national identity less than did debates over U.S. history.[1] Even so, leaders on the right worried that too much study of "other cultures" besides Europe and North America would discourage young Americans from embracing a common heritage and diminish their commitment to traditional western ideals and values.

Multiculturalists argued that the curriculum should include Islam and other world religions, not because world history does not make sense without them, but because Muslims and others now form significant groups within the American population. Though multiculturalists consistently ranged themselves against the dominance of western heritage studies, the issue of which ethno-religious communities should be included and how much time should be allotted to each took on a reductionist logic as immigrant constituencies of various origins multiplied and had to be accommodated in the curriculum the school year would have to be sliced into finer and finer bits. Critics on the right responded to this social calculus by crying, "Enough!" The curriculum is slipping into chaos, they warned. Fragmentation of social education, and ultimately the fabric of the nation, can be averted only by returning to the unitary narrative of western civilization, well spring of democracy and universal values. Room might be found for detailed study of a few "non-western cultures," but students who do not see themselves and their forebears reflected in the mainstream version of the past should just be grateful for the chance to adopt the western heritage as their passport to the American way of life. On the other hand, the educational community was quietly winning the struggle for a history curriculum that included more social history of minority groups, working people and women, and that had a more internationalist scope.

Another factor affecting coverage of Islam among world religions has been the successful movement to forge a national consensus on teaching about religion within a legal and social framework that honors religious diversity. After the Second World War, majority sentiment among educators favored the idea that ignoring religion in schools was a good way to avoid conflict. Consequently, religions were nearly written out of many social studies programs altogether. This trend contrasted sharply with the situation in post-war Britain, where religious education was the one subject required by parliamentary statute in all state-maintained schools.

Public discontent in the United States over this trend came to a head in the 1970s. Critics charged that school policies designed to avoid religious issues were based on faulty interpretation of the First Amendment to the U.S. Constitution, the clause forbidding establishment of religion. Gradually, consensus developed among historians, theologians and educators that study of religions is not only constitutional but highly desirable: it promotes understanding among peoples of diverse faiths and takes account of the significance of religion in history and culture. The most important factor in achieving consensus was the promulgation of classroom criteria that clearly differentiate between teaching religion and teaching about religion (Nord 1995; Piediscalzi and Collie 1977). A milestone in this project was the 1988 Williamsburg Charter, a public statement that set forth principles regarding the meaning and social implications of the First Amendment. Two U.S. presidents, two chief justices of the Supreme Court and over two hundred political and civic leaders attended the charter's signing ceremony. One of the signatories was Warith Deen Muhammad, a Muslim who had brought most of the body of the Nation of Islam into the fold of Sunni Islam (Haynes and Thomas 1994, 2:1-8).

Also in 1988, seventeen religious and educational organizations, including the Islamic Society of North America, approved guidelines that articulate the distinctions between "teaching religion" and "teaching about religion" (Haynes and Thomas 1994, 6:1, 10:1). In brief, these criteria require an academic, not devotional, approach to religious study, the goal being student understanding of various belief systems and their history. Schools may sponsor study, but not practice of religion; assign sacred scriptural texts as primary source readings and discuss them within appropriate historical and cultural contexts, but not simulate religious observances; and teach about various beliefs and practices, but not reduce them to sociological or psychological phenomena or explain them away as manifestations of "cultural relativism." The 1988 guidelines have become widely accepted in American schools, and they provide standards for assessing educational materials (Douglass 1994, 79-122). There is no doubt that since the 1960s American educators have made enormous progress in reintegrating education about religion into the schools (American Textbook Council 1994, 32-4; Nord 1995, 138-59; Douglass 2000, passim).

Islam in World History Textbooks

. . . The time an average student spends studying about Islam and Muslim history in American schools amounts to just a few weeks in twelve years of schooling. This instruction usually takes place in the context of world history or world culture/geography surveys between grades six and twelve (ages 11-18). The prescribed textbook sets forth not only the factual information students are expected to learn but also the conceptual framework by which they will relate history involving Islam and Muslims to the history of their community, their nation, western civilization and the world as a whole. Even the sequencing of chapters influences the degree to which students perceive Muslim history and culture either as a dimension of the human community to which young Americans belong or as antiquarian, essentialist and exotic. It guides students toward or away from the Orientalist paradigm, which disconnects the history of Islam from the Judaeo Christian tradition.

In the past thirty years, no publishing firm has marketed a textbook entitled "World History" that recounts exclusively the history of western countries. In the 1970s, publishers quickly hoisted sail to catch the breezes of educational ideology favoring internationalism and multiculturalism. Consequently, world history textbooks had to include more than cursory coverage of major African, Asian and American "cultures." Recent textbooks therefore reflect educators' demand for increased sensitivity to cultural or ethno-racial diversity, including all the cultural and religious traditions whose absence might be noticed by interested groups.

On the other hand, textbooks do not stimulate social studies educators to rethink conceptions of world history or to integrate the narrative along more global-scale lines. Texts have paid little attention to major processes of change that cannot be confined within the experience of one "culture group" or another. Such a unitary approach, what André Gunder Frank (1991) has called "humano centric history," might effectively satisfy the inclusionary demands of multiculturalists and at the same time be more relevant to the interactive, deterritorialized, globalizing world in which we live.

If a coherent and engaging paradigm for a more unified version of the human past is some years off, the victory of multiculturalist sentiment and the movement to include teaching about religion has meant that all widely used textbooks include lessons on Islam and Muslim history. This is also true of the eleven textbooks reviewed here, including their most recent revisions (Armento et al. 1991, 1994; Banks et al. 1997; Beck et al. 1999; Bednarz et al. 1997; Boehm et al. 1997; Ellis and Esler 1997; Farah and Karls 1997, 1999; Garcia et al. 1997; Hanes 1997, 1999; Krieger et al. 1997; Wallbank 1997). In these books the introductory chapter on Islam and early Muslim civilization appears somewhere in the second third of the book, but in varying juxtaposition to narratives on the breakup of Rome, the Byzantine empire and medieval Europe. This placement tends to inhibit attention to world-scale chronologies or connections among peoples across space.

For example, lessons on Byzantium usually end with the "fall" of Constantinople to the Ottomans in 1453, though introductions to Islam, the Abbasid Caliphate and the Turkic expansion may come much later in the book. Consequently, historical explanations of events in the Eastern Mediterranean–Black Sea basin that incorporate the entire aggregate of peoples and social forces of that region are sacrificed to coverage of Byzantine civilization as a self-contained phenomenon. In the older books, students may even study the Crusades and Italian maritime expansion in the Mediterranean before they read about Islam. In three of these texts the Ottoman Empire is sent into decline before students read about the early modern Iberian expansion or the development of bureaucratic states and religious wars in sixteenth-century Europe. Most books contain information about the growth of Muslim communities in East and West Africa, but not in connection with interregional factors of cause and effect (such as the maturing of the Indian Ocean commercial economy or long-distance gold trade). Rather, students read a chapter on "Africa," which includes paragraphs on Neolithic farming, Nok sculpture, Christian Ethiopia, Zimbabwe, Mali, Songhay, Benin, the East African city-states and various other subjects in a single sequence. This largely incoherent chapter, which in two of the eleven books is grouped in a unit with pre-Columbian America, meets the multicultural requirement for an answer to the question, "What was happening in Africa?" but leaves peoples of the continent disconnected from wider spheres of world-historical meaning.

Coverage of Muhammad, Mecca, and the Rise of Islam

The 1988 guidelines for teaching about religion challenge textbook authors to explain "how people of faith interpret their own practices and beliefs," using language that clearly attributes these tenets to their adherents. Though introductory chapters on Islam in the world history books have improved considerably in this respect over the past decade or so, most still fall short of the guidelines. Our review of these books reveals that Islam is generally not interpreted as its adherents understand it but as the editors believe will be acceptable to textbook adoption committees. Moreover, certain fundamental facts are ignored, while other details are selectively emphasized.

Critics on the right responded. . . . Fragmentation of social education, and ultimately the fabric of the nation, can be averted only by returning to the unitary narrative of western civilization . . . .

Most of the textbooks address similarities among Judaism, Christianity and Islam. They point out links, common elements or shared scriptural understandings that do not necessarily imply Islamic "borrowing" from the two antecedent faiths. Six of the eleven books include a few sentences on interfaith linkages, and three of them compare and contrast beliefs of the three religions fairly extensively (Armento et al. 1994; Ellis and Esler 1997; Hanes 1997, 1999). Most of the books explain that all three faiths share a common monotheism, that is, belief in "one God" (two books) or "the one true God" (two books). Four books declare that Muslims believe in "the same God" as Jews and Christians. Most of them define the Qur'an as a scripture held by Muslims to be the word of God. Seven of the books contain direct quotations from the Qur'an.

On the whole, however, the texts do not demonstrate continuity among the monotheistic faiths or invite direct comparison and contrast. Rather, coverage seems to compartmentalize the three traditions. Abraham, Jesus and Muhammad are characterized as founding figures, scriptures are mainly viewed as discrete, and the history of the traditions is described as following separate paths. Intentionally or otherwise, Judaism, Christianity and Islam each appear as autonomous cultural packages. Moreover, subtle and not so subtle statements denigrate or "explain away" Islam in clear violation of the 1988 guidelines.

In discussing major world religions (including Buddhism, Hinduism, Confucianism and others), the texts generally avoid references to continuities and connections that might cause discomfort to parents, officials or interest groups that oppose religious ecumenism in public schools. Typically, the books characterize each world religion in terms of a founder figure, an origins story, a holy scripture, a set of basic tenets and practices, and identification with a particular historical period or cultural tradition. This approach accords well with multicultural precepts, the aim being mainly to stress how these religions differ from one another and to encourage understanding and toleration of dissimilar worldviews and practices. These objectives are not undesirable, but they do produce troublesome byproducts. Treating each religion as a cultural entity situated within a bounded period of the past leads easily to its being perceived as homogeneous ("all Muslims do this, all Christians do that"), essentialized ("If you are a Muslim, here is how you will think and act") and made ahistorical ("Muslims think and behave this way because they have done so for fourteen hundred years").

Textbooks often use the term "new" to introduce the origins story of monotheistic belief systems. Five of the eleven books describe Islam as a "new" religion. In the other five books the implication is the same, since none of the texts make clear Muslims' belief that Islam is religion per se or that it is the faith of Adam and all the subsequent prophets, despite the clarity of Islamic doctrine on this point. In fact, Adam and Eve are virtually excluded from all world history texts, even as cultural referents. This primordial pair is presumably of little use when the aim is to dwell mainly on the dissimilarities among Judaism, Christianity and Islam. The origin of Islam, rather, is described not as Muslims would likely do it but in relation to two historical matrices that intersect in the seventh century. The first matrix is the society and culture of the Arabs. The second is the life, beliefs and actions of Muhammad as "founder" of Islam.

Explanations of Islam as the religion of the Arabs typically begin by describing an arid, harsh physical environment inhabited by nomadic camel herders, traders and townspeople. The Arabian Peninsula is depicted as a remote, bounded locality, and nomadic culture is made the root of Islam. Some texts use romantic language, as in this extreme example: "They lived as desert wanderers, these Arab traders. . . . Lacking a permanent home, these nomads, or wanderers, called themselves Arabs" (Armento et al. 1991, 50, 53). All of the books emphasize nomadism as a primary lifestyle of the Arabs, some older texts barely mentioning towns. Text illustrations offer images of modern Bedouin survivals and camels projected backward fourteen hundred years. The dry Arabian steppe is featured over arable or rainwatered terrain, and little reference is made to interactions between Arabs and peoples of Syria Persia, East Africa or India before Islam. Only three of the books mention Roman or Sassanid relations with Arabia or with the cities of Petra and Palmyra. Some books describe the symbiotic relationship between sedentary and nomadic Arab groups, and four mention, or illustrate on maps, the long-distance trade routes that crossed Arabia (Armento et al. 1991, 53; Banks 1997, 267).

Some accounts note a Jewish and Christian presence in Arabia but do not elaborate this point, except to set up the possibility that Muhammad, at home or on his trading journeys, might have become familiar with some of the beliefs of these faiths and subsequently absorbed their ideas into "his" new religion. The religious context of Arabia, and particularly of Quraish as the leading tribe, is described in most of the accounts as pagan, paganism being part and parcel of nomadic Arab culture. Two of the texts mention the hanif tradition, one with strong ethnic overtones: "Holy men known as *hanifs* denounced the worship of idols. They rejected Judaism and Christianity, preferring to find a uniquely Arab form of monotheism" (Farah and Karls 1997, 271). The origins of Islam and Judaism are characterized in distinct but also parallel ways — the story of an ethnic group's spontaneous departure from a prevailing polytheistic belief system.

Mecca is the focal point of information on the Arabian religious context, the texts typically describing it as an oasis on the trade route between the Arabian Sea and the major cities of the Middle East. Some texts explain that Mecca was becoming a more prominent commercial center around the time Muhammad lived. All the texts describe the town as the location of a religious shrine housing the Arabs' tribal idols. One book states that the Ka'ba was "like the Pantheon of Rome." Another asserts that Islamic monotheism in some way grew out of Meccan polytheism:

> Before Muhammad, the Bedouins and the townspeople worshipped hundreds of gods and spirits. Spirits called jinn were thought to reside in rocks and other natural objects. Mecca was the home of the most sacred of these rocks. The Black Stone of Mecca was [still is] embedded in the wall of a shrine called the Kaaba. . . . The Kaaba also contained idols representing 360 gods, including one deity called Allah. (Krieger et al. 1997, 186)

Most of the texts draw attention to the Black Stone as an important and distinctive Islamic symbol. Some books even suggest that it is an object of worship. The emphasis is on the stone's quaintness and obscurity—one of the icons that makes Islam "different"—rather than on its symbolism or spiritual meaning.

Seven of the eleven accounts acknowledge that Muslims believe in the prophethood of Jesus, Moses and Abraham, or mention the doctrine that the Qur'an completes the chain of earlier revelation. This information, however, is often placed in a concluding section on doctrines and practices, rather than being linked to the "origins story." Consequently, the texts consistently manage to gloss over the idea that Islam richly shared the Abrahamic tradition with Judaism and Christianity. Until the most recent editions of these textbooks, and then under repeated prodding from reviewers, discussions of Mecca's origins have excluded references to Abraham, Isma'il and Hajar. Two of the texts allude to the association between Abraham and the building of the Ka'aba, one book noting, slightly incorrectly, that "Muslims today believe [it] was built by the prophet Abraham" (Banks et al. 1997, 187; see also Ellis and Esler 1997, 256). Another text quotes the cry of modern pilgrims, "Here I am, O God, at Thy command!" but fails to note that this cry commemorates Abraham's reply to God's call as quoted in the Bible (Genesis, chapter 22). The same book states, following the account of Mecca's origins, that "Muslims believe that Abraham rebuilt the original Ka'abah," attributing this to Muhammad's saying, or to "tradition" (Armento et al. 1994, 184). None of the lessons mentions Abraham and Hajar's journey or their connection to Mecca. None of the texts explains Muslims' belief that Isma'il was the son Abraham was prepared to sacrifice, despite its importance in the major Islamic celebration 'Id al-Adha.

It is difficult to escape the conclusion that the world history textbooks deliberately downplay or exclude connections between Islam and Abraham in order to maintain neat partitions among the symbols, beliefs and major figures of the three monotheistic faiths. Muslim and other scholarly reviewers of textbooks have repeatedly argued that the Abrahamic tradition must be a part of the basic account of Islam's origins and practice. Many publishers continue to disregard the advice, though some new editions indicate that they are beginning to change. Indeed, the omission is made in clear violation of the 1988 guidelines for teaching about religion. Editors may have concluded that the textbook adoption market in politically and religiously conservative states will not bear ambiguity about Abraham's strict identification with the Old Testament and the Judaeo Christian tradition.

The second matrix for explaining the origins of Islam is the biography of Muhammad, which all the texts recount. None of these narratives expressly describes Qur'anic teachings on the beginnings of Islam. Explicitly or subtly, all the texts define Muhammad as the founder of Islam, just as Abraham, Jesus and the Buddha are cited as the founders of their respective religions. Four of the books apply the terms "founded" or "founder" to characterize Muhammad's career (Banks et al. 1997, 271; Bednarz et al. 1997, 78; Hanes 1997, 47; Wallbank et al. 1987, 34, 137). None of them gives a definition of the term, though many students would likely understand it as synonymous with "inventor," one who brings something into existence, rather than one who established something or caused it to be recognized and accepted. None of these books reflects the Muslims' belief that God is the source of revelation, rendering the concept of a founder extraneous, or the fact that Muhammad is not considered the first prophet of Islam. This presentation of a foregone conclusion about Muhammad's role belies an intrusion of irreligious assumptions that contradict the guidelines by failing to portray the views of believers neutrally. Similar assumptions apply to coverage of other religions in these texts.

The biographic details in the books are fairly uniform. Most make Muhammad's orphanhood, mercantile profession, and marriage to the older, wealthy Khadijah as the defining features of his life before prophethood. A few mention his reputation for honesty and simplicity and his dislike of the idols that the Arabs worshipped. All of the books relate the story of the cave of Hira' as the site where Islam "began." On this point, most of the accounts are quite authentic, though brief. They quote the Iqra' verses or the words of Jibril as recorded in the hadith, carefully attributing these statements to Muslim beliefs. Some of the books directly acknowledge Muhammad's prophethood, though others distance the reader from the concept that God conferred revelation on him. The distancing term of choice in some of the books is "vision," a word that is not used to describe revelation or contact with God in the discussions of early Judaism or Christianity. One account features multiple repetitions of the term.

At the age of 40, Muhammad's life was changed overnight by a vision. . . . In his vision, the angel Gabriel told him that he was a messenger of God. Muhammad had other visions in which Gabriel appeared with messages from Allah (Arabic for God). Who was Allah? Muhammad believed Allah was the same God worshipped by Christians and Jews. (Krieger et al. 1997, 186)

Islam, presented as separate from the Abrahamic tradition, is shown to have picked up similarities with Judaism and Christianity through alleged imitation or borrowing. Three of the accounts state unequivocally that the earlier traditions were absorbed into the later religion as doctrine. One of the statements is particularly crass, "explaining away" Islam in violation of the guidelines: "In his travels [Muhammad] met many people of different cultures, including Jews and Christians. These contacts were to have a profound influence on the religion that he later developed" (Wallbank et al. 1987, 188). Other statements imply unambiguously that Muhammad incorporated certain Jewish or Christian beliefs into Islam simply to fulfill some worldly motive. The decision to change the Kiblah (orientation when praying) from Jerusalem to Mecca for example, is often explained in such a way that divine revelation and political maneuver become thoroughly confused:

In Mecca, Muhammad had emphasized that he was continuing the tradition of Jewish and Christian prophecy. When Jewish tribes in the oasis of Medina refused to acknowledge him as a prophet, however, he began to move away from Jewish and Christian practices. Instead of facing the holy city of Jerusalem while praying, for example, in Medina a new revelation commanded the Muslims to face Mecca and the Kaʿabah instead. (Hanes 1997, 249)

Such simple turns of phrase can be loaded statements, because if true, they mean that the religion is false.

Though all of the texts present the Hijra in 622 CE as the consequence of intense persecution by the Meccans, the writers often portray Muhammad's acts in Medina as willful, artful, and calculated. A few of the accounts, after admitting that Muslims endured persecution in Mecca for their beliefs, imply that the subsequent battles were motivated by Muhammad's aggression. In these same texts, this theme forms the central motif in the account of Islam's spread. The newer texts tend to sidestep the issue of Muhammad's motives while he was in Medina, either by ignoring the question altogether or by invoking the young Muslim community's faith, effort and struggle without attempting to explain what happened between 622 and 630 CE The texts miss many opportunities to describe the dynamics of tribal relations or the events by which the Muslims checkmated the Quraish. Most accounts skip quickly to the victory over Mecca and the end of Muhammad's life.

The problem with these accounts is not that they characterize Muhammad as a political and military leader, which of course he was. The objection, rather, is that they present the conclusion that political willfulness, calculation, and purely personal ingenuity on Muhammad's part are sufficient explanations for these events, contradicting the Muslim belief that God guided His prophet to make particular decisions through revelation. Such assumptions or conclusions about Muhammad's motives are therefore anything but neutral. They support a between-the-lines interpretation that Muhammad's personality and willpower are sufficient to explain the origin of Islam, and that his assertion of will was not tempered by his principles or even linked in any way to actions by the opposing side, as in these examples:

> With Medina now under Muslim control, Muhammad set about conquering his enemies at Makka. For eight years, Muhammad's small forces fought the larger Meccan forces. (Armento et al. 1991, 60)

> From Medina, Muhammad began to convert the desert tribes. With their help, Muslims raided Meccan caravans. In 630, after several years of warfare, the people of Mecca gave in. (Hanes 1997, 249)

Another remarkable feature of the texts is that they relegate the community of Muslims and especially the companions (sahabah) to the background until after Muhammad's death. Apart from Khadijah, who acquires some vital dimension in the accounts, no figure in the community comes to life. The reader barely senses the presence of a community at all. The narratives focus relentlessly on Muhammad and his acts, decisions and responses. Because they must cover so much world history, textbook narratives on the early ummah are necessarily brief; but the uniformity of this approach across the whole range of books suggests a particular interpretative slant. Islam is portrayed as the work of a "great man" leading a group of murkily defined Others, rather than a community of real human beings expressing their Abrahamic faith and struggling to defend it.

Coverage of Muslim History after Muhammad's Death

Placement of basic Islamic teachings varies, but all of the books present the "five pillars" as the centerpiece of Islamic doctrine. The descriptions are fairly accurate, though simplistic. None of the texts situates the pillars in a cultural context, showing how each had strong communal aspects or gave rise to lasting institutions. They are described simply as ritual acts of worship in which the personal obligation predominates. Other frequently mentioned Muslim practices are dietary prohibitions, jihad, slavery, marriage, divorce, and male and female rights. Some of the older texts imply that Islam sharply circumscribes women's roles, but newer ones list their rights and duties, a few offering a more differentiated discussion within the context of the early centuries. All of the books indicate in some way that Islamic practice embraces a way of life. Indeed, some praise values such as racial equality, help for the poor, respect toward parents, and women's rights as compared with their status in other societies in these early centuries, though not today.

Descriptions of the Qur'an and hadith as the two major sources of Islamic knowledge and practice vary widely in quality. Many provide murky or inaccurate definitions of the hadith and the sunnah, and only one book describes how the Qur'an or the hadith were transmitted to succeeding generations. The most common statement regarding the transmission or transcription of the Qur'an is that it was essentially fragmentary and oral during Muhammad's lifetime, being collected into a book only some time after his death. An example of strategic omission, and one firmly grounded in the Orientalist sources, is the practice of telling readers that the Qur'anic suras were put in order (often described as longest to shortest) after Muhammad's death. The unsuspecting reader is not told about the important role of those who had memorized the Qur'an during Muhammad's lifetime, or the fact that most of the chapters were not revealed at a single time, so that ordering individual ayat (verses) into suras would have been by far the greater task. Readers are not encouraged to consider that if the ordering had not been accomplished before Muhammad's death, the chances of the community's agreeing on one version of the Qur'an would have been virtually nil. By subtle means, the textbooks give students the impression that the Qur'an's manifestation need not be considered as taking place any differently from the way the Bible and Torah evolved. Moreover, none of the text books notes the consensus of scholarship that the Qur'an remains essentially unchanged today.

The question of religious tolerance among Muslims is often portrayed in muddled terms that may reinforce cultural stereotypes. The topic is usually covered as part of the narrative on the spread of Islam. Some books describe the right of People of the Book to worship and live according to their religious law as an initiative of individual rulers rather than as a permanent feature of the Shari'a. Some narratives offer a confusing picture, indicating in some passages that other religions were tolerated, and in others that Muslims forced people to convert (Armento et al. 1991, 62, 64, 66, 80). Much of the mystification over the significance of both tolerance and jihad in the seventh and eighth centuries results from failure to draw a chronological or conceptual distinction between the rapid territorial expansion of the Muslim state, and the actual spread of Islam among populations within the state, a much slower process that went on for centuries. The texts rarely draw attention to Islam's minority status in the early period but rather conflate the military expansion of Arab armies and conversion to the faith as part of a single, conquest-driven process.

A broad interpretative thread in all the textbooks is use of the terms "Islam" and "Islamic." In most of the books the word is applied to all manner of historical phenomena: "Islamic empire," "Islamic trade routes," "Islamic art and science," "Islamic men and women" are some examples of usage suggesting that anything that happened in regions where Muslim populations predominated may reasonably be attributed to religion. This practice is of course fairly pervasive in the scholarly literature generally. None of the texts uses the term "Christian" in the same way. In critically reviewing textbooks, Muslim scholars have tried to impress on publishers the marked difference between Islam—its beliefs, practices, and principles and the shared cultural and historical experience of both Muslim believers and non-Muslims who lived among them. Marshall Hodgson defined societies where Muslims were preponderate and set the cultural and social style as

"Islamicate." In the most recent revisions, many textbook writers have acquiesced to using "Muslim" as an adjective to convey a similar meaning to Hodgson's term, "Islamicate" being too abstract or unconventional for young readers.

Particularly misleading is the practice of assigning religious causation to historical developments that must largely be explained in other ways. For example, a few of the texts attribute early scientific advances in Muslim culture almost exclusively to the need to pray at accurate times, establish the direction of prayer and *hajj* routes, calculate inheritances, and fulfill various other conditions of Islamic practice. Similarly, certain social attitudes and behavior toward women are framed in terms of Islam, though their roots may lie in cultural habits that contradict Islamic teachings. Some Muslim historical figures whom the texts characterize as villains are associated with Islam, but their acts are not dissociated from it. A good example of this type of mixed attribution of Islamic-ness is an account of Shah Abbas the Great of Persia that appeared in a draft textbook manuscript. In one sentence, the Shah is described as the greatest leader of his time, his law giving and his construction of beautiful mosques offered in evidence. On the next page, he is shown touring the bazaar in the interest of economic and social justice. Finding a butcher who cheated his customers, Shah Abbas is said to have ordered him roasted on his own charcoal spit. The inference? Such punishment was perfectly acceptable practice for "Islamic" rulers. Religious teachings regarding such behavior remained unexamined. Though the editors omitted the story in the published text, the incident illustrates how textbooks can be minefields of misinformation and Orientalist stereotyping. Obviously, the whole range of human flaws—militarism, greed, cruelty, corruption—are easy to find in the historical record of any religious or social group. The guidelines for teaching about religion, however, require that the distinction between the tenets of religions and the acts of their adherents be clearly made.

All of the books assign one chapter or less to the origins of Islam, with a second section on the high culture and achievements of Muslim civilization. They follow political developments from the early successors of Muhammad to the period of the *fitna* and the establishment of the Umayyad state, ending with an account of the Abbasid state. In all of the books, the lesson on Muslim history concludes with cultural events, usually under the rubric of the "golden age" of the Abbasid Caliphate and often including al-Andalus. For eras of world history following this "golden age," Muslims walk on to the textbook stage mainly in small roles in accounts of the European Crusades or West African empires and in larger roles in brief narratives of the Ottoman, Mughal and Safavid empires. Most texts still conform to the traditional Orientalist habit of defining Islam as the civilization of the Arabs of the "Near East," that is, the people and territory immediately next door to Christian Europe. As Marshall Hodgson pointed out many years ago, this tendency has detracted attention from the larger-scale patterns of conquest, trade, conversion, intellectual life and urbanization that characterized the emergence of Muslim civilization as a trans-hemispheric phenomenon between 1000 and 1500 CE (Hodgson 1974, 96-7).

A conspicuous aspect of the "golden age" approach in these books is a listing of each civilization's special achievements. Ever since the 1970s, when multiculturalist ethno-racial critics protested the common schoolbook claim that Europe possessed a monopoly on scientific genius, publishers have included mention of inventions and other achievements as standard fare in chapters on premodern, non-western cultures. The most commonly cited Muslim achievements are astronomical knowledge, medical advances, algebra, bank cheques and lateen sails, described in many books as "Arab." Some recent texts now credit India with "Hindi-Arabic numerals" and the concept of zero, though this innovation is said to have "passed through" the Muslim Middle East en route to Europe. Students are given a list of items "we" got from "them," but they learn little about the setting, circumstances or individuals involved in the transfer of ideas and technology. Because the multicultural model treats each civilization's narrative in isolation, few cross-references to seminal inventions and discoveries are made in adjoining chapters on Europe.

Muslim scholars, . . . questing for knowledge in fulfillment of one of the prime values of their own faith, achieved a sweeping new synthesis of the mathematical sciences between the eighth and the fourteenth century.

An exception is the transfer of Greek philosophical and scientific works to the West by way of Muslim scholars and their enlightened patrons. Revised 1999 editions of a few textbooks demonstrate change in this direction, including discussion of Ibn Rushd's influence on Thomas Aquinas's work, for example, in the chapter on medieval Europe (Beck et al. 1999, 351; Hanes 1999, 297). Even here, however, most of the books give students the impression that scientific and philosophical documents were merely refrigerated in Muslim libraries until rationalist European thinkers thawed them out. Reference to Muslims might appear in a chapter on the European High Middle Ages or Renaissance but not in connection with the Scientific Revolution. One text explains how Thomas Aquinas managed successfully to join faith with reason, while Muslim thinkers suppressed such investigation and chose faith—and consequently backwardness over progress—for all time (Hanes 1997, 258, 297-98, 402). The most recent revision omits these overt misconceptions (Hanes 1999, 258, 297). None of the books, however, has caught up with the current academic view that Muslim scholars, drawing on Indian, Persian and Greek sources and questing for knowledge in fulfillment of one of the prime values of their own faith, achieved a sweeping new synthesis of the mathematical sciences between the eighth and the fourteenth century.

Almost all the textbooks state or at least imply that the Muslim "golden age" exhausted itself by about the eleventh century; few texts acknowledge any contributions thereafter except tiles and tulips. One recent secondary book is a notable exception. The chapter on Islam closes with an essay entitled "Author's Commentary: A Dynamic Civilization," which notes how recent historical studies have revised the earlier notion of an Abbasid "golden age." Historians, concludes the essay, now acknowledge that Muslim civilization has played an expansive role in world history (Hanes 1997, 1999, 268). The essay is all the more remarkable because it is the only such feature in the book, and because no other publisher has seen fit to draw attention to such changes in the field of scholarship. More typical is the statement in one of the older texts: "Under the Abbasids, the Islamic Empire enjoyed a brief but brilliant golden age in arts and sciences" (Krieger et al. 1997, 192). Ironically, that statement is juxtaposed against an image of Muslim scholars using astronomical instruments, though the caption fails to identify the illustration as a seventeenth-century Ottoman miniature.

Most of the books have little to say about shifts in the direction of Muslim history, or about world-historical developments involving Muslims during the period from 1000 to 1500 CE. The most common exceptions are paragraphs on the Crusades, the Mongol Empire, the Ottoman state, West African empires and East African city-states. These topics appear discontinuously and incoherently in several different chapters, so that the dynamic growth of the Dar al-Islam, as well as the transformative actions of Muslims across the entire central two-thirds of the Afro-Eurasian region, is almost totally obscured. For example, the fourteenth-century Muslim traveler and legal scholar Ibn Battuta appears in almost all the recent texts. Publishers have recognized his story as a multicultural counterpoint to Marco Polo, a major icon in the conventional narrative of western exploration and discovery. The record of Ibn Battuta's adventures serves mainly as a source of interesting but brief primary document quotes inserted to describe one non-western region or another, often the sultanate of Mali. Writers miss the opportunity to show students how Ibn Battuta was a world-historical figure whose venture illustrates trans-hemispheric patterns of communication, trade, scholarship and urban cosmopolitanism. Rather, the point made is culture-specific: Europe has its Marco Polo, Islam has its Ibn Battuta, and in the newest books, China has its Cheng Ho (whose Muslim affiliation usually escapes mention). Only one book places these three travelers in the context of hemispheric trade during the period from 1000 to 1500 CE and exemplifies an integrated account of cultural transfers and interconnections (Boehm et al. 1997, 336-94).

The multiculturalist scheme of textbook writing rests on the premise that once a major civilization or region (Africa) has been introduced and its formative era and cultural achievements set forth, then not much more need be said about it, leaving the authors free to devote the second half of the book to the history of Europe and Europeans abroad. Developments in Muslim regions, or even more importantly the historical agency of Muslims in effecting world-scale change, earn virtually no discussion for the period from the sixteenth to the mid-nineteenth century. Most of the books offer lessons on the Ottoman, Safavid and Mughal states within a lesson on "three empires." Coverage is devoted almost exclusively to political developments, with cultural achievements confined to court-sponsored arts. The content is nearly always framed in terms of a telescoped sequence of rise, decline and fall, ending with a summary of events to the twentieth century. These lessons appear before the reader has been exposed to developments in Europe beyond the Renaissance. As a result, these states come across largely as historical artifacts lacking any concrete connection to main trends of the fifteenth through to the seventeenth century, such as demographic transformations, developments in the world economy, the rise of "gunpowder empires," advancements in bureaucratic organization, or the continuing growth of Islam in parts of Asia, Africa and Europe. Most of the texts present these Turkic-ruled states as the executors of a latter-day Muslim "golden age" centered on the early sixteenth century, exemplified by the Blue Mosque and the Taj Mahal as iconographic illustrations of high cultural achievement. Social history in these chapters is limited to portrayals of religious conflict between Hindu and Muslim, Turk and Christian, Sunni and Shi'a. This discussion lays the groundwork for later coverage of ethno-racial and religious animosities among nonwestern groups in the twentieth century.

Lessons on "three Muslim empires" bring to a close almost all discussion of Muslim peoples as independent agents of change in the modern world. Muslims appear haphazardly in chapters on the nineteenth century as minor characters in the drama of Europe's overseas enterprises and the "new imperialism." The texts describe nineteenth- and early twentieth-century colonialism in Africa and Asia in a generic way, with little specific focus on Muslim regions. Muslim personalities such as Selim III, Muhammad Ali, Abd al-Qadir or Samori Turé may appear as ethnic leaders, militant figures or political failures, but not as significant historical agents. European overseas expansion and settlement are seldom set in the context of change in the world economy or in terms of encounters among different peoples. Rather, paragraphs on Europe's imperial expansion take the form mainly of sentences with transitive verbs whose grammatical subjects are Portugal, Spain, France, Britain or some other European power.

In the chapters devoted to the twentieth century, Islam figures mainly in connection with the themes of world war, modernization, oil politics, women's roles and Islamic resurgence. Departing only modestly from the "sick-man-of-Europe" formulation of Orientalist inspiration, recent books usually relate the demise of the Ottoman Empire to the diplomatic and political arrangements that followed the First World War. The Arab-Israeli conflict is given considerable space in all the books, but the depth of coverage varies widely. A few newer texts provide some background on the Zionist movement, while others portray the creation of the Israeli state and the influx of Jewish settlers almost solely as a result of the Holocaust. The Mandate period is often mentioned only briefly as background to this issue. Coverage of the Arab-Israeli conflict is mainly a recital of wars and disturbances—including the Intifada—interspersed with milestones in the U.S.-sponsored peace process. The hallmark of these lessons is avoidance of thought-provoking questions and critical thinking, though coverage has become more even-handed in recent books.

As a world religion in the twentieth century, Islam comes across as a traditional holdover, as anti-western, and often as merely militant and extremist. By contrast, the westernizing secularization programs of Atatürk, Nasser, and the Shah of Iran are more positively portrayed. The status of women in contemporary Muslim societies is usually described within the framework of a dichotomy between tradition and modernity. The culture-bound structure of textbooks and the intellectual commitments reflected in the sources used by textbook researchers make interregional and global patterns of the century, especially since the Second World War, appear irrelevant to Muslim countries. The twin foci of Middle East conflict and Islam dominate coverage in such a way that they almost symbolize the entire region. Nor is the resurgence of Islam placed in comparative context with trends in Buddhism, Judaism and various Christian churches, despite the importance of these patterns as world-scale cultural developments.

Conclusion

... Though textbook authors and editors bring considerable good will to the process of portraying religions, many of them fail to paint a consistent or thoroughly accurate picture of the faith or its adherents' history. The willingness of publishers more systematically to seek the advice of knowledgeable reviewers is a hopeful sign. While significant improvement has taken place over the past decade or so, the most important condition for achieving further progress is to convince publishers and curriculum writers to adopt a humanocentric structure for world history that helps students understand particular peoples and religious traditions not as homogeneous and separate "worlds" of historical reality, but as embedded in contexts of change across time and space that ultimately include all of humanity. Another condition for progress is to raise the level of scholarship upon which textbook accounts are based, including critical use of primary source documents and fundamental understanding that all historical writing, including textbooks, inevitably involves interpretation, judgment, and social reconstruction of the past. Finally, if educators attend carefully to accepted standards for teaching about religion, more authentic and less confusing accounts will result. Textbook authors should write about Islam and all other faiths not to induce belief or disbelief, but to record as accurately as they can both the findings of modern scholarship and the understandings that Muslims have of doctrine, moral behavior, spiritual aspiration and the origins and establishment of their faith. The U.S. Supreme Court argued that the central reason for teaching about religion is that without it neither the long run of human history nor contemporary global culture will make sense to future generations. This is a simple and obvious proposition, but putting it to a full test will require abandoning the current habit in American education of essentializing religions, civilizations and ethno-racial groups in the interests of either patriotism or cultural self-esteem. A human-centered and dynamic global history in the schools holds some promise of counteracting and ultimately bringing to an end the caricatures and misrepresentations of Islam that flow from the popular media.

Note

1. An important exception has been public contention over Afrocentric claims of ancient Egypt's "blackness" and its primacy in the diffusion of ancient civilization (see Nash et al. 1997, 117-22).

References

Ahmad, I., Brodsky, Crofts and Ellis 1995. *World Cultures: A Global Mosaic*. Upper Saddle River, NJ: Prentice Hall.

American Textbook Council 1994. *History Textbooks: A Standard and Guide*. 1994—5 edn. New York: Center for Education Studies/American Textbook Council.

Armento, B.J., Kior de Alva, J.J., et al. 1994. *To See a World: World Cultures and Geography*. Boston: Houghton Mifflin.

Armento, B.J., Nash, G.B., et al. 1991. *Across the Centuries*. Boston: Houghton Mifflin.

Banks, J.A., et al. 1997. *World: Adventures in Time and Place*. New York: Macmillan McGraw-Hill.

Barlow, E. (ed.) 1994. *Evaluation of Secondary-Level Textbooks for Coverage of the Middle East and North Africa: A Project of the Middle East Studies Association and the Middle East Outreach Council*. 3rd edn. Ann Arbor, MI: Center for Middle Eastern and North African Studies, University of Michigan.

Beck, R.B., et al. 1999. *World History: Patterns of Interaction*. Evanston, IL: McDougal Littell.

Bednarz, S., et al. 1997. *Discover Our Heritage*. Boston: Houghton Muffin.

Bennett, W.J. 1992. The *De-Valuing of America: The Fight for Our Culture and Our Children*. New York: Summit Books.

Boehm, R.G., et al. 1997. *Our World Story*. Orlando, FL: Harcourt Brace.

Commonwealth of Virginia Board of Education 1995. *Standards of Learning for Virginia Public Schools*. Commonwealth of Virginia Board of Education.

Council on Islamic Education 1995. *Teaching About Islam and Muslims in the Public School Classroom*. 3rd edn. Fountain Valley, CA: Council on Islamic Education.

Department for Education, Great Britain 1995. *History in the National Curriculum*. January. London: Department for Education.

Douglass, S.L. 1994. *Strategies and Structures for Presenting World History, with Islam and Muslim History as a Case Study*. Beltsville, MD: Council on Islamic Education/Amana Publications.

———. 2000. *Teaching About Religion in National and State Social Studies Standards*. Nashville, Tennessee: Council on Islamic Education and First Amendment Center.

Ellis, E.G. and Esler, A. 1997. *World History: Connections to Today*. Upper Saddle River, NJ: Prentice Hall.

Farah, M.A., et al. 1994. *Global Insights: People and Cultures*. New York: Glencoe.

Farah, M.A. and Karls, A.B. 1997. *World History: The Human Experience*. New York: Glencoe/ McGraw-Hill.

Frank, A.G. 1991. A plea for world system history. *Journal of World History* 2: 1-28.

Friedlander, J. 1981. *The Middle East: The Image and the Reality*. Berkeley: University of California Press.

Garcia, J.R., et al. 1997. *The World and Its People*. Parsippany, NJ and Needham, MA: Silver Burdett Ginn.

Gingrich, N. 1995. *To Renew America*. New York: HarperCollins.

Gitlin, T. 1995. *The Twilight of Common Dreams: Why America is Wracked by Culture Wars*. New York: Henry Holt.

Hanes, W.T. III (ed.) 1997, 1999. *World History: Continuity and Change*. Austin, TX: Holt, Reinhart and Winston.

Haynes, C.C. and Thomas, O. (eds), 1994. *Finding Common Ground*. Nashville, TN: Freedom Forum First Amendment Center, Vanderbilt University.

Heywood, A. 1997. *The Muslim Way*. London: Hodder and Stoughton.

Hodgson, M.G.S. 1974. *The Venture of Islam*. Vol. 1. Chicago: University of Chicago Press.

Krieger, L.S., Neill, K. and Jantzen, S.L. 1997. *World History: Perspectives on the Past*. Lexington, MA: D.C. Heath.

Nash, G.B., Crabtree, C. and Dunn, R.E. 1997. *History on Trial: Culture Wars and the Teaching of the Past*. New York: Alfred A. Knopf.

National Center for History in the Schools 1994. *National Standards for World History: Exploring Paths to the Present*. Expanded edn. Los Angeles: University of California, Los Angeles.

——— 1995. *National Standards for History*. Basic edn. Los Angeles: University of California, Los Angeles.

New Hampshire Department of Education 1997. *New Hampshire K-12 Social Studies Curriculum Framework*. New Hampshire Department of Education.

Nord, WA. 1995. *Religion and American Education: Rethinking a National Dilemma*. Chapel Hill: University of North Carolina Press.

Pankhania, J. 1994. *Liberating the National Curriculum*. London: Fahner Press.

Piediscalzi, N. and Collie, WE. (eds), 1977. *Teaching About Religion in Public Schools*. Niles, IL: Argus Communications.

Schlesinger, A.M. Jr 1991. *The Disuniting of America: Reflections on a Multicultural Society*. New York: W.W. Norton.

Shaheen, J.G. 1980. *The Influence of the Arab-Stereotype on the American Children*. Washington, DC: American-Arab Anti Discrimination Committee.

———. 1984. *The TV Arab*. Bowling Green, OH: Bowling Green State University Popular Press.

Wallbank, T.W., et al. 1987. *History and Life: The World and Its People*. 3rd edn. Glenview, IL: Scott, Foresman.

Islam and Muslims in the Mind of America

By
FAWAZ A. GERGES

This article examines the ways in which the U.S. public, media, interest groups, and foreign-policy elites, including Congress, influence the making of American policy toward political Islam. It focuses on the domestic context of American politics, especially the linkages among society, politics, and government. Following an analysis of the historical, cultural, and current political developments that inform Americans' attitudes on Islamic resurgence, this article argues that contemporary security and strategic considerations, not merely culture and ideology, account for America's preoccupation with Islamism.

Keywords: Middle East policy; public opinion; security; terrorism; stereotyping

Accceding to the eminent French scholar Maxime Rodinson, "Western Christendom perceived the Muslim world as a menace long before it began to be seen as a real problem" (1987, 3). This view is echoed by the late British historian Albert Hourani, who argued that Islam from the time it appeared was a problem for Christian Europe. Looking at Islam with a mixture of fear and bewilderment, Christians could not accept Muhammad as a genuine prophet or the authenticity of the revelation given to him. The most widely held belief among Christians,

Fawaz A. Gerges holds the Christian A. Johnson Chair in International Affairs and Middle East Studies at Sarah Lawrence College. He was educated at Oxford University and the London School of Economics and has previously been a research fellow at Harvard and Princeton universities. He is the author of The Superpowers and the Middle East: Regional and International Politics, *and his articles have appeared in several of the most prestigious journals in the United States, Europe, and the Middle East. Gerges is researching a follow-up book tentatively entitled* The Islamists and the West: Ideology versus Pragmatism?

NOTE: "Islam and Muslims in the Mind of America" by Fawaz A. Gerges was originally published in *America and Political Islam: Clash of Cultures or Clash of Interests?* (London: Cambridge University Press, 1999). Reprinted with the permission of Cambridge University Press.

DOI: 10.1177/0002716203255398

noted Hourani, was that "Islam is a false religion, Allah is not God, Muhammad was not a prophet; Islam was invented by men whose motives and character were to be deplored, and propagated by the sword" (1991, 7–8, 10). As the thirteenth-century Crusader and polemicist Oliver of Paderborn claimed, "Islam began by the sword, was maintained by the sword, and by the sword would be ended" (Daniel 1960, 127).

Centuries of interaction have left a bitter legacy between the world of Islam and the Christian West, deriving largely from the fact that both civilizations claim a universal message and mission and share much of the same Judeo-Christian and Greco-Roman heritage (Rodinson 1987, chapter 1). Separated by conflict and held together by common spiritual and material ties, Christians and Muslims presented a religious, intellectual, and military challenge to each other (Hourani, 8; Esposito, 25; Lewis, 89). The nineteenth-century German thinker Friedrich Schleiermacher argued that Christians and Muslims were "still contending for the mastery of the human race" (*The Christian Faith* 1928, 37). However, this portrait of unremitting Western-Muslim hostility is misleading. The pendulum of Western-Muslim relations has swung between rivalry/confrontation and collaboration/accommodation. Although conflict arising from cultural, religious, and ideological factors has been the norm, realpolitik and interstate interests have also shaped the relationship between the two civilizations.

Historically, Western powers felt no qualms about aligning themselves with Muslims against fellow Christian powers. Throughout the nineteenth century, the French, British, and Germans joined ranks with the Ottoman Muslims against their European opponents. Despite its inherent weakness, the Ottoman empire was an integral player in the inter-European balance-of-power system. The destruction of the empire in 1918 occurred as a result of its joining Germany in World War One against the Allied powers. The British and French also entered into alliances with Arab Muslims to counterbalance the Ottomans and Germans. Between 1919 and the 1950s, European interest in Muslim societies was more influenced by the requirements of colonial policy and decolonization than by religious sentiment (Fuller and Lesser, 19–20). British and French officials collaborated with whomever was willing to serve their interests, whether Islamist or nationalist. Political control and economic expediency, not religious or cultural variables, were the driving forces behind the Near East policy of Paris and London.

Unlike Europe, the United States did not engage in any prolonged, bloody encounters with Muslim states and societies. It never directly ruled over Arab and Muslim lands or developed Europe's complex imperial system. In the first part of the twentieth century, the United States, unrestrained by colonial and geographic requirements, established dynamic and cordial relations with Arabs and Muslims, who viewed America as a progressive island amid European reaction.

Even after it became a superpower, the United States was much less constrained by colonial, historical, and cultural factors than its European counterparts. Political and economic control have been the driving force behind Washington's Near East policy. Furthermore, in contrast to the Europeans, Americans do not appear to be concerned about the presence of a large immigrant Muslim community in their midst; in the United States, it is the Hispanics who are the focus of assimilationist fears concerning the "immigrant threat" (Halliday, 182–84). Although the religious and intellectual challenge of Islam continues to seize the imagination of many people in the United States, it is the security and strategic implications of the mass politics of Islam that resonates in the minds of Americans . . . .

A Brief Historical Sketch

The emergence of a U.S. global role after World War Two dramatically changed the foreign-policy elite's attitudes toward rapid sociopolitical change in the third world. Although U.S. officials in the first part of the twentieth century supported the concept of self- determination and opposed the perpetuation of colonialism, in the second half of the century they looked with suspicion on populist third-world movements and ideologies. By the late 1940s, containing the perceived Soviet threat and ensuring the security of pro-Western Middle Eastern regimes was higher on the U.S. foreign-policy agenda than coming to terms with third-world nationalisms. True, some officials in the Truman, Eisenhower, and Kennedy administrations advocated an alliance between the United States and local nationalist forces to contain Soviet expansionism, but they were a minority (Acheson 1969; Gerges 1995, 1–20).

The scale became weighted in favor of those U.S. policy advocates who mistrusted third world nationalists and suspected them of being allied with the Soviets in order to overthrow the existing regional order. On the whole, between 1955 and 1970, U.S. policy in the Arab world was framed in opposition to secular Arab nationalism led by President Gamal Abdel-Nasser of Egypt. In U.S. eyes, revolutionary nationalism, not political Islam, represented a security threat to the pro-Western, conservative monarchies. Symbolic representations, such as "extremist" and "satellite," were applied to radical nationalist elements throughout the Middle East (Russell 1989, 86, 142; Cottam 1990, 267–70).

Ironically, in the 1950s and 1960s, the United States hoped to construct an alliance of Islamic states with sufficient prestige to counterbalance "godless communism" and the secular nationalist forces as represented by Nasser. In the mid-1960s, one of the reasons for the deterioration of U.S.-Egyptian relations was Nasser's belief that President Lyndon Johnson had encouraged King Faisal ibn 'Abd al Aziz of Saudi Arabia to sponsor a holy Islamic alliance to isolate Egypt in the Arab world (*Foreign Relations of the United States, 1955–1957*). As importantly, in the 1950s and 1960s, the United States exhibited an ambivalent and hostile attitude toward revolutionary Arab nationalism, whereas the politics of Islam was seen to serve Western interests. In the struggle between Islam and populist nationalism, the United Stated sided with the former. American policy was driven by Cold War considerations and strategic calculations, not by history, culture, or any intrinsic fear or hatred of Islam.

The U.S. perception of the Middle East situation and the nature of the threat, however, underwent a radical shift in the 1970s, largely because of the explosion of

Islamic politics onto the scene. Regional events—the 1973 Arab-Israeli war, the consequent Arab oil embargo, and the 1978–79 Iranian revolution and ensuing hostage crisis—shocked many American officials into viewing Islam as a threat to Western interests (Esposito, 17; Cottam, 277; Said, x). Again, security calculations, along with related political and economic concerns, lie at the heart of the shift in U.S. perceptions.

Whereas Nasser had fought the 1967 Arab-Israeli war under the ideological banner of Arab nationalism, his successor, Anwar Sadat, could be argued to have fought the 1973 Ramadan War under the banner of Islam. The new Islamic asser-tiveness was accompanied by the OPEC oil boycott, which triggered escalating oil prices and inflation and, according to Zbigniew Brzezinski, Assistant for National Security Affairs for President Jimmy Carter, "had an acute effect on the daily life of virtually every American; never before had we felt such an impact in peacetime" (Brzezinski, 532–33). For the first time since the dawn of colonialism, the U.S. government had to contend with a return of the power of Islam (Esposito, 17; Said, x, 33).

Furthermore, in the early 1970s, Libyan President Mu'ammar al Qaddafi employed Islamic symbols to legitimize his populist rule and to assist revolutionary movements throughout the Middle East and Africa. According to a U.S. official who served then as an ambassador to a Central African state, American diplomats, whether in Washington or Africa, became preoccupied with Qaddafi's proclama-tion of an Islamic state, his promotion of Islam as the religion of the "black man" in Africa, and his spreading of Islamic "radicalism" and "terrorism" worldwide. They feared that radical Islam was moving southward to engulf the whole desert. In fact, Qaddafi's Islamic campaign influenced U.S. official perceptions of Islamic revival-ism long before the Iranian revolution.[1]

The Impact of the Islamic Revolution in Iran

Of all the regional developments in the 1970s, the Iranian revolution and the hostage crisis had the most formative effect on the U.S. foreign-policy establish-ment and the public's views of Islam. Accustomed to seeing their country as the most democratic and generous, Americans were shocked to hear Iran's Ayatollah Khomeini call it the "Great Satan." As one U.S. official noted in 1995, "the Iranian experience extremely conditioned U.S. thinking about the violent, anti-American nature of fundamentalist Islam."[2]

Never before had the U.S. government been subjected to this type of confronta-tion, which it deemed uncompromising and "irrational." President Carter described his negotiations with the Iranian mullahs thus: "We are dealing with a crazy group" (Sick, 277). By holding 52 Americans hostage for 444 days, Khomeini's Iran inflicted daily humiliation on the United States, eliciting an intense degree of hostility and a deep and unfamiliar sense of powerlessness. Even-tually Iran became a national obsession (ibid., 275).

As with Arab nationalism in the 1950s and 1960s, such labels as "extremist," "terrorist," and "fanatical" were applied to the Islamic revolution in Iran (Carter 1982, 12, 499, 506). In a poll of mainstream Americans conducted in 1981, 76 percent of the respondents indicated that they had a low opinion of Iran; 56 percent cited "hostage" as coming to mind when Iran was mentioned; after "Khomeini," "oil," and "the Shah," many also cited "anger," "hatred," "turmoil," and "troublesome country."[3] Iran's brand of revolutionary Islam appeared to be on a collision course with the United States. It was under the impact of the Iranian revolution, then, that Islamism replaced secular nationalism as a security threat to U.S. interests, and fear of a clash between Islam and the West crystallized in the minds of Americans.

Although the religious and intellectual challenge of Islam continues to seize the imagination of many people in the United States, it is the security and strategic implications of the mass politics of Islam that resonates in the minds of Americans.

One of the major reasons given by former U.S. Secretary of State Cyrus Vance for his objection to a military mission to rescue American hostages in Iran was the specter of an Islamic-Western war: "Khomeini and his followers, with a Shi'ite affinity for martyrdom, actually might welcome American military action as a way of uniting the Moslem world against the West" (Vance 1983).

On a practical level, the real damage to the U.S. presence in the Middle East was the loss of the Shah of Iran, a staunch American ally whom President Richard Nixon and his Secretary of State, Henry Kissinger, once counted on to police the Persian Gulf.[4] Meanwhile, U.S. fears that the Iranian revolution would destabilize neighboring Gulf states were reinforced by Khomeini's vehement denunciation of Saudi Arabia and other Gulf monarchies as "un-Islamic" and his disdainful characterization of their ties with the United States as "American Islam." He further called on the Gulf countries to "follow the path of revolution, resort to violence and continue their struggle to regain their rights and resources" (Cottam, 276; Goldberg 1986, 242–43).

Events of the following years only sharpened U.S. fears of the power of resurgent Islam. At the end of 1979, Saudi Arabia, America's most valued client in the Middle East, was rocked by the two-week takeover of the Grand Mosque at Mecca by rebellious Islamists who denounced the Saudi royal family's monopoly on political and economic power. The 1981 assassination of President Sadat of Egypt and the bloody attacks against U.S. personnel and installations in Lebanon, Kuwait, and elsewhere, heightened U.S. officials' concern over the export of Iranian "fundamentalism" (Brzezinski, 484, 533; Esposito, 21–22).

The Islamic revolution in Teheran colored U.S. attitudes toward political Islam. The result, note some observers, is that Iran's brand of revolutionary Islam overshadows much of the current U.S. debate about the rise of political Islam. The above-mentioned poll shows the extent to which Islam and Iran were linked for mainstream Americans. When asked what comes to mind when the words "Muslim" or "Islam" are mentioned, the two most common responses, which received an equal number of votes, were "Muhammad" and "Iran" (Slade, 148–49, 157).[5] The politics of Islam were confused with the politics of Iran, with many Americans unable to imagine relations with an Islamist government in which the United States was not cast in the role of the Great Satan (Fuller and Lesser, 22). "U.S. perceptions of the Iranian experience," conceded one State Department official, "were projected to our experience of the Arab Middle East" (continuation of interview, 27 May 1995).

The Fear of Terrorism and Its Effects on U.S. Policy

Terrorism has emerged as one of the most important political issues in the United States. Some U.S. officials and commentators have linked it to Islamic militancy, particularly to Iran. Secretary of State Warren Christopher said that "Iran is the foremost state sponsor of terrorism in the world," representing "one of the greatest if not the greatest threats to peace and stability in the region" (Christopher, 1995, 1).

Unlike its European partners, the United States virtually escaped the horror of terrorism during the Cold War era. This is no longer true. Terrorists now select targets in the United States itself. A series of explosions shattered America's peace of mind, raising fears about further attacks and calls for punitive action against the perpetrators and their alleged state sponsors. Perhaps the most memorable of these instances was the February 1993 World Trade Center bombing, as a result of which ten Muslims were convicted of waging "a war of urban terrorism" against America and of plotting to kill President Mubarak (*New York Times*, 2 October 1995). The subsequent trial—coupled with the revelations that the perpetrators had conspired to carry out a bloody campaign to destroy the United Nations and other New York landmarks and force the United States to abandon its support for

Israel and Egypt—deepened Americans' fears about the security threats associated with Islamists.

According to Professor Richard Bulliet of Columbia University, Americans have quite readily accepted the notion that acts of violence committed by some Muslims "are representative of a fanatic and terroristic culture that cannot be tolerated or reasoned with." Bulliet expressed his fear that the United States might be witnessing the growth of a new kind of anti-Semitism, based not on theories of Semitic race but on Islam: "We at some point are going to reach a threshold where people no longer need evidence to believe in a generic terrorist threat from religious Muslim fanatics" (Bulliet 1994, iii, see also 4, 11).[6] Some observers added fuel to the fire by warning of the existence of a coordinated international network of "Islamic terrorist" groups through out the United States with its guns aimed against Western interests (PBS, 21 November 1994).

Although no evidence emerged about the existence of an "Islamic Internationale," the World Trade Center bombing did considerable damage to the Muslim image and presence in the United States. As James Brooke commented in the *New York Times*, by linking "Muslims and domestic terrorism in the minds of many Americans," the bombing made Muslims vulnerable targets for racism and political discrimination (*New York Times*, 28 August 1995). For example, in the first of two surveys on American attitudes toward Islam taken just after the bombing, more than 50 percent of the respondents said that "Muslims are anti-Western and anti-American."[7] In the second survey, the respondents were asked to rate various religious groups from favorable to unfavorable; Muslims topped the most unfavorable list.[8]

The explosion in New York City had broader implications for U.S. foreign policy. As a senior State Department official remarked, the World Trade Center bombing represented a setback to the Clinton administration's efforts to define a positive, accommodationist policy toward Islam and because of its link to the growth of Hamas on the West Bank and Gaza, of Hezbollah in Lebanon, and of other militant Islamists in Sudan and Algeria (continuation of interview, 27 May 1995). Some Middle Eastern regimes, particularly Israel and Egypt, sought to capitalize on the bombing by pressing the United States to support them further in the struggle against local Islamist opposition groups. In the United States, those subscribing to variations of the clash-of-civilizations hypothesis used it to advocate a tough policy toward Islamists.

Therefore, the World Trade Center blast provided confrontationalists in the United States and overseas with a golden opportunity to lobby the Clinton administration to formulate a forceful policy toward Islamists. Before the dust had settled in the April 1995 bombing of a federal building in Oklahoma City, some of the media's "terrorism experts" were linking Arabs, Muslims, and Middle Easterners to the explosion.[9] A *New York Times* commentator asserted that although the Oklahoma massacre was the work of American terrorists, most "other attacks against Americans came from the Middle East" (*International Herald Tribune* 26

April 1995). The evidence supplied to the FBI and the State Department shows otherwise, however.

According to FBI sources for the year 1993, radicals with Muslim backgrounds were responsible for the World Trade Center bombing; as reprehensible as it was, this was the only violent act committed domestically by people from Muslim background for that year. In contrast, the FBI reported the following terrorist attacks during the 1982–1992 period: Puerto Ricans, 72 attacks; left-wing groups, 23 attacks; Jewish groups, 16 attacks; anti-Castro Cubans, 12 attacks; and right-wing groups, 6 attacks (FBI 1995). An analogous pattern can be seen with regard to anti-U.S. terrorist attacks abroad: In 1994, 44 took place in Latin America, 8 attacks in the Middle East, 5 in Asia, 5 in Western Europe, and 4 in Africa (U.S. Department of State 1995, 67).

. . . Iran's brand of revolutionary Islam overshadows much of the current U.S. debate about the rise of political Islam.

It was within this charged atmosphere that Muslims in the United States became targets of harassment after the 1995 Oklahoma City bombing. In the following three days, more than 200 violent attacks against Muslim Americans were recorded (Brooke 1995). The Oklahoma City bombing further exposed the latent negative imagery that characterizes and colors U.S. public views of Islam and Muslims. It also showed the media's willingness, when it comes to Arabs/Muslims, to abandon their principle of fair and accurate reporting. It should be stressed that the media's history of stereotyping Arabs/Muslims taps into a receptive political culture that feels skeptical and ambivalent about unfamiliar "others."

In moments of crisis, confrontationalists gain the upper hand and dominate the airways and media. It is at such a juncture that Americans' attitudes toward Arabs/Muslims harden. Several of the polls mentioned above confirm this reality. Instead of treating terrorist incidents as an aberration, some commentators exaggerate their importance and portray them as part of a systematic war against Western civilization. Instead of seeing terrorism for what it really is—a desperate and isolated act—these observers view it as part of a pattern of anti-Westernism and anti-Americanism. In this sense, terrorism has further poisoned Americans' perceptions of Islam and Muslims.

To his credit, President Bill Clinton was quick to caution against leaping to conclusions in the face of initial accusations that the Oklahoma City bombing bore the marks of Middle East–style terrorism: "This is not a question of anybody's country of origin. This is not a question of anybody's religion. This was murder, this was evil, this was wrong. Human beings everywhere, all over the world, will condemn this out of their own religious convictions, and we should not stereotype anybody" (*New York Times* 21 April 1995).

Nonetheless, a direct consequence of the Oklahoma City bombing was the new lease on life given to the 1995 Omnibus Counterterrorism Act, passed by the House of Representatives and the Senate and signed into law by President Clinton. One of the law's provisions allows the U.S. government to use evidence from secret sources in deportation proceedings against aliens suspected of terrorist involvement, without having to disclose the sources of the information. A second provision allows the government to deport aliens who have made charitable contributions to organizations branded as terrorist by the authorities.[10]

Despite the denials by Clinton administration officials, observers note that this counterterrorism legislation was partly aimed against "Mideast terrorism," a synonym for "Islamic terrorism" (Lewis 1995).[11] At a Senate hearing in April 1993, Acting Coordinator for Counter-Terrorism Laurence Pope noted, "Twenty years ago in the Arab world, secular nationalism was the preferred ideology. And so it was the ideology that terrorists adopted as a cover for their actions. Increasingly, it's Islamic ideology, extremist Islamic ideology, which provides that cover" (*Hearings* 1993). An American official who works on terrorism at the National Security Council (NSC) corroborated this interpretation: In U.S. eyes, Islamists have replaced pan-Arab nationalists as the driving force behind terrorism in the Middle East; today terrorism is basically religiously inspired, lacking any nationalist inspiration (interview 29 March 1995).[12]

Although in agreement with the above assessment, two other NSC officials remarked that while individuals and states who practice terrorism do not represent Islam, they might succeed in doing so if the United States comes to be seen as anti-Islamic. Although the Clinton administration, according to these officials, does not accept the claims of the Israeli, Egyptian, and Algerian governments that the mainstream Islamist opposition fosters terror, the administration fails to distinguish effectively between Islamists who participate in the political field and those who carry out violence. The blurring of the lines between the two groups may explain the ambiguity in U.S. policy statements on political Islam (interview 29 and 30 March 1995).

The Role of the Media

Although observers of the American scene agree that the mainstream media's negative news coverage of Islam and Muslims conditions public perceptions of and attitudes toward Muslim societies, they find it difficult to delineate the complex relationship between the mainstream media and U.S. policy. To some, the "dominant media are themselves members of the corporate-elite establishment," so fundamental tensions between the foreign-policy and media establishment seldom arise (Herman 1993, 25; Sigal 1973, 42–49). In this view, a number of factors contribute to the situation, including the media's overwhelming dependence on government sources for their news stories; the lack of public contestation of government propaganda campaigns; and the government's use of ideological weapons like anticommunism, a demonized enemy, or potential national-security threats. Only rarely do offbeat reporters dare to challenge the fundamentals of official policy (Sigal, 42–60; Herman, 26).

A slightly different perspective holds that the media subordinated their usual interests to Cold War requirements in the name of national security, resulting in a "journalism of deference to the national security state."[13] In the aftermath of the Cold War, Leon Hadar argues that the media, following either their own initiatives or the footsteps of the foreign-policy elite, speculated about the rise of new global enemies. This explains, in his view, the press's fascination with political Islam and Iran, or what he calls "the Green Peril" (Hadar, 64).

In this view, the press is not part of the foreign-policy establishment but has been a willing participant in foreign-policy making insofar as it helps "establish the boundaries within which policy can be made" (Dorman, 289, 291). This is evident in the case of Islam and of Muslims, who are often portrayed in a negative light, thus placing them at a considerable disadvantage in U.S. public opinion. Although mass public opinion may not count much in the foreign-policy equation, elite opinion does; decision makers and members of the policy elite get much of their information from the press (ibid., 297).[14] Both views—on the one hand, of the media as a supportive arm of the state, whose negative coverage of Islam reinforces and reflects U.S. policy makers' fears and prejudices, and on the other, of the press as an indirect participant in the process insofar as it contributes to the climate in which policy is made—have this in common: the notion that the media's coverage of Islam and Muslims sheds much light on the making of U.S. policy.

Many U.S. officials deny any connection between the negative portrayal of Islam in the press and American policy. Assistant Secretary of State Robert Pelletreau, for example, sharply criticizes the media for coverage that fosters the tendency, both in scholarship and public debate, to equate Islam with Islamic fundamentalism and extremism, but he does not consider the impact of the media's coverage on foreign-policy making, or vice versa (Pelletreau, 2). Other U.S. policy makers, while agreeing that a flow of information exists on a multiplicity of levels between nongovernmental and policy-making agencies, assert that the desire of American decision makers to exchange ideas with the media and academia depends on the situation and the need for crisis management. A comment frequently heard is that U.S. officials base their decisions on their perception of national interests (Interview, NSC officials, Washington DC, 30 March 1995).

Moreover, the way in which U.S. officials define national interests is related closely to their perception of reality, and policy is not formulated in a vacuum. The role of Congress, the media, and domestic considerations all drive policy and influence opinion within the foreign-policy community, especially on such issues as the Arab Israeli conflict and political Islam (Interview, State Department Official, Washington, DC, 30 March 1995). Samuel Lewis, former director of the State

Department's Policy Planning Staff, acknowledges that the media's hostile cover-age of "extremist Islamist groups" reinforces American perceptions of Islam, thus complicating the task of U.S. policy makers (Interview, Chicago, 23 February 1995). In fact, the media's negative portrayal of Muslims, according to the poll mentioned above, has become an integral part of public consciousness (Slade, 144–45, 147, 150, 157).

The Role of Israel and Its Friends

According to the Israeli writer Haim Baram, since the collapse of the Soviet Union and the fall of communism, Israeli leaders have attempted to enlist the United States and Europe in the battle against Islamic fundamentalism, portraying it as a larger-than-life enemy; their strategy is designed to convince U.S. public opinion and policy makers of Israel's continuing strategic value in a turbulent world (Baram 1994, 8). A cursory review of Israeli politicians' pronouncements illustrates their strongly held views on political Islam. For example, as early as 1992, former President Herzog of Israel told the Polish Parliament that "the disease [of Islamic fundamentalism] is spreading rapidly and constitutes not only a danger to the Jew-ish people, but to humanity in general (Reported in the *Guardian*, 19 June 1992).

In his frequent visits to the United States, the late Prime Minister Yitzhak Rabin often referred to the "Islamic peril" in order to convince Americans that "Iran is posing the same threat as Moscow in the good old days." Visiting the United States a few days after the World Trade Center bombing, Rabin told Clinton that "funda-mentalism incited by Iran is infiltrating Muslim institutions in the West" (Reported in the *New York Times*, 23 February 1993). Shimon Peres, Israel's former Prime Minister, was more direct: "After the fall of Communism, fundamentalism has become the greatest danger of our time." In another speech, Peres recalled the evils of Nazism and Communism, warning against the current threat of Islamic fundamentalism, which, he said, "like Communism adopted the Machiavellian slo-gan that ends justify means, which is a license to lie, to subvert, to kill" (Sciolino 1996; Purdum 1995).

According to Elaine Sciolino and to Arthur Lowrie, a former State Department official, the momentum of the anti-Islamist campaign in the United States suggests that "the purported views of Israeli leaders have been increasingly adopted by their supporters and others" (Sciolinio, ibid.; Lowrie, 212). To what extent have Israeli views and lobbying efforts influenced the making of American policy on political Islam? Most U.S. officials at the State Department and NSC deny any Israeli con-nection in the formulation of American policy toward Islamists, contending that U.S. national interests are the sole consideration (Interview, member of U.S. State Department's Policy Planning Staff, Washington, DC, 27 March 1995; Interview, NSC official, Washington, DC, 30 March 1995).

There were, however, a few dissenters. According to a senior State Department official, "we are very much influenced by the Israeli definition of Islamists. To a large extent, Israel's view of Islamic fundamentalism shapes U.S. officials' perception of this phenomenon" (Princeton interview, 27 May 1995). Another member of the State Department noted that U.S. suspicions of Islamists is related partly to the latter's opposition to peace with Israel, a very important foreign-policy issue to the United States (Interview, member of State Department's Policy Planning Staff, 27 March 1995).

President Clinton's vow before the Jordanian parliament in October 1994 to resist "the dark forces of terror and extremism" is a clear reference to militant Islamist groups, who oppose the Arab Israeli peace process (Clinton 1994, 1). The impression conveyed by American officials is that the various U.S. administrations are well aware and responsive to Israel's definition of its security in the Middle East. Arthur Lowrie, a former State Department official, asserted that Clinton's dual-containment policy of Iran and Iraq and his subsequent 1995 announcement of a complete trade embargo on Iran were influenced by the lobbying efforts and political pressures of Israel's friends (Lowrie, 215–16). Similarly, the author of an article in the *Economist* suspected Clinton of relying partly on information supplied by Israel to appear personally tough on the issue of the day—terrorism (6 May 1995).[15] The *Economist*'s point raises critical questions about the input of interest or pressure groups in shaping policy.

Congressional Influence on U.S. Foreign Policy

More than anywhere else in the world, Congress plays a determining influence on U.S. policy toward the Middle East, having emerged as a decisive player in the last three decades. Although the President has much more leverage and leeway in that geopolitical sphere. Clinton administration officials whom I interviewed expressed their anxiety over the general atmosphere in the Congress. One NSC official remarked that Congress and the public hold "simplistic" and "prejudiced" views toward Islam and Muslims (Interview, Washington, DC, 29 March 1995). According to Elaine Sciolino of the *New York Times*, "In the absence of other compelling threats to the United States, Islamic radicalism has also seized the imagination of some in Congress" (21 January 1996).

A cursory review of statements by some Congressmen reveals deep concern about security threats associated with the rise of political Islam. These include terrorism, acquisition of nuclear weapons, and the security of Israel and the Gulf states. Former House Speaker Newt Gingrich has called for "a coherent U.S. strategy for fighting Islamic totalitarianism" (cited in Sciolino, ibid.). Congressional hearings are rife with questions about the threat that Middle East and Islamic "terrorism" pose the United States and Western security.[16] Representative Ileana Ros-Lehtinen accused the State Department of underestimating the uniform nature of "Islamic extremism" and of stressing instead its diffused and eclectic character; in her view, Islamic groups represent a monolithic movement "sworn to fight the Great Satan America for global supremacy of Islam" (ibid.).

The chairman of the House International Relations Committee, Benjamin Gilman, a New York Republican, attacked the Clinton administration's terrorism policy as ineffectual, using the security lapse in the World Trade Center bombing to demand radical changes in U.S. immigration laws: "We cannot continue to allow these people [Omar Abd al-Rahman and his followers] into our country. The laws are wrong. We've allowed our U.S. to become a dumping ground for hoodlums, terrorists, and people who are not interested in any good. They merely wish to destroy the U.S. I demand changes be made, and tomorrow will not be too soon."[17]

. . . In U.S. eyes, Islamists have replaced pan-Arab nationalists as the driving force behind terrorism in the Middle East; today terrorism is basically religiously inspired, lacking any nationalist inspiration.

As to whether Congress has had an impact on the U.S. approach toward political Islam, some American officials have intimated that public and congressional perceptions of Islam do influence and set constraints on the policy-making process.[18] Demonizing Islamic movements, asserted a retired State Department official, complicates the United States' ability to adopt a constructive policy (Lowrie, 215). One striking example is the Clinton administration's approval in December 1995 of $20 million in covert aid to change the Iranian government or at least change its behavior (Weiner 1996).

Speaker Gingrich, an ex-officio member of the House Intelligence Committee and the one who appoints its Republican members, used his great influence over government spending to force the President to fund the "secret mission," despite administration and CIA convictions that there is no viable alternative to the current Iranian leadership and that such a policy is likely to fuel paranoia and anti-Americanism in Teheran (ibid.). The result is that Congress tied the President's hands, forcing him to pursue a course of action that might have negative repercussions on U.S. interests. By agreeing to Gingrich's "secret" plan, however, Clinton bowed to Congress's wishes on an important foreign-policy issue. This is one way in which Congress indirectly participates in the making of U.S. foreign policy.

Another example was President Clinton's decision in April 1995, first announced before the World Jewish Congress, to impose a total trade embargo on Iran in an effort to change its behavior. Again, the President's decision, as Todd S. Purdum of the *New York Times* remarked, was suffused with domestic politics. Clinton administration officials were fully aware that anti-Iranian sentiment was building "in the Senate and House, with some proposals aimed at punishing not only Iran but also foreign companies that continue to do business with it. By acting on its own, the White House hoped to seize the initiative and preempt the tougher anti-Iran Republican bills in the Congress" (Purdum 1995).

The President's actions, however, did not mollify influential Senate and House members. During a Capitol Hill hearing, Representative Gilman took credit for the additional sanctions against Iran by reminding Assistant Secretary of State Pelletreau that the administration would not have acted without sustained pressure from Congress. Gilman also stated that the Congress views the economic ban as "the beginning and not the end of the process," demanding a showdown with foreign companies that continue to trade with Iran (Hearings 1995, 4). Again, the President bowed to Congress's wishes when the latter passed legislation stipulating the punishment of any foreign company that invests $40 million or more in the Iranian oil and industrial sector. Despite warnings by Europe and Japan, Clinton signed this new legislation into law in summer 1996.

The effective pressure applied by Congress on the Clinton administration shows the extent of the legislative influence in foreign-policy making. The case of Iran is just one example in which Congress keeps a watchful eye on foreign policy as well as participates in its formulation.

Notes

1. According to a State Department official, interviewed in Princeton, NJ, 27 May 1995.

2. Ibid. Other U.S. officials, with whom John Esposito had met, saw political Islam through the prism of Iran/Khomeini. See Esposito (1983, 9).

3. A corrective should be added here. This poll showed that the low opinion of Arabs/Muslims was largely due to Americans' perception that Arabs/Muslims are hostile to the United States and are anti-Christian. This finding indicated that Americans' low opinion of Muslims was a merely defensive reaction. For example, of those Americans who believed that Muslims have a respect for Christianity, 45.8 percent had a high opinion of Arabs. Conversely, of those respondents who believed that Muslims have contempt for Christianity, a mere 28.5 percent had a high opinion of Arabs. See Shelley Slade (1981, 148–49, 158).

4. Kissinger said that "Iran under the Shah, in short, was one of America's best, most important, and most loyal friends in the world." See his *White House Years*, p. 1262.

5. Iran's hostility toward the United States, coupled with its emphasis on the conflict between Islam and the West, only furthers the perception of Arabs and Muslims as inherently anti-Christian and anti-Western.

6. Ironically, Medieval Christians believed that Muslims were barbaric, irrational creatures, and Muhammad's actions were often invoked as examples of how Islam encouraged and praised the use of force. Jacques de Vitry wrote the "use of force in Islam derived from Muhammad's own practices." Cited in Daniel (1960, 123–24).

7. Survey sponsored by the National Conference on Inter-Group Relations, the Ford Foundation, and the Joyce Foundation. It was conducted between 6 and 8 August 1993 by L. H. Research. The number of the respondents was 2,755.

8. Survey sponsored by the American Muslim Council and conducted between 16 and 23 March 1993 by the John Zogby Group International. The number of the respondents was 905.

9. CBS Evening News, 19 April 1995; New York Times, 20 April 1995; Washington Post, 20 April 1995; International Herald Tribune, 26 April 1995. See also Lowrie (1995, 213).

10. For background on the complex issues surrounding the counterterrorism legislation, see relevant articles in the New York Times, 21, 24, 27, 29, and 30 April; 8 and 9 June; and 3 October 1995.

11. Some Zionist groups said that they hoped the measure could be used to dry up potential contributions in the United States for terrorist groups like Hamas, as reported in the New York Times, 21 April 1995.

12. A similar point was made by the State Department senior official interviewed 27 May 1995 in Princeton.

13. William Dorman (1993, 289, 291–92, 304) qualifies this assertion by noting that the U.S. media are not a monolith and that journalists do not take their orders from official Washington; rather, "the effects of ideology work their way more through cultural osmosis than directive."

14. On another level, Andrea Lueg (1995, 7, 15–16) asserts that the Western media's portrayal of Islam is the primary source for Western conception of Islam and the region in which it predominates.

15. See "Punishing Iran," in The Economist, 6 May 1995. In testimony before the House Foreign Affairs Committee in July 1993, Undersecretary for Global Affairs Timothy Wirth acknowledged that the U.S. government has "very, very good contacts with Israeli intelligence," especially on Iran. See U.S. House of Representatives, The Future of U.S. Anti-Terrorism Policy, p. 23.

16. According to Representative Ileana Ros-Lehtinen, chairperson of the Subcommittee on Africa, "Islamic militancy has emerged as one of the most serious threats to Western security." See Ros-Lehtinen (1995, 1).

17. According to Gilman, this quote was taken from a letter sent to him by one of his New York constituents, as cited by Laurence Pope during the hearing of the Senate Judiciary Committee," Terrorism and America, p. 2. Gilman's point should be interpreted in a larger context. The World Trade Center and Oklahoma City bombings, noted sociologist Nathan Glazer of Harvard, focused attention in the United States on "Middle Eastern immigrants and their political activities, though the guilt [in the case of Oklahoma] turned out to lie elsewhere." See Nathan Glazer (1995).

18. Nevertheless, these diplomats have insisted that U.S. policy toward political Islam is ultimately determined by official statements, which are not "sensational and panic-stricken." Drawn from interview with a member of the State Department's Policy Planning Staff, Washington, DC, 27 March 1995; and interview with an NSC official, Washington, DC, 30 March 1995.

References

Acheson, Dean. 1969. Present at the creation: My years in the State Department. New York: New American Library.

Baram, Haim. 1994. The demon of Islam. Middle East International. 2 December.

Brooke, James. 1995. Attacks on U.S. Muslims surge even as their faith takes hold. New York Times. 28 August.

Brzezinski, Zbigniew. 1983. Power and principle: Memoirs of the national security adviser, 1977-1981. New York: Farrar, Straus and Giroux.

Bulliet, Richard W. 1994. Under siege: Islam and democracy. Occasional Papers 1. New York: The Middle East Institute of Columbia University.

Carter, Jimmy. 1982. Keeping faith: Memoirs of a president. New York: Bantam Books.

Clinton, William J. 1994. Remarks by President Clinton to the Jordanian Parliament. The White House, Office of the Press Secretary, Amman, Jordan, 26 October.

Cottam, Richard W. 1990. U.S. and Soviet responses to Islamic political militancy. In Nikki R. Keddie and Mark J. Gasiorowski. eds. Neither East nor West: Iran, the Soviet Union and the United States New Haven, CT: Yale University Press.

Daniel, Norman. 1960. Islam and the West: The making of an image. Edinburgh: Edinburgh University Press.

Der Christliche Glaube. 1842. In Samliche Werke,. 2nd ed. vol. 3. pt 1. Berlin. *The Christian Faith*. 1928. English trans. Edinburgh.

Dorman, William. 1993. Media, public discourse, and U.S. policy toward the Middle East. In H. Amirahmadi. ed. *The United States and the Middle East: A Search for New Perspectives*. Albany: State University of New York Press.

Esposito, John L. ed. 1983. *Voices of resurgent Islam*. New York: Oxford University Press.

———. 1992. *The Islamic threat: Myth or reality?* New York: Oxford University Press.

Federal Bureau of Investigation. 1995. Terrorist research and analytical section.

Foreign Relations of the United States, 1955-1957: Arab-Israeli Dispute, January 1–July 26, 1956. 1989. vol. 15. Washington, DC: U.S. Government Printing Office.

Fuller, Graham E., and Ian O. Lesser. 1995. *A Sense of siege: The geopolitics of Islam and the West*. Boulder, CO: Westview Press.

Gerges, Fawaz A. 1995. The Kennedy Administration and the Egyptian-Saudi conflict in Yemen: Co-opting Arab Nationalism. *Middle East Journal* 49 (Spring):1-20.

Glazer, Nathan. 1995. Debate on aliens flares beyond the melting pot. *New York Times*. 23 April.

Goldberg, Jacob. 1986. The Shi'i minority in Saudi Arabia. In Juan K. I. Cole and Nikki R. Keddie, eds., *Shi'ism and social protest*. New Haven, CT: Yale University Press.

Hadar, Leon. 1994. The media and Islam. In Bulliet.

Halliday, Fred. 1985. *Islam and the myth of confrontation: Religion and politics in the Middle East*. London: I. B. Tauris.

Hamroush, Ahmed. 1984. *Qissa taura 23 Yulio: Karif Abdel-Nasser* [The story of 23 July revolution: The autumn of Abdel Nasser], vol. 5. Cairo: Maktaba al-madbuli.

Herman, Edward S. 1993. The media's role in U.S. foreign policy. *Journal of International Affairs* 47, no. 1 Summer.

Hourani, Albert. 1991. *Islam in European thought*. New York: Cambridge University Press.

Interview, Washington, DC, 29 and 30 March 1995.

Kissinger, Henry. 1979. *White House years*. Boston: Little, Brown & Company.

Lewis, Anthony 1995. This is America. *New York Times*. 1 May.

Lowrie, Arthur L. 1995. The campaign against Islam and American foreign policy. *Middle East Policy* 4, nos. 1 and 2 (September).

Lueg, Andrea. 1995. The perception of Islam in Western debate. In Hippler, Jochen, and Andrea Lueg. eds. *The next threat: Western perceptions of Islam*. Boulder, CO: Pluto Press, 1995.

Pelletreau , Robert. 1995. Symposium: Resurgent Islam. Op-ed article. *New York Times*. 2 October.

Purdum, Todd. 1995. Clinton to order a trade embargo against Tehran. *New York Times*. 1 May.

Rodinson, Maxime. 1987. *Europe and the mystique of Islam*. Trans. by Roger Veinus. London: I. B. Tauris.

Rosenthal, A. M. 1995. Things America can do to curtail terrorism, domestic and foreign. *New York Times* column. Reprinted in the *International Herald Tribune*, 26 April.

Ros-Lehtinen, Ileana 1995. The threat of Islamic extremism in Africa. Prepared Testimony of the Honorable Ileana Ros-Lehtinen, Committee on International Relations, U.S. House of Representatives, *Federal News Service*, 6 April.

Russell, Francis J. 1989. U.S. policies toward Nasser. Paper delivered by the Secretary of State's Special Assistant on 4 August. In *Foreign Relations of the United States: Suez Crisis, 1956*, vol. 16. Washington, DC: U.S. Government Printing Office.

Said, Edward. 1981. *Covering Islam: How the media and the experts determine how we see the rest of the world*. New York: Pantheon Books.

Sciolino, Elaine. 1996. The red menace is gone. *New York Times*. 21 January. Week in Review section.

Sick, Gary. 1985. *All fall down: America's fateful encounter with Iran*. London: I. B. Tauris.

Sigal, Leon V. 1973. *Reporters and officials: The organization and politics of newsmaking*. Lexington, MA: D.C. Heath.

Slade, Shelly. 1981. The image of the Arab in America: Analysis of a poll on American attitudes. *Middle East Journal* 35 (Spring).

U.S. Department of State. 1989. Memorandum of conversation. Subject: U.S.-UAR Relations, 17 September 1965. In The Lyndon B. Johnson National Security Files, the Middle East: National Security Files, 1963-1969. Frederick, MD: University Publications of America. Reel 8 of 8.

U.S. Department of State. 1995. *Patterns of global terrorism*. Washington, DC: U.S. Government Printing Office.

U.S. House of Representatives. 1995. Hearing with Defense Department personnel; House International Relations Committee; International Economic and Trade Subcommittee—U.S. sanctions on Iran. *Federal News Service* 2 May.

U.S. House of Representatives. 1993. *The Future of U.S. Anti-Terrorism Policy*. Hearing Before the Subcommittee on International Security, International Organizations, and Human Rights of the Committee on Foreign Affairs, 13 July. Washington, DC: U.S. Government Printing Office.

U.S. Senate. 1994. *Hearing of the Senate Judiciary Committee. Terrorism and America: A Comprehensive Review of the Threat, Policy, and Law*, 21 April 1993. Washington, DC: U.S. Government Printing Office, Serial No. J-103-9.

Vance, Cyrus. 1983. *Hard choices: Critical years in American foreign policy*. New York: Simon & Schuster.

Weiner, Tim. 1996. U.S. plan to change Iran leaders is an open secret before it begins. *New York Times*. 26 January.

White Slaves, African Masters

By
PAUL BAEPLER

This article introduces narratives by American captives during and after the Barbary Wars (1801-1805, 1815). Set against a background of American imperial pursuits, the accounts reveal the hypocrisy and double-standards common among early Americans (who accepted black slavery in America but reacted strongly against the idea of white slaves in the custody of the North African Muslims). The accounts were largely works of fiction, but were accepted as fact. Arabs are presented as bizarre, gruesome, and primitive. The stories were sold by the thousands, so members of almost every household were exposed to these negative portrayals.

Keywords: Barbary captivity; North African history; slavery; race; stereotypes; narratives; eighteenth-and nineteenth-century America

Although Barbary privateers began to take North American colonists as early as 1625, the written genre of the Barbary captivity narrative didn't flourish in the United States until the early nineteenth century. During these years, several survivors of Barbary captivity published immensely popular accounts of their suffering in North Africa, and the story of Barbary captivity became a common tale that involved hundreds of men and women, invoked public subscriptions for ransom funds, forced the government to pay humiliating tributes in cash and military

Paul Baepler is a lecturer for the Continuing Education Department of the University of Minnesota. He received his Ph.D. in English from the University of Minnesota. His book White Slaves, African Masters (University of Chicago Press, 1999) *explores the little-known Barbary captivity narrative. His related article, "The Barbary Captivity Narrative in American Culture" will be published in* Early American Literature *this fall (39.1). Two of his short nonacademic pieces appear in* Thus Spake the Corpse: An Exquisite Corpse Reader 1988-1998 *(ed. Andrei Codrescu, Black Sparrow Press, 1999).*

NOTE: "White Slaves, African Masters" by Paul Baepler was originally published in *White Slaves, African Masters: An Anthology of American Barbary Captivity Narratives* (University of Chicago Press, 1999). Reprinted with the permission of the University of Chicago and Paul M. Baepler.

DOI: 10.1177/0002716203255399

arms to African rulers, stimulated the drive to create the U.S. navy, and brought about the first postrevolutionary war. Among other things, these narratives reveal some of the earliest impressions Americans had of Africa at a time when the issue of chattel slavery in the United States increasingly divided the country. The account by Captain James Riley, for example, sold nearly a million copies, and Abraham Lincoln's biographers credit Riley's narrative for helping to change the future president's stance on slavery.[1]

The word *Barbary*, which Europeans consistently used to mark the Maghreb or North Africa, evolved out of a place that Mary Louise Pratt has called a "contact zone," "a social space where disparate cultures meet, clash, and grapple with each other, often in highly asymmetrical relations of domination and subordination"; and consequently the word has a particularly revealing etymology.[2] While its derivation is uncertain, there are several likely theories. Most scholars agree that *Barbary* originated from the Greek *barbaros* or the Latin *barbarus* to signify non-Greeks or non-Romans, and thus uncivilized populations. Lotfi Ben Rejeb remarks that "the Arabs in the seventh century are reported to have used . . . *berbera* (to mumble) in reference to the natives' unintelligible language."[3] Similarly, Paulo Fernando de Moraes Farias suggests that *Barbara* was a categorical label used to denote African tribes who opposed communication and trade and thus "whose nature was like the nature of animals. . . . Behind such classifications is the notion of trade as a metaphor for language or vice versa, i.e., the symbolic equivalence of the exchange of messages and the exchange of goods."[4] So it is not strange that Saint Augustine, himself a native of North Africa, used the term *barbarus* to refer to his fellow natives who resisted Roman rule and Christianity. If we accept this derivation, then from virtually the beginning of its use in Africa, *Barbary* had not only pejorative connotations but a sense of commercial and cultural resistance; Africans were called "barbarians" because they refused to communicate and were reluctant to cooperate. The Barbary corsairs themselves originated in part from the need to defend North Africa from European aggression.[5]

Although the Barbary captivity narrative in English existed for more than three centuries, it caught the attention of United States readers primarily during the first half of the nineteenth century. Between John Foss's 1798 narrative and the numerous printings of James Riley's 1817 account, which continued to be offered into the second half of the century, American publishers issued over a hundred American Barbary captivity editions. The rise in popularity of the Barbary captivity narrative coincides not only with the growing number of U.S. sailors held in North African bondage during these years, but also with the resurgent demand for Indian captivity tales during the revolutionary period.[6] At the time of the War for Independence, colonists increasingly viewed themselves as captives to a tyrannical king rather than as protected royal subjects, and Indian captivity narratives, like those of John Williams and Mary Rowlandson, enjoyed a renewed readership after having been out of print for decades. In 1779, *The Narrative of Colonel Ethan Allen's Captivity*, the first American prisoner-of-war account, modeled after tales of Indian captivities, sold nearly twenty thousand copies in its first year of publication and then appeared in nineteen editions between 1779 and 1854. The fact that in 1776, Jefferson,

Franklin, and Adams proposed a captivity motif for the Great Seal of the United States in which Israelites are depicted safely crossing the Red Sea as their Egyptian captors drown illustrates the pervasiveness and propagandistic power of the collective captivity metaphor.[7]

After the Revolution, Indian captivity narratives still proved immensely popular, though the frontier where abductions took place gradually receded to the West. By the 1830s, the attitude in New England toward American Indians had slowly shifted from overt hatred to a sentimental interest as the threat of local Indian wars faded with the decline in population and presence of Indian nations in the East. Those who once represented a menacing savage presence now symbolized America's national heritage, or at least an antiquarian relic from the bloody past.[8] The new Barbary captives, on the other hand, were almost exclusively mariners from the East, and while North Africans posed no personal threat to the safety of the average citizen, they greatly disrupted shipping. The Revolutionary War had put the new nation at odds with its former trading partners—Britain (including the British West Indies), France, and Spain—and while the Baltic states and the Orient seemed like promising new markets for American merchants, the increasingly important trade was based in the Mediterranean. At a time when overseas trade was becoming more important for the United States, the North African corsairs promised to become a greater problem and, at the same time, a test of the country's diplomatic and military independence. While the removal of Indian nations from the East seemed exemplary of American vitality and domestic strength, Barbary captivity represented public humiliation and signaled the new nation's vulnerability in international affairs. The Tripolitan War, which resulted in the forced release of over three hundred U.S. captives, however, would change this perception, and North Africa would eventually become a world theater where Jefferson's navy could flex its new muscle.

The development of the Barbary captivity narrative also coincides with the dramatic increase in the number of black slaves held in the United States. The one million Africans and African-Americans owned by whites in 1807 doubled in just thirty years. At the same time, the country witnessed the emergence of an organized antislavery response as the abolitionist movement matured and promoted the cause of free blacks through the American slave narrative. More than one hundred former slaves wrote of their flight to freedom before the end of the Civil War, speaking for the tens of thousands who made that same perilous journey. Many of these accounts, like the 1845 *Narrative of the Life of Frederick Douglass, an African Slave*, quickly became bestsellers and endured as testaments to the cruelty of slavery, testaments that continue to inform American culture.

While the question of black slavery increasingly divided the country, white intellectuals also battled over the concept of "race" as a significant category. Racial theorizing had been spurred on by advances in the study of heredity as well as by the rise of the study of physiology and physiognomy, what was then known as the science of ethnology. (Ethnology; a "new" science, rose, in part, from the epistemological rupture that Michel Foucault has traced to the seventeenth century, wherein discrimination or difference took precedence over similitude and resemblance in modes of scientific inquiry.[9]) No immediate consensus emerged on the question of whether race was a biological determinant or whether it was a rhetorical ordering principle imposed on people to make sense of economic and political hierarchies. Dana Phillips has suggested that the central paradox concerning the nineteenth century's notion of race was that "everything seemed to be racial, or 'racy'; but (especially in polyglot America) no one thing by itself seemed to be 'race.' "[10] It is within this unstable context—a time in which the question of black slavery increasingly divided the country and contesting theories of race competed for dominance—that the Barbary captivity narrative grew in prominence.

As a form of exploration and adventure literature, the narrative of captivity in Africa translated local issues of race and slavery onto a removed setting that had been made exotic by European lore about the "Dark Continent." Typically, the account is structured as a journey that through some ill fortune—kidnapping, war, shipwreck—leads the narrator off her original course and into Africa and consequently into slavery. The narrator recounts her discoveries, once she has been captured, much as an explorer does, noting the lay of the land, the climate, the natural resources, and particularly the manner and appearance of her barbarous captors as well as the other Africans she encounters. While eventually presented as the ostensible memoir of an American in Africa, the narrative actually stages a larger drama about racial struggle.

For nineteenth-century readers in the United States, the plight of the captive in Africa appeared to transpose the traditional roles of black and white bodies. Karen Sanchez-Eppler has argued that in general the black body was marked as subservient. For instance, Dr. Samuel Cartwright, a southern physician writing in midcentury, suggested that the slave's body was particularly suited for genuflection: "in the anatomical conformation of [black slave's] knees, we see 'genu flexit' written in his physical structure, being more flexed or bent than any other kind of man."[11] In this case, the white doctor inscribed ancient Latin upon the "physical structure" of the black slave to illustrate white superiority. In the captivity narrative, however, such a formula does not obtain. White bodies no longer possess full authority; indeed, they be come the property of their captors and subservient to black desire.[12] These texts thus create a site in which once-privileged white flesh can suddenly be whipped, maimed, coerced into labor, traded for other slaves, exchanged for money, and even killed. At the same time, the captive-narrator never loses control over the range of narrative strategies he can deploy to tell his story. He engages in what James Clifford has called a kind of "cultural *poesis*" or "the constant reconstitution of selves and others through specific exclusions, conventions, and discursive practices."[13] Thus while the status of black and white bodies actually changes, the capacity to "decode and recode" the situation remains under the control of the white narrator.[14]

White slaves actually suffered greatly in captivity and were forced to live under humiliating conditions, eat rancid food, sleep with droves of vermin, bake under the desert sun, strain at the galley oars, cart massive boulders, and face inhuman punishments. The captive life, for some slaves, could be infernal; yet it would be wrong to equate it with institutionalized chattel slavery in the United States. Barbary slaves were not born into captivity or stolen from their homeland; they ventured into danger as travelers engaged in mercantile or military enterprises. Furthermore, many white captives were eventually ransomed and liberated from their slavery. They could return to the intact family and social structures into which they were born.[15] Freedom for a slave in America, however, most often disrupted family ties, relocating the slave far from her natal home and never liberating her from the material and psychological effects of hegemonic racism. Thus while the Barbary captivity narrative might seem to mirror a slave narrative, the situations of white and black slaves differed, just as the ability of the narrators varied.

The image of the white captive in Africa nevertheless evoked comparison to the black slave in America. Most often, the captive used the situation to indirectly justify slavery in the United States or altogether denounce Africans as "barbarous." Archibald Robbins, for instance, who was shipwrecked off the coast of Morocco in 1815, felt fully justified in withholding his sympathy for U.S. slaves given his protracted captivity in the desert: "These Africans, of every name and feature and complexion, take delight in enslaving each other; . . . it can hardly be expected that an American, who has for months and years been enslaved by them, can feel so much compassion towards a slave *here* as those do who have always enjoyed the blessings of humanity and liberty."[16] Even James Riley, who captained the ship upon which Robbins served, and who in his immensely popular narrative eventually vowed to fight for the freedom of American slaves when he returned home, initially portrayed his African captor as a subhuman cannibal:

> He appeared to be about five feet seven or eight inches high, and of a complexion between that of an American Indian and negro. He had about him, to cover his nakedness, a piece of coarse woollen cloth, that reached from below his breast nearly to his knees; his hair was long and bushy, resembling a *pitch mop*, sticking out every way six or eight inches from his head; his face resembled that of an ourang-outang more than a human being; his eyes were red and fiery; his mouth, which stretched nearly from ear to ear, was well lined with sound teeth; and a long curling beard, which depended from his upper lip and chin down upon his breast, gave him altogether a most horrid appearance, and I could not but imagine that those well set teeth were sharpened for the purpose of devouring human flesh!!"[17]

Less frequently, captives, or those who wrote about white slavery, were tempted to reveal the hypocrisy of the American slave system. In *The Selling of Joseph*, the first antislavery tract written and printed in New England in 1700, the famous judge and diarist Samuel Sewall commented upon the duplicitous nature of complaints made against Barbary in the light of American slavery: "Methinks, when we are bemoaning the barbarous Usage of our Friends and Kinsfolk in *Africa:* it might not be unreasonable to enquire whether we are not culpable in forcing the *Africans* to become Slaves amongst our selves."[18] In 1786, at the time of the first postrevolutionary captivity crisis, John Jay, the secretary of foreign affairs, issued a complaint against English authorities for "carrying away" from New York several African-Americans. In questioning the denominating of Africans as "goods and chattels," he invoked the example of Algerian captives: "Is there any difference between the two cases than this, that the American slaves at Algiers were WHITE people, whereas the African slaves at New York were BLACK people?"[19] In 1797, James Wilson Stevens echoed this sentiment in *An Historical and Geographical Account of Algiers:* "With what countenance then can we reproach a set of barbarians, who have only retorted our own acts upon ourselves in making reprisals upon our citizens? For it is manifest to the world, that we are equally culpable, and in whatever terms of opprobrium we may execrate the piratic disposition of the Africans, yet all our recriminations will recoil upon ourselves."[20] Much later, in 1853, the ardent abolitionist Charles Sumner wrote a short history entitled *White Slavery in the Barbary States* in order to detail the antislavery battle in Africa and to illustrate the injustice of such practices in the United States: "The interest awakened for the slave in Algiers embraced also the slave at home. Sometimes they were

---

At a time when overseas trade was becoming more important for the United States, the North African corsairs promised to become a greater problem and, at the same time, a test of the country's diplomatic and military independence.

---

said to be alike in condition; sometimes, indeed, it was openly declared that the horrors of our American slavery surpassed that of Algiers."[21] That the Barbary captivity narrative is used to portray African "barbarity" (just as accounts of Indian captives conjure portraits of Indian "savagery") as well as critique slavery in America (work more often associated with the traditional American slave narrative) suggests the semiotic plasticity of the Barbary narrative and the interconnections among all three genres.

When Tripoli declared war on the United States in 1801, John Adams authorized William Eaton's dramatic march across the desert to help install a friendlier bashaw—an event memorialized in "The Marine's Hymn": "From the halls of Montezuma to the shores of Tripoli." Fewer than a dozen U.S. marines, however, actually invaded Tripoli, a minor incursion compared to that of the French occupation of Algeria, which began in 1830. By the turn of the century, most of the region would be European colonial territories.[22] Though the United States never had a grand design to invade North Africa, this did not preclude many captives from musing about the eventual conquest of the Barbary coast. James Cathcart, for one, dreamed that France would march into Africa and overpower his own Algerian captors, whom he saw as unjust and capricious: "What a pity such a character as Napoleon Bonaparte, with one hundred thousand men under his command, had not a footing in Barbary; with that force he would subdue the whole of the Barbary States from Salu to Derna in less than twelve months."[23] Archibald Robbins, writing after the Tripolitan War, lamented the difficulty of invading Africa while recalling how the U.S. Navy used Tripoli as a proving ground to demonstrate its imperial muscle: "Destroy [Tripoli's] naval armaments, and batter down their capitals," Robbins complained, and "they still have a safe retreat in their mountains and in their deserts, where a civilized army cannot subsist. The mention of *Tripoli* calls up the proud recollection of the infancy of the *American Navy*. It was upon the coast of that country, that Americans began to learn how to conquer upon the ocean."[24] The fictional narrative attributed to Thomas Nicholson, which also reflects a strong desire to subdue Africa, suggests that military force would have to be combined with diplomatic guile in order to succeed: "An absolute conquest of the Algerine territory cannot be effected but by invasion from the interior, through the co-operation of the Grand Seignior or the assistance of the other Barbary states."[25]

The reason for bringing up these "conquest" reveries is not to suggest that the United States would have invaded North Africa if it had had the military wherewithal to do so, but to illustrate that the nation participated in the eventual subjugation of North Africa through narrative. Insofar as imperialism is a theory and practice of domination, it must also be understood as a cultural project expressed in myriad ways and by assorted nations, institutions, and individuals. As Edward Said points out, the imperialist struggle is not exclusively about territorial boundaries:

> The main battle in imperialism is over land, of course; but when it came to who owned the land, who had the right to settle and work on it, who kept it going, who won it back, and who now plans its future—these issues were reflected, contested, and even for a time decided in narrative. . . . The power to narrate, or to block other narratives from forming and emerging, is very important to culture and imperialism, and constitutes one of the main connections between them.[26]

The Barbary captivity narrative engages in this textual battle through a variety of rhetorical strategies that reinforce the image of the dominated captive as culturally superior. In this sense, these accounts both created and dramatized the conflict between Western "civilization" and African "barbarity." What we must keep in mind is that every captive who wrote a narrative survived the ordeal. We name these accounts "captivity" narratives, but they might just as easily be called "survival" narratives, a special form of the adventure story, because a survivor has, in most cases, returned home or to a place of refuge to write about her past experience as a captive. Her success—measured by her native ability to stay alive until such time as her compatriots can arrange for her redemption—illustrates her ability to overcome great hardship at the hands of barbarous captors and bring honor to her home. The text begins with the supposition that the captive's superior culture, and sometimes her superior devotion to God, has provided her with the fortitude to overcome the ordeal. That the writer has returned to a place where she is free to record and represent her experience is evidence of her success and the greatness of her society—as well as her God—in the face of barbarous circumstances.

The unbalanced relationship between captive and master plays a key role in establishing a defining boundary between the captive's own identity and that of her African captor. From the moment of first contact, the writer can clearly establish a moral and cultural difference based on the "unmoral," "unlawful," "inhuman" act of abduction itself, which begins to define a widening gulf between the civilized and the barbaric. The aggrieved captive can then easily insist upon other differences between herself and her new masters, differences that are usually framed in terms of something lacking and something a civilized country could eventually supply: rationality, progress, history, self-control, etc. To tell her story, the author relies not only upon the adventure tale but on the elements of travel narrative and ethnography that give her license to present "Africa" to her readers from the standpoint not only of a person of strong character in dismal conditions, but of a careful, even scientific, observer. Frequently, these observations offered a negative portrait of Africans while proposing the need for further study, assessment, and exploration.

[T]hese accounts both created and dramatized the conflict between Western "civilization" and African "barbarity."

A case in point comes from the opening pages to Judah Paddock's narrative about his 1800 captivity, which includes a letter of support from one Thomas Eddy, urging the former captive to write his narrative. Eddy suggests that Paddock's experience would be welcomed by the public because of a growing curiosity about Africa: "The civilized world is now looking towards that country with increasing interest, and any genuine information can hardly fail to be favourably received."[27] The "civilized" world's burgeoning fascination with Africa took several forms.

Western contact with Africa had largely been restricted to the coastal trading areas—the slave coast, the gold coast, the ivory coast, the pepper coast, etc. As a result of the Enlightenment and the scientific revolution, a growing curiosity arose about the African interior, a space filled by confused fiction on most maps. Questions often centered around geographic problems such as the sources of the Zaire and Nile Rivers and the course of the Niger River. The same British African Association that quizzed Adams (later to be known as the Royal Geographical Society) sponsored scientific expeditions like that of Mungo Park's excursion up the Gambia

River in 1795. Other explorers, such as the famous David Livingstone, sought not only to survey the continent but to convert and eventually to "civilize" its inhabitants. Several Protestant missions established themselves in Africa by the first decade of the nineteenth century, although the Moravian Brethren first arrived in what is now South Africa as early as the 1730s. These same religious forces helped to curtail the British slave trade, and the first act banning slavery in Great Britain came into effect in 1772. By 1807, Britain had forbidden its citizens to trade in slaves, and by 1833 it had outlawed slavery in all of its colonies except India. With the decline in the slave trade came a concomitant increase in the demand for industrial raw materials such as rubber, ivory, beeswax, gum, coffee, and palm oil. Abolitionists viewed the shift to commodity exchange and a wider, more profitable trade in resources as necessary to reduce the incentive to market slaves, but the demand had grown primarily out of an expanding middle class, particularly in Britain, and the evolution of modern industrial capitalism based on wage labor. It was largely the middle class that sponsored the African Association and helped to finance exploration while feeding public interest in the continent. The United States, eager to develop its overseas markets, found the possibilities presented by Africa no less interesting.

Many captives noted the continent's well-known natural potential and marveled over the land's great possibilities in the hands of an industrial society. John Foss, for one, observed that although Algiers had seven principal rivers, none was currently navigated: "It is however likely that they might be made use of for this purpose, were the inhabitants of a more intelligent and industrious character, for some of them are of a tolerable depth. Such is the gross ignorance of the natives in whatever concerns domestic improvements, that there is not a single bridge over any of those rivers."[28] In Tripoli, several years later, William Ray noted that under Roman rule the land had been called "the garden of the world" but could scarcely lay claim to such fecundity any longer. He declared the town of Tripoli inferior to both Algiers and Tunis, and this owing to no fault of the soil: "The fertility of the soil cannot be controverted; for were it not extremely prolific, the exanimate inhabitants, oppressed by tyranny, and abandoned to indolence, could not possibly subsist."[29] A decade later, in Morocco, Archibald Robbins put it more succinctly:

> Although Africa holds the third rank in point of size among the four great continents that constitute our globe, in a moral, political, and commercial point of view, it is decidedly inferior to them all. While the continents of Europe and America have been making rapid progress in civilization, the arts and sciences, Asia may be said to have been, for the most part, stationary and Africa retrograding.[30]

For Foss, Ray, and Robbins, African land presented wondrous possibilities, while African people posed daunting impediments.

Before they wrote their narratives, several of the captives had researched what had already been written about Africa. Many wrote brief histories of Africa, never failing to measure the apogee of African civilization in terms of the rise of the Roman Empire. Writers usually interpreted the years after the Roman decline as a

period of stagnation or regression, certainly not one of great development or innovation. Thus North Africa was usually viewed as a decayed world built upon the
ruins of Western civilization. Two examples must stand in for many. James Riley
claims to have been keenly observant of his surroundings; his experience as a seagoing captain, he mentions, made him extremely conscious of geography and gave
him a natural curiosity about foreign places. Near the end of Riley's captivity, when
his strength was at its nadir, he claims that he could not help but speculate on the
desert's lustrous past: "Notwithstanding my frame was literally exhausted, yet my
imagination transported me back to a time when this region might have been
inhabited by men in a higher state of civilization, and when it was probably one of
the fairest portions of the African continent."[31] Riley's nostalgia for a more civilized
past appears almost benign in contrast to William Ray's depiction of the heavily
armed Tripoli harbor. To Ray's sensibility, what had followed the Roman legacy
wrought only Gothic horror:

> For here [the Tripoli beachhead] bribery, treachery, rapine, murder, and all the hedious
> [sic] offspring of accursed tyranny, have often drenched the streets in blood, and dealt, to
> the enslaved inhabitants, famine, dungeons, ruin and destruction. On yonder noddling
> tower, once waved the banners of the all-conquering Rome, when these fruitful regions
> were styled the Eden of that empire, now Gothic ruins, and barbarous inhabitants curse
> the half-tilled soil.[32]

Both Riley's and Ray's descriptions refuse any idea of progress, a notion particularly important to Enlightenment philosophers.[33] They recall Roman greatness and
the potential for future wealth, but to them the present suggests only ruins and
desert wastes. Their descriptions conjure a static picture of a society headed
nowhere. Is it any wonder that Riley wrote of his captors as "wandering" Arabs?[34]
The rhetorical gesture of erasing local history serves as a way to deny a sense of
"movement toward a destiny." David Spurr has argued that Western travelers
engage in an imperial rhetoric when they describe a country as having no legacy or
worthy past: "This way of defining the African, as with out history and without progress, makes way for the moral necessity of cultural transformation. The colonizing
powers will create a history where there was none."[35]

Much of colonial discourse creates the imperative for "cultural transformation"
in the manner Spurr describes and thus reproduces a notion of the African other as
outside humanity; Christopher Miller, for instance, has noted how "Africa has been
made to bear a double burden, of monstrousness and nobility."[36] Nowhere is this
polarized account of Africa more apparent than in James Riley's narrative. We have
already seen how Riley depicted his captors as monstrous cannibals, but much later
in the narrative Riley's impression of Africans expands. Nearing the border of
Morocco, Riley meets with Rais bel Cossim, an emissary for the British consul.
Riley confesses that he feels extremely weak and that he fears he will die before
ever regaining his freedom. Rais bel Cossim listens patiently and then chastises the
Christian for doubting a merciful God who had preserved Riley through such trials.
Riley is astonished:

To hear such sentiments from the mouth of a Moor, whose nation I had been taught to consider the worst of barbarians, I confess, filled my mind with awe and reverence, and I looked up to him as a kind of superior being, when he added, "We are all children of the same heavenly Father, who watches over all our actions, whether we be Moor, or Christian, or Pagan, or of any other religion; we must perform his will."[37]

In this passage, Riley describes Rais bel Cossim as a superior being who understands all humanity as equal under the eyes of God. Commenting on similar passages, Spurr argues that the ultimate aim of colonial discourse is not to maintain a radical difference between colonizer and subject but to foreground their common humanity: "[imperial discourse] seeks to dominate by inclusion and domestication rather than by a confrontation which recognizes the independent identity of the Other."[38] This is the logic that allows the colonizer to see his subjects as sympathetic to imperial aims. The colonizer can rationalize his civilizing mission—often violently implemented—as one that brings humanity together.

Depictions of Africans as noble or exemplary are infrequent, indeed rare. "Monsters," "savages," "cannibals," and "torturers" typify the descriptions captives give of the Africans they encounter. Judah Paddock, for instance, confessed that his reading of travel literature had done little to prepare him for his first contact with Africans: "Their figure, and ferocious look, to say nothing of their behaviour, were as savage, and even exceeded in savageness, any thing that I ever have read in narratives of voyages. . . . Before I proceed further, I will describe, as well as I can, these monsters."[39] John Foss portrayed his Algerian captors as more hostile than the indigenous wild animals: "Indeed a considerable part of the back country is a savage desert, abounding with Lions, Tigers, Leopards, Jackalls, Buffaloes, wild Boars, Porcupines, &c. And it must be acknowledged, that these animals are not the least amiable inhabitants of this country."[40]

Soon after his capture, Riley describes an interesting scene in which two groups of Arabs clash over who properly owns the American captives. Eight Arabs jump off their camels with their scimitars "naked and ready for action." They lay hold of the Americans, pulling and hauling in every direction, claiming them as their own. Soon, the disagreement escalates to blows:

They cut at each other over my head, and on every side of me with their bright weapons, which fairly whizzed through the air within an inch of my naked body, and on every side of me, now hacking each other's arms apparently to the bone, then laying their ribs bare with gashes, while their heads, hands, and thighs, received a full share of cuts and wounds. The blood streaming from every gash, ran down their bodies, colouring and heightening the natural hideousness of their appearance.[41]

This passage is of particular interest because Jonathan Cowdery describes almost an identical scene when the Tripoli navy boarded the U.S.S. *Philadelphia*. After the flag was lowered, "the Tripolitan chiefs collected their favourites, and, with drawn sabers, fell to cutting and slashing their own men, who were stripping the Americans and plundering the ship."[42] These scenes of mutual mutilation among captors are particularly important not only for how they define barbarity but for their larger implications for self-governance. They represent in miniature what has been implied about the political corpus; that is, individuals who exhibit a lack of self-discipline and a strong proclivity toward self-destruction are the products of a society that is unable to govern itself. Primitive passions that go unrestrained reflect the utter debasement of an entire culture as well as moral and intellectual degradation.

In addition to such wild melees, the Barbary captivity narrative writers create a pool of bizarre episodes and images: spectacularly gruesome punishments, meals of camel sores and human urine, "ourang-outang" men, etc. Barbary becomes a safe repository for the grotesque and bizarre.[43] James Riley, for instance, is convinced that many inhabitants of the desert live to be two hundred years old.[44] His claim imbues the desert with mysterious, life-granting properties, even though its harsh climate threatens to kill Riley at every moment. This description reinforces the notion that Barbary is a land of extremes, a country either lush or barren and rarely conventional. We see this again in James Cathcart's depictions of the notorious prison, the bagnio belique, as he conjures an image of utter bedlam. In this portrait of Algiers, the world is turned upside-down and the comfort of wild animals is prized over the health and safety of civilized men:

> The greatest inconvenience in this prison is in consequence of the lions and tigers being kept there which creates an insufferable stench, which joined to the common shore of the hospital which communicates with that of the prison corrodes the atmosphere that in the summer season it is nearly suffocating. I have known twenty-seven animals of this description to have been kept at once in this prison which are maintained at the expense of the Christian tavern keepers. They frequently break loose and have killed several of the slaves as they dare not destroy them even in their own defense, and if very ferocious, an order must come from the Dey and some of his guards are then dispatched to shoot them before the evil can be removed. The offals from their dens serve to maintain an enormous number of rats, the largest I ever saw, which frequently serve to satisfy the craving appetite of some of the poor slaves. Cats are likewise eaten from mere necessity, and once in particular I asked a Frenchman what he was going to do with it after skinning, he laconically answered, "Ma foi it [sic] faut Manger." During the plague this prison, in consequence of its communication with the hospital, had the greatest number of its inhabitants destroyed with that contagion.[45]

For James Riley, the exotic took many forms, including the very desert terrain that caused him such sustained agony. When we recall that most captives wrote or rewrote their narratives as survivors, the fact that they could retrospectively take pleasure from the vistas they encountered as if they were on the Grand Tour should not come as a surprise. Their expression of a cultivated aesthetic reaffirms the captive's position as a civilized person. This ability to recognize "beauty" in the "wild" appears in several guises, most notably in the captive's aesthetic appreciation for the African landscape. While often the landscape appears horrid and inhospitable to the suffering captive, she frequently comes upon a view that astounds her. This is particularly the case for the shipwrecked captives who were forced to travel across great expanses of desert and mountains. Note how James Riley writes about the encroaching mountains as he approaches them from the south:

> We had seen these mountains for several days past, in the distant horizon, when we were on the high ridges, which we were obliged to pass; but we now beheld them from this wide-spreading plain in all their awful magnitude: their lofty summits, towering high above the clouds in sharp peaks, appeared to be covered with never-melting snows. This sight was calculated to fill the mind of the beholder with wonder and astonishment.[46]

Once again Riley expresses a particularly Romantic appreciation for the "lofty" and "towering" vista. His observation that the view was "calculated" to fill him with "wonder and astonishment" reminds us that the "calculation" was formulated as an invisible aesthetic imposed upon the scene and describes Riley's own cast of mind.

These scenes of mutual mutilation among captors are particularly important not only for how they define barbarity but for their larger implications for self-governance.

If what Riley saw filled him with visual rapture, then his ears delighted him no less. All captives wrestled with communication problems and were forced to make do with hand signals and gesticulations. Riley, however, claims to have learned a form of Arabic tolerably well and thanks his creator that he "endowed me with intelligence to comprehend a language I had never before heard spoken."[47] To Riley, however, who aestheticizes the experience, comprehension is less important than the images that are called to his mind when he listens only to the sound of his captors' speech: "Their language . . . thrills on the ear like the breathings of soft wind-music, and excites in the soul the most soothing sensations; but when they speak in anger, it sounds as hoarse as the roarings of irritated lions, or the most furious beasts of prey."[48] Riley's shipmate, Archibald Robbins, was similarly awed by his captors' voice and claimed "there is a kind of peculiar mystery in their language."[49]

This mystification of language is particularly important when we recall the etymology of the term *barbary*, traced earlier, which refers to unintelligibility. According to this history, Africans were named *barbarians* because they refused to communicate. Riley and Robbins, who are not invaders per se but strangers in a foreign land, do not expect the burden of communication to be placed on their captors—it is they themselves who must learn the lingua franca. In essence, they are the "barbarians" who cannot speak the native tongue. Unintelligibility thus takes on a Romantic cast and is translated into melody and mystery. For Riley, rudimentary language acquisition becomes a source of intellectual pride and a new sphere of mastery.

A danger exists, however, as we see in Robert Adams's narrative. To Joseph Dupuis, who was one of the first to meet Adams upon his return from captivity, Adams's speech represented a form of contamination. Dupuis writes in a letter included in the introduction to the narratives:

> I had difficulty at first in believing him to be a Christian. When I spoke to him in English, he answered me in a mixture of Arabic and broken English, and some times in Arabic only. . . . Like most other Christians after a long captivity and severe treatment among the Arabs, he appeared upon his first arrival exceedingly stupid and insensible.[50]

Dupuis's remarks suggest a fear that the boundary of identity is closely linked to language and that language acquisition—particularly under the duress of captivity—comes perilously close to cultural assimilation.

Perhaps it was a real source of fear since as many as two-thirds of the Algerian corsair *reis* or captains in the seventeenth century were Christian renegades who had served in the professional armies of France, England, or the United Netherlands. We also know that many Christian slaves never returned home and likely "took the Turban," but we know very little about them. Kathryn Zabelle Derounian-Stodola and James Levernier have noted that transculturated Indian captives often chose to remain silent because of their decision to disassociate themselves from their natal culture, and this may have been the case with returning renegades who chose not to write of their conversions. In addition, Western publishers were less likely to publish accounts of Barbary that went against the prevailing image of a sinister North Africa.[51] Nabil Matar has suggested that during the Renaissance at least, captive Christian apostates were the rule, not the exception. Many were forced under penalty of death to convert. Others who lived among Muslims slowly grew accustomed to the habits and rituals of Islamic life and gradually chose to accept the dominant culture as their own. Certainly many chose to renounce their faith to receive better treatment and avail themselves of Islamic privileges: freedom from slavery and opportunities for marriage and employment. "Evidently," Matar notes, "Mohammad was more attractive than Christ because he paid higher wages to those who served him."[52]

Occasionally, a captive does document the presence of a renegade. Adams, for instance, describes the miserable condition of two of his fellow mariners, Williams and Davison, who regretfully renounced their religion, believing there was no other alternative. For their conversion, they were given a horse, a musket, a blanket, and the opportunity to marry a Muslim woman. It is likely that they were eventually ransomed and partly responsible for contesting the veracity of Adams's account because of their own embarrassment. Other captives may have "turned Turk" and lived quite a good, long life. That their stories are not reported is a sign of the troubling picture a "white barbarian," like a "white Indian," posed. "What 'civilized' person would voluntarily join an 'inferior' culture?" What white American would allow his whiteness to be symbolically erased?[53] For theologians, the figure of the Christian apostate might suggest the possible superiority of Islam and the legitimacy of the prophet Muhammad.[54] While ostensibly about African barbarity; these accounts delimit the boundary of the civilized United States as they discuss matters of history, rationality, aesthetic development, cultural degradation, theological hegemony, and transculturation.

In many ways, the captive writer participates in and is encircled by a culture grounded in imperial pursuits. I do not mean to suggest that Foss, Riley, and the other captives should have been expected to write differently. On the contrary, they wrote within a climate that limited their vision, and that, as Mary Louise Pratt has suggested of the European travel writer, invested the captive with "imperial eyes [that] passively look out and possess."[55] Basil Davidson characterized the general myopia of early travelers in Africa when he wrote, "If they tried to understand the minds and actions of Africans they knew, it was by the way, and it was rare. Nearly all of them were convinced they were faced by 'primeval man,' by humanity as it had been before history began, by societies which lingered in the dawn of time."[56] These narratives, then, must be read with an awareness of the writers' immersion in imperialist culture if both their confining limits and how they expressed a dominating attitude are to be understood.

Notes

1. See McMurtry, "The Influence of Riley's *Narrative* upon Abraham Lincoln." For a longer discussion of Riley, see Alig, *Ohio's Last Frontiersman.*

2. Pratt, *Imperial Eyes,* 4.

3. Ben Rejeb, "To the Shores of Tripoli," 2.

4. Fernando de Moraes Farias, "Models of the World and Categorical Models," 39.

5. The term *barbarian* is often used by Indian captives to describe Native Americans; more interestingly, however, the entire Christian/Muslim conflict seems to have been superimposed onto the conflict between South American natives and European settlers in order to deny their humanity and label them "infidels." See Haberly, "Captives and Infidels"; and Frederick, "Fatal Journeys, Fatal Legends."

6. In some instances, publishers issued both Indian captivity narratives and Barbary captivity narratives. Matthew Carey in Boston, for example, published several of each, as well as a number of travel accounts about North Africa and Susanna Rowson's drama "Slaves of Algiers."

7. The great seal was rejected not because of the captivity image but because it was thought the image was too busy. See Sieminski, "The Puritan Captivity Narrative and the Politics of the American Revolution."

8. See Derounian-Stodola and Levernier, *The Indian Captivity Narrative, 1550-1900,* 36.

9. In *The Order of Things,* Foucault suggests that the seventeenth century marks the close of the "age of resemblance" and is replaced by an analysis of "identity and difference." Following Descartes's line of thought in his *Regulae,* Foucault writes:

> Comparison, then, can attain to perfect certainty: the old system of similitudes, never complete and always open to fresh possibilities, could, it is true, through successive confirmations, achieve steadily increasing probability; but it was never certain. Complete enumeration and the possibility of assigning at each point the necessary connection with the next, permits an absolutely certain knowledge of identities and differences: . . . The activity of the mind . . . will therefore no longer consist in *drawing things together,* in setting our on a quest for everything that might reveal some sort of kinship, attraction, or secretly shared nature within them, but, on the contrary, in *discriminating,* that is, in establishing their identities, then the inevitability of the connections with all the successive degrees of a series. (55)

10. Phillips, "Nineteenth-Century Racial Thought and Whitman's 'Democratic Ethnology of the Future,' " 299.

11. Sanchez-Eppler, "Bodily Bounds," 30. Cartwright originally published his theory in "Diseases and Peculiarities of the Negro Race," *De Bow's Review* II (1851), which is excerpted in Breeden, *Advice among Masters*, 173. Sanchez-Eppler comments on this passage, suggesting that "God writes 'subservience' upon the body of the black" just as the bodies of women were read against them ("Bodily Bounds," 30). Breeden notes that Cartwright was a prominent spokesman for southern nationalism. How he used racial theory to political ends is apparent in an article he first published in the *New Orleans Medical and Surgical Journal* in May 1851 which was reprinted widely in the South. Stephen Jay Gould cites theories concerning black inferiority, which Cartwright traced to inadequate decarbonization of blood in the lungs, a condition he termed "dysesthesia." The disease was characterized by carelessness and insensitivity, and, not surprisingly, part of the cure included a form of whipping with a broad leather strap and hard work to stimulate blood flow. For more on Cartwright, see Breeden, "States-Rights Medicine in the Old South."

12. In several instances black Americans were captured and treated as slaves in Africa. In each case, they were highly prized as workers because they were black and never were allowed, so far as I know, to return to the United States. For instance, Richard Delisle, the black cook aboard the *Commerce*, was never returned despite Riley's pleas to be permitted to ransom him. Similarly, the Bedouins who captured the crew of the *Oswego* refused to ransom Jack and Sam, two black seamen who served with Judah Paddock. Paddock attempted to intercede on their behalf: "I assured Ahamed [his new master] . . . that if these men were of any more value to their masters than the rest of us, the surplus of their value our consul would pay for them," but Ahamed refused to believe Paddock, whom he accused of conducting a slaving voyage. Paddock, *Narrative of the Shipwreck of the Ship Oswego*, 68. In these cases, the strength and endurance of black bodies are highly prized attributes compared to the weak and withering white bodies. It is highly likely that a great number of African-American sailors were taken captive in North Africa, for seafaring was one of the few employments where northern black men could thrive, and their numbers aboard ship were large in comparison to their population in the northern states. For more on African-American men in the maritime trade, see Bolster.

13. Clifford, "Partial Truths," 24.

14. Most of the Barbary captivity narratives can be read as African ethnographies. For instance, the entire second half of James Riley's narrative is given over to the description of the manners and customs of the Moroccans that he has observed. While they appear under the guise of scientific observation, these accounts are more closely related to imaginative writings, as James Clifford has observed: "Ethnographic writings can properly be called fictions in the sense of 'something made or fashioned,' the principal burden of the word's Latin root, *fingere*. But it is important to preserve the meaning not merely of making, but also of making up, of inventing things not actually real" ("Partial Truths," 6).

15. James Wilson Stevens, in his *An Historical and Geographical Account of Algiers*, comments on the varied conditions of Barbary slaves as well as the hyperbolized reports of their treatment that circulated in the United States:

> The condition of those who are slaves to private individuals, depends very much upon the disposition of their master, and the slaves' own conduct. Some of them fare better in Algiers, than ever they did in their own countries, and if they are good for anything, are entertained rather as companions than servants; though by far the greater number are barbarous masters, who treat their slaves with great cruelty. . . . While the Americans were enslaved in Algiers, the most exaggerated accounts were circulated respecting the severity of their afflictions. It was reported that the tongues of some were cut out, that others were emasculated; and captain Lawrence of the Hull Packet, who is said to have obtained his information at Cadiz, informs us that the Americans had their heads shaved close, and were not permitted to wear any kind of covering on their heads. Their calamities were indeed without a parallel, but the above accounts were entirely unfounded. (242-43)

16. Robbins, *A Journal*, 91.

17. Riley, *An Authentic Narrative*, 18. James Riley's son William published a sequel to his father's narrative that included journal entries and letters. Although James Riley was eventually elected to the House of Representatives, he appears never to have fought for emancipation. It seems, however, that Riley supported

the recolonization movement and was willing to undertake an exploratory expedition along the African coast to find a suitable harbor to land former American slaves. See Riley, *Sequel to Riley's Narrative*, 55-56.

18. Sewall, *The Selling of Joseph*, 11. As early as 1688, Germantown settlers had signed a petition denouncing slavery in America, comparing it to slavery of Christians in North Africa. See "Germantown Friends' Protest against Slavery, 1688."

19. Quoted in Sumner, *White Slavery in the Barbary States*, 88.

20. Stevens, *An Historical and Geographical Account of Algiers*, 235.

21. Sumner, *White Slavery in the Barbary States*, 83.

22. The events of the Tripolitan War helped to foster nationalist pride and homespun prestige. If we have long ago forgotten this war, the fact that the United States now has more than twenty-five towns named either Eaton or Decatur testifies to the former popularity of these men and the pervasiveness of their stories. Despite the pride the country took in its military action against Tripoli, the United States sought and accepted financial and tactical aid from the British. That the nation with its brand-new navy saw itself as acting in the interest of international commerce suggests the degree to which the war might be viewed as both a nationalistic and internationalistic affair.

23. Cathcart, *The Captives*, 1.

24. Robbins, *A Journal*, 147.

25. Nicholson, *An Affecting Narrative*, 19.

26. Said, *Culture and Imperialism*, xii-xiii.

27. Paddock, *Narrative of the Shipwreck of the Ship Oswego*, vii.

28. Foss, *A Journal of the Captivity and Sufferings*, 41.

29. Ray, *Horrors of Slavery*, 173.

30. Robbins, *A Journal*, 38.

31. Riley, *An Authentic Narrative*, 223.

32. Ray, *Horrors* of Slavery, 164.

33. Peter Hulme has remarked that the Enlightenment notion of history "was the idea of 'progress,' initially from 'savagery' to 'civilization,' but then through the stages of a more complex developmental model based on distinctions between hunting, pastoralism, and agriculture" (8). For John Locke, the mere existence of food mattered little. Locke made a key distinction between people who simply gathered and those who cultivated the land. Those who failed to improve the land or their material conditions and refused to learn what reason readily taught could be viewed as irrational or animalistic. To neglect reason was an indictment of moral lassitude and further evidence that a society had not progressed out of its savage past or had lapsed into a state of barbarity. This was also the argument used to discount American Indian agricultural practices as irrational. See Hulme and Jordanova, *The Enlightenment and Its Shadows*. See also Matar, "John Locke and the 'Turbanned Nations.' "

34. John Foss also imagines the indigenous people to be aimless wanderers: "The people in the country, have no houses, but live intents, and remove from one place to another, as they want pasture, or as any other accidental circumstance may happen" (34).

35. Spurt, *The Rhetoric of Empire*, 98-99.

36. Miller, *Blank Darkness*, 5.

37. Riley, *An Authentic Narrative*, 209.

38. Spurr, *The Rhetoric of Empire*, 32.

39. Paddock, *Narrative of the Shipwreck of the Ship Oswego*, 47-48.

40. Foss, *A Journal of the Captivity and Sufferings*, 41-42.

41. Riley, *An Authentic Narrative*, 55.

42. William Ray, who was aboard the *Philadelphia* at the time, disputes Cowdery's account. He admits that there was "a sort of mutiny" among the Tripolitans but nothing to the extent Cowdery describes: "For my part I never saw any hands amputated, nor do I believe there were any lives lost, for myself and a hundred others were in the ship much longer than the Doctor, and none of us ever saw or heard of this carnage amongst themselves." Ray, *Horrors of Slavery*, 79. In this section of his account, Ray aims to discredit Cowdery and call attention to the doctor's cowardice; his correction may indeed be a much more accurate picture of what actually occurred.

43. David Spurr has suggested that

[t]he Third World continually provides what writers call "material" of a special nature: the exotic, the grotesque, the bizarre, the elemental. . . . The atavism of the Third World becomes the object of interest and attraction, as if it offered an image of our own more primitive being. Madness, revolution, barbarism, natural disaster—all seem closer to the surface there, offering a constant source of pathos. But, like Proust at his breakfast table, one can experience this pathos safely by virtue of an aesthetic mediation whose transforming power increases with cultural distance. (Spurr, *The Rhetoric of Empire*, 46)

44. See Riley, *An Authentic Narrative*, 313-14.
45. Cathcart, *The Captives*, 56-57.
46. Riley, *An Authentic Narrative*, 201.
47. Ibid., 256.
48. Ibid., 316.
49. Robbins, *A Journal*, 72.
50. Adams, *The Narrative of Robert Adams*, xxiii-xxiv.
51. See Derounian-Stodola and Levernier, *The Indian Captivity Narrative*, 73-74.
52. Matar, "Turning Turk," 38.
53. See Axtell, "The White Indians of Colonial America."
54. Many Christians resisted apostasy. One extreme form of resistance involved tattooing newborn children on the face with the sign of the cross so that the child's body was indelibly marked as Christian flesh. See Matar, "Turning Turk," 38-39.
55. Pratt, *Imperial Eyes*, 7.
56. Quoted in Said, *Culture and Imperialism*, 99.

References

Adams, Robert. *The Narrative of Robert Adams, A Sailor who was wrecked on the Western Coast of Africa, in the Year 1810, was detained three years in slavery by the Arabs of the Great Desert, and resided several months in the city of Tombuctoo*. Ed. S. Cook. London: William Bulmer and Co., 1816.

Alig, Joyce L. *Ohio's Last Frontiersman, Connecticut Mariner: Captain James Riley*. Celina, OH: Messenger Press, 1996.

Allison, Robert J. *The Crescent Obscured, The United States and the Muslim World 1776-1815*. New York: Oxford UP, 1995.

Austin, Allan D. *African Muslims in Antebellum America: A Sourcebook*. New York: Garland, 1984.

———. *African Muslims in Antebellum America: Transatlantic Stories and Spiritual Struggles*. New York: Routledge, 1997.

Axtell, James. "The White Indians of Colonial America." In *The European and the Indian: Essays in the Ethnohistory of Colonial North America*. New York: Oxford UP, 1981.

Baepler, Paul. "The Barbary Captivity Narrative in Early America." *Early American Literature* 30, no. 2 (fall 1995): 95-120.

———. "Rewriting the Barbary Captivity Narrative: The Perdicaris Affair and the Last Barbary Pirate." *Prospects* 24, 2000: 175-211.

Ben Rejeb, Lotfi. "'To the Shores of Tripoli': The Impact of Barbary on Early American Nationalism." Diss., Indiana U, 1981.

Bolster, W. Jeffrey. *Black Jacks: African American Seamen in the Age of Sail*. Cambridge: Harvard UP, 1997.

Bradley, Eliza. *An Authentic Narrative of the Shipwreck and Sufferings of Mrs. Eliza Bradley, the Wife of Capt. James Bradley of Liverpool, Commander of the Ship Sally, which was wrecked on the coast of Barbary in June 1818*. Boston: James Walden, 1820.

Braudel, Fernand. *The Mediterranean and the Mediterranean World in the Age of Philip II*. Trans. Sian Reynolds. New York: Harper & Row, 1972.

Breeden, James O. "States-Rights Medicine in the Old South." *Bulletin of the New York Academy of Medicine* 53 (March-April 1976): 348-72.

————, ed. *Advice among Masters: The Ideal in Slave Management in the Old South*.Westport, CT: 1980.

Carr, Helen. *Inventing the American Primitive: Politics, Gender and the Representation of Native American Literary Traditions*. New York: New York UP, 1996.

Castiglia, Christopher. *Bound and Determined: Captivity, Culture-Crossing, and White Womanhood from Mary Rowlandson to Patty Hearst*. Chicago: U of Chicago P, 1996.

Cathcart, James Leander. *The Captives, Eleven Years a Prisoner in Algiers*. Compiled by J. B. Newkirk. La Porte, IN: Herald Print, 1899.

Clifford, James. "Partial Truths." In *Writing Culture: The Poetics and Politics of Ethnography*. Eds. James Clifford and George E. Marcus. Berkeley: U of California P.1986.

Cooper, James Fenimore. *The History of the Navy of the United States of America*. Ed. R. D. Madison. Del Mar, NY: Scholar's Facsimiles & Reprints, 1988.

Cowdery, Jonathan. *American Captives in Tripoli; or, Dr. Cowdery's Journal in Miniature. Kept during his late captivity in Tripoli*. 2d ed. Boston: Belcher and Armstrong, 1806.

Davis, William. "A True Relation of the Travels And most miserable Captivity of WILLIAM DAVIS, Barber-Surgeon of London, under the Duke of Florence." In *A Collection of Voyages and Travels*. Ed. Awnsham Churchill. London, 1704.

Derounian-Stodnla, Kathryn Zabelle, and James Arthur Levernier. *The Indian Captivity Narrative, 1550-1900*. New York: Twayne, 1993.

Dobson, Joanne. "Reclaiming Sentimental Literature." *American Literature* 69, no. 2 (June 1997): 263-88.

Ebersole, Gary. *Captured by Texts: Puritan to Postmodern Images of Indian Captivity*. Charlottesville: U of Virginia P, 1995.

Elias, Robert H., and Eugene D. Finch. *Introduction to Letters of Thomas Atwood Digges*. Raleigh: U of South Carolina P, 1982.

Estes, J. Worth. "Commodore Jacob Jones: A Doctor Goes to Sea." *Delaware History* 24, no. 2 (1990): 109-22.

Fernando de Moraes Farias, Paulo. "Models of the World and Categorical Models: The 'Enslavable Barbarian' as a Mobile Classificatory Label." In *Slaves and Slavery in Muslim Africa*. Vol. 1, *Islam and the Ideology of Enslavement*. Ed. John Ralph Willis. London: Frank Cass, 1985.

Foss, John D. *A JOURNAL, of the Captivity and Sufferings of JOHN FOSS; several years a prisoner in ALGIERS: Together with some account of the treatment of Christian slaves when sick:—and observations on the manners and customs of the Algerines*. Newburyport, MA: A. March, 1798.

Foucault, Michel. *The Order of Things: An Archaeology of the Human Sciences*. New York: Random House, 1970.

Franklin, Benjamin. *Benjamin Franklin, Writings*. New York: Library of America, 1987.

Frederick, Bonnie. "Fatal Journeys, Fatal Legends: The Journey of the Captive Woman in Argentina and Uruguay." In *Women and the Journey: The Female Travel Experience*. Ed. Bonnie Frederick and Susan H, Mcleod. Pullman, WA: Washington State UP, 1993.

Gee, Joshua. *Narrative of Joshua Gee of Boston, Mass., While he was captive in Algeria of the Barbary pirates 1680-1697*. Intro. Albert Carlos Bates. Hartford: Wadsworth Atheneum, 1943.

"Germantown Friends' Protest against Slavery, 1688." In *Am I Not a Man and a Brother?: The Antislavery Crusade of Revolutionary America 1688-1788*. Ed. Roger Bruns. New York: Chelsea House, 1977.

Gomez, Michael A. "Muslims in Early America." *Journal of Southern History* 60 (November 1994): 671-709.

Gould, Stephen Jay. *The Mismeasure of Man*. New York: Norton, 1981.

Haberly, David T. "Captives and Infidels: The Figure of the *Cautiva* in Argentine Literature." *American Hispanist* 4 (October 1978): 7-16.

Hulme, Peter, and Ludmilla Jordanova. *The Enlightenment and Its Shadows*. New York: Routledge, 1990.

Huntress, Keith. *Introduction to An authentic narrative of the shipwreck and sufferings of Mrs. Eliza Bradley, the wife of Capt. James Bradley of Liverpool, commander of the ship* Sally *which was wrecked on the coast of Barbary, in June 1818. . . . Written by herself*. Fairfield: Ye Galleon Press, 1985.

Irwin, Robert. *The Arabian Nights: A Companion*. New York: Penguin, 1994.

Jefferson, Thomas. *The Papers of Thomas Jefferson*. Eds. Julian Bond et al. 25 vols. Princeton UP, 1950.

Judy, Ronald T. *(Dis)Forming the American Canon: African-Arabic Slave Narratives in the Vernacular*. Minneapolis: U of Minnesota P, 1993.

Kitzen, Michael. "Money Bags or Cannon Balls: The Origins of the Tripolitan War, 1795-1801. *Journal of the Early Republic* 16, no.4 (winter 1996): 601-24.

Knight, Francis. *A Relation of Seven Years Slavery under the Turks of Algier, Suffered by an English Captive Merchant.* In *A Collection of Voyages and Travels.* Ed. Awnsham Churchill. London, 1704. 465-89.

Laranda, Viletta. *Neapolitan Captive: Interesting Narrative of the Captivity and Sufferings of Miss Viletta Laranda, A Native of Naples, Who, with a Brother was a passenger on board a Neapolitan vessel wrecked near Oran, on the Barbary coast, September 1829, and who soon after was unfortunately made a Captive of by a wandering clan of Bedowen Arabs, on their return from Algiers to the Deserts—and eleven months after providentially rescued from Barbarian Bondage by the commander of a detached Regiment of the victorious French Army.* New York: Charles C. Henderson, 1830.

Lewis, James R. "Images of Captive Rape in the Nineteenth Century." *Journal of American Cultures*, no. 2 (summer 1992): 69-77.

Martin, Lucinda [Maria Martin]. *HISTORY OF THE Captivity and Sufferings of MRS. MARIA MARTIN, who was six years a slave in ALGIERS: two of which she was confined in a dark and dismal dungeon, loaded with irons.* Boston: W Crary, 1807.

Matar, Nabil I. "John Locke and the 'Turbanned Nations,' " *Journal of Islamic Studies* 2 (1991): 67-78.

———. " 'Turning Turk': Conversion to Islam in English Renaissance Thought." *Durham University Journal* 86 no. 1 (January 1994): 33-41.

Mather, Cotton. *A Pastoral Letter to the English Captives in Africa.* Boston: B. Green and J. Allen, 1698.

———. *The Glory of Goodness. The Goodness of God Celebrated in Remarkable Instances and* Improvements *thereof And more particularly in the REDEMPTION Remarkably obtained for the English Captives, Which have been Languishing under the Tragical, and the Terrible, and the most Barbarous Cruelties of BARBARY. The History of what the Goodness of God, has done for the Captives, lately delivered out of Barbary.* Boston: T. Green, 1703.

McMurtry Gerald R. "The Influence of Riley's *Narrative* upon Abraham Lincoln." *Indiana Magazine of History* 30 (1934): 133-38.

Miller, Christopher L. *Blank Darkness: Africanist Discourse in French.* Chicago: U of Chicago E 1985.

Munday, Anthony. "The worthie enterprise of John Fox an Englishman in delivering 266 Christians out of the captivitie of the Turkes at Alexandria, the 3 of Januarie 1577." In *The Principal Navigations, Voyages, and Discoveries of the English Nation.* Ed. Richard Halduyt. Cambridge: Cambridge UP, 1965.

Namias, June. *White Captives: Gender and Ethnicity on the American Frontier.* Chapel Hill: U of North Carolina P, 1993.

Nicholson, Thomas. *An Affecting Narrative of the Captivity and Sufferings of Thomas Nicholson [A Native of New Jersey] Who has been Six years a Prisoner among the Algerines, And from whom he fortunately made his escape a few months previous to Commodore Decatur's late Expedition. To which is added a Concise Description of Algiers of the Customs, Manners, etc of the Natives—and some particulars of Commodore Decatur's Late Expedition, Against the Barbary Powers.* Boston: Printed for C. Walker, 1816.

Okeley, William. *Eben-Ezer or a Small Monument of Great Mercy Appearing in the Miraculous Deliverance of John Anthony William Okeley William Adams, John Jephs and John Carpenter.*London, 1675.

Paddock, Judah. *Narrative of the shipwreck of the ship Oswego, on the coast of south barbary, and of the sufferings of the master and the crew while in bondage among the arabs; interspersed with numerous remarks upon the country and its inhabitants, and concerning the peculiar perils of that coast. In An Authentic Narrative of the loss of the American Brig Commerce, Wrecked on the Western Coast of Africa, in the Month of August, 1815. With An Account of the Sufferings of her Surviving Officers and Crew, who were enslaved by the wandering arabs on the Great African Desert, or Zahahrah; and Observations historical geographical, &c. Made during the travels of the author while a slave to the arabs, and in the empire of Morocco.* By James Riley. 3 ed. New York: Collins & Co. i8i8.

Paine, Ralph D. *The Ships and Sailors of Old Salem: The Record of a Brilliant Era of American Achievement.* New York: Outing Publishing, 1908.

Perdicaris, Ion H. "In Raissuli's Hands: The Story of My Captivity and Deliverance May 18 to June 26, 1904." *Leslie's Magazine* 58 (September 1904): 510-22.

Phillips, Dana. "Nineteenth-Century Racial Thought and Whitman's 'Democratic Ethnology of the Future.' " *Nineteenth Century Literature* 49, no. 3 (1994): 289-320.

Pratt, Mary Louise. *Imperial Eyes: Travel Writing and Transculturation*. New York: Routledge, 1992.

Rawlins, John. "The wonderful recovery of the Exchange of Bristow, from the Turkish Pirats of Argier, published by John Rawlins, here abbreviated." In *Hakluytus Posthumus or Purchas His Pilgrimes*. Ed. Samuel Purchas. Glasgow: James MacLehose and Sons, 1905.

Ray, William. *Horrors of Slavery or the American Tars in Tripoli*. Troy, NY: Oliver Lyon, 1808.

Riley, James. *An Authentic Narrative of the loss of the American Brig* Commerce, *wrecked on the western coast of Africa, in the month of August, 1815, with an account of the sufferings of her surviving officers and crew, who were enslaved by the wandering Arabs on the great African desert, or Zahahrah; and observations historical geographical &c. made during the travels of the author, while a slave to the Arabs, and in the empire of Morocco*. Hartford: Published by the author, 1817.

Riley, William Wilshire. *Sequel to Riley being a sketch of interesting incidents in the life voyages and travels of Capt. James Riley from the period of his return to his native land, after his shipwreck, captivity and sufferings among the Arabs of the desert, as related in his narrative, til his death*. Columbus: G. Brewster, 1851.

Robbins, Archibald. *A Journal, Comprising an Account of the Loss of the Brig Commerce, of Hartford (Con.) James Riley, Master, Upon the Western Coast of Africa, August 28th, 1815 of the Slavery and Sufferings of the Author and the Rest of the Crew Upon the Desert of Zahara, In the Years 1815, 1816, 1817; with Accounts of the Manners, Customs and Habits of the Wandering Arabs; also, A brief Historical and Geographical view of the Continent of Africa*. 20th ed. Hartford: Silas Andrus, 1831.

Roberts, Nicholas. "A Letter contayning the admirable escape and glorious Victorie of Nicholas Roberts Master, Tristram Stevens his Mate, and Robert Sucksbich Boatson of a Ship of Dover, taken by Algier Pyrates." In *Hakluytus Posthumus or Purchas His Pilgrimes*. Ed. Samuel Purchas. Glasgow: James MacLehose and Sons, 1905.

Rowlandson, Mary. *The Sovereignty and Goodness of God*. Ed. Neal Salisbury. New York: Bedford Books, 1997.

Rowson, Susanna. *Slaves in Algiers; or a Struggle for Freedom: A Play, interspersed with songs, in three acts*. Philadelphia: Wrigley and Berriman, 1794.

Said, Edward. *Culture and Imperialism*. New York: Vintage Books, 1993.

Sanchez-Eppler, Karen. "Bodily Bounds: The Intersecting Rhetorics of Feminism and Abolition." *Representations* 24 (1988): 28-59.

———. *Touching Liberty: Abolition, Feminism, and the Politics of the Body*. Berkeley: U of California P 1993.

Sekora, John. "Black Message/White Envelope: Genre, Authenticity; and Authority in the Antebellum Slave Narrative." *Callaloo* 10, no. 3 (fall 1987): 482-515.

Sewall, Samuel. *The Selling of Joseph: A Memorial*. Ed. Sidney Kaplan. Amherst: U of Massachusetts P, 1969.

Sha'ban, Fuad. *Islam and Arabs in Early American Thought: The Root of Orientalism in America*. Durham: Acorn Press, 1991.

Shaw, Elijah. *A short sketch of the life of Elijah Shaw, who served for twenty-two years in the Navy of the United States, taking an active part in four different wars between the United States & foreign powers; namely first—with France, in 1798; second—with Tripoli, from 1802 to 1805; third—with England from 1812 to 1815; fourth—with Algiers, from 1815 to 1816: and assisted in subduing the pirates from 1822 to 1826*. Rochester: Strong & Dawson, 1843.

Sibley, John Langdon. *Biographical Sketches of Harvard University, In Cambridge, Massachusetts*. Vol. 2. Cambridge: Charles William Sever, 1881.

Sieminski, Greg. "The Puritan Captivity Narrative and the Politics of the American Revolution." *American Literature* 42, no. 1 (March 1990): 35-56.

Smith, John. *The True Travels, Adventures, and Observations of Captaine John Smith*. In *The Complete Works of Captain John Smith (1580-1631): in Three Volumes*, vol 3. Ed. Philip L. Barbour. Chapel Hill: U of North Carolina P, 1986.

Snader, Joe. "The Oriental Captivity Narrative and Early English Fiction." *Eighteenth-Century Fiction* 9, no. 3 (April 1997): 267-98.

Sofka, James. "The Jeffersonian Idea of National Security: Commerce, the Atlantic Balance of Power, and the Barbary War, 1786-1805." *Diplomatic History* 21, no. 4 (fall 1997): 519-44.

Springer, Haskell. "The Captain's Wife at Sea." In *Iron Men, Wooden Women: Gender and Seafaring in the Atlantic World 1700-1920*. Eds. Margaret S. Creighton and Lisa Norling. Baltimore: Johns Hopkins UP, 1996.

Spurr, David. *The Rhetoric of Empire: Colonial Discourse in Journalism, Travel Writing, and Imperial Administration*. Durham: Duke UP, 1993

Stevens, James Wilson. *An Historical and Geographical Account of Algiers; comprehending a novel and interesting detail of events relative to the American Captives*. Philadelphia: Hogan & M'Elroy: 1797.

Sumner, Charles. *White Slavery in the Barbary States*. Boston: John P. Jewett, 1853

Toulouse, Teresa A. " 'My Own Credit': Strategies of (E)Valuation in Mary Rowlandson's Captivity Narrative." *American Literature* 30, no. 4 (December 1992): 656-76.

Tucker, Glen. *Dawn like Thunder: The Barbary Wars and the Birth of the US. Navy*. Indianapolis: Bobbs-Merrill, 1963.

Turkistanj, Abdulhafeez Q "Muslim Slaves and Their Narratives: Religious Faith and Cultural Accommodation." Diss., Kent State U, 1996.

Velnet, Mary. *The Captivity and Sufferings of Mrs. Mary Velnet, Who was Seven Years a Slave in Tripoli, three of which she was confined in a dungeon, loaded with irons, and four times put to the most cruel tortures ever invented by man. To which is added, The Lunatic Governor, and Adelaide, or the Triumph of Constancy, a Tale*. Boston: T. Abbot, 1828.

Winter, Kari. *Subjects of Slavery, Agents of Change: Women and Power in Gothic Novels and Slave Narratives, 1790-1865*. Athens: U of Georgia P. 1992.

Wolf, John B. *The Barbary Coast: Algiers under the Turks 1500-1830*. New York: Norton, 1979.

Crusades and Jihads: A Long-Run Economic Perspective

By
ALAN HESTON

Crusades and jihads have been a part of the histories of Christianity and Islam for more than a century. This article examines this often-violent history from several perspectives, focusing heavily on the period between 1000 and 1300, and on the factors that allowed Europe and its overseas extensions in North America and Australia to economically overtake the rest of the world by 1600. While some weight is given to religion in the discussion, many of the effects seem to have been accidental, both negative and positive. These include the reforms in marriage and family formation introduced by the Catholic Church; demographic pressures in Europe; and the development of institutions in Northern Europe that provided continuity in commerce, administration, and archiving of intellectual advances. The factors that favored the economies of Northern Europe and/or held back other parts of the world do not appear to be related to anything inherent in Christianity or Islam.

Keywords: religion; economic growth; crusades; jihads

We are following with great interest and concern the preparation of the crusaders to launch war to occupy a former capital of Islam, to pillage the wealth of Muslims and install a puppet government that follows the dictates of its masters in Washington and Tel Aviv.
> —Reported translation of a statement in Arabic attributed to Osama bin Laden on *Al Jazeera*[1]

To understand many current attitudes and conflicting worldviews centering on the Eastern Mediterranean, it is important to keep the economic and political events of 1000 to 1200 firmly in view. This argument is hardly new; Karen Armstrong in *Holy War* (1991) has provided a rich and provocative analysis of the conflict and cooperation between followers of the three religions that consider themselves children of Abraham and regard the Temple Mount/Al-Harram

Alan Heston is a professor of economics and South Asia at the University of Pennsylvania. His research interests include economic history and development and international comparisons of economic growth, output, and relative prices.

DOI: 10.1177/0002716203255393

Al-Shariff as their sacred space. Armstrong sums up by saying, "I now believe that the Crusades were one of the direct causes of the conflict in the Middle East today" (p. xiii). Tariq Ali (2002), in *The Clash of Fundamentalisms*, has made similar links and uses the subtitle, *Crusades, Jihads and Modernity*. President George W. Bush, in a number of justifications for attacking Iraq, harks back to a tradition of crusading and holy war, though the word *crusade*, itself, has apparently been retired from his public vocabulary after its first use.

Most Christians learn a colorful, romantic, and chivalrous account of the Crusades in Sunday school or similar settings. The crusading tradition of Christianity as seen by Muslims and Jews was probably unknown to the founders or most members of the Campus Crusade for Christ. *Jihad* as used in the vocabulary of those identifying themselves as militant Muslims is far from its original meanings; and *jihad* has now entered the international vocabulary. The many meanings given to words like *crusade* and *jihad* suggest the long and tortured relationships between Christians, Jews, and Muslims. It is a consequence of this often bitter history that while many Muslims attribute 9/11 to a Zionist conspiracy, there are many in America who brand Muslims, Arab or not, as suspect.

Economic factors are frequently mentioned when it comes to sources of conflict in the Middle East or the causes of terrorism. Two short-term factors, for example, are the asserted collective responsibility of sports utility vehicle drivers for financing terrorists and the supposed connection between poverty and terrorism. With respect to oil dependence, Iraq and many others argue that the focus of the Bush administration on regime change has less to do with weapons of mass destruction than with maintaining cheap supplies of petroleum products to the United States. The administration, of course, denies this; but one of the powerful arguments of bin Laden with his followers is how the willingness of Saudi Arabia to permit bases in its territory compromises the most important shrines of Islam. These bases are viewed as primarily safeguarding Middle East oil supplies to the United States and protecting Israel while keeping Palestinians from their nationhood and rightful territory.

Similarly, a supposed economic cause of terrorism is the lack of hope of suicide bombers who suffer from economic deprivation. Some would scuttle economic explanations of terrorism by noting that most of the 9/11 actors were from middle-class families and not economically deprived. But an important distinction to be kept in mind is that economic deprivation is more a relative concept than absolute and may be the product of both short-term and long-term factors. Certainly, many middle-class Muslim families in recent years have named their sons Osama as some type of nonreligious protest statement.

Rather than short-run economic factors, this article looks at the role of long-run economic factors in explaining what Huntington (1996) has termed the *Clash of Civilizations*. By *long-run economic factors*, I mean institutions, innovations, and other factors that allowed average incomes and total economic resources in the West in the past millennium to catch up to and surpass those of the Muslim world and other Eurasian areas. The first part of the article looks at why the Crusades of the eleventh and twelfth centuries are so much more important in the collective memory of Arabs than of other Muslims or of Christians and Jews. The second part examines the relationship of the Crusades to contemporary and later economic and political developments and, particularly, the question of why Europe was able to overtake the rest of the world economically after 1600. Moving forward, the third part of the article briefly looks at fundamentalism, which is often seen as antithetical to explanations based on economic factors. The discussion draws heavily on the fundamentalism project of Marvin Marty and Scott Appleby (1992). These diverse strands are then brought together in the concluding section. There I argue that the economic framework of economies, particularly institutions with continuity and minimal restraints on decision making, appears to be a more important influence on economic growth than culture or religion.

A point about language is that, while appreciative of Said's *Orientalism* (1978), the vocabulary in this article has a heavily Western slant, and readers are left to sort this out. Terrorism, like piracy, is a label of the speaker or writer, as illustrated in the following anecdote. When Alexander captured a notorious pirate, he berated him as a scourge who pillaged the seas. The pirate supposedly responded, "But, sir, you pillage the world."

Holy Wars and Crusades

Some background

The focus here is on how the economic growth in Europe and North America allowed these areas to surpass those of the Middle East and other parts of the world by the nineteenth century. This, in contrast to the fact that from the eighth to twelfth centuries, the Islamic world (and much of Asia) was substantially ahead of Europe in terms of scientific knowledge, technology, and economic levels. The emergence of three major empires with non-Arab Muslim leaders in the fifteenth and sixteenth centuries still made Asia the economic center of the world. This reversal of economic fortunes referred to by Landes (1998), Maddison (2002), and others as the "West and the Rest" has been subject to a variety of explanations. Some explanations involve religion, some culture, and some technology, while most offer alternative perspectives from which to view the continuing tensions in the Middle East and the relationship of terrorism, protest, and religion.[2]

One recurring theme is the set of institutions and ideology that have supposedly operated in favor of the economic success of Europe and its colonial extensions after 1600. These same factors were presumably somehow absent in the Muslim world and elsewhere. The discussion views the various holy wars and crusades of the period from 1000 to 1300 as essential background to what followed. This leads to an examination of the role of institutions like private property and the economics of warfare, a digression on the effects of Dutch Disease, and the role of unintended consequences.

The initial Arab conquests during the century after Mohammed's death in 632 extended westward from Mecca to North Africa, Sicily, and Spain and to the east through Iran to the Indian subcontinent and Bukhara and Samarkand in Central Asia. However, by 800, many of these empires were under a variety of non-Arab rulers. The ensuing period labeled by the Orientalists as the "Classical Era of Islam" was roughly from 800 to 1200, when Europe was beginning to emerge from the Dark Ages. During this period, not only did Baghdad, Alexandria, and other cities under Muslim rule become the intellectual centers of European classical tradition, they also fostered major centers of contemporary science, medicine, and scholarship. Chinese technological advances may have been more important in the long run, but for Europe in the period after 800, the contributions of archives and scholarship from the Muslim world in areas like medicine, mathematics, and science were critical.

Muslim Spain is especially interesting because of its high level of culture and learning, as contrasted with what was a much less sophisticated culture to the north. The library of the ruler of Cordoba in the tenth century was said to have contained four hundred thousand volumes, more than all the books in Europe at the time. Cordoba had a population of perhaps one hundred thousand, twice that of Paris, and third to Baghdad and Constantinople. And Cordoba had seven hundred mosques, three hundred public baths, and other public buildings.

Spain is also interesting because it illustrates the very fluid coalitions that easily crossed religious lines when secular interests were at stake. Cordoba, for example, split from Baghdad and had its own caliph of Al-Andalus. The Abbasid dynasty in Baghdad was not itself capable of putting down Cordoba, so it asked Charlemagne to attack its brethren in Spain. Similarly, the Eastern Christians and Latin Christians sought help from Muslim rulers and vice versa. It is also interesting how religious barriers could often be crossed at ease in social relationships. In Al-Andalus, there was intermarriage and integration of Christians, Jews, and Muslims, and religious differences were not a major issue. In fact, Jews had welcomed Muslim rule as more tolerant than that of Christians, with many Jews migrating from other parts of Europe to Al-Andalus.

But empires seem to always overextend themselves like investment bubbles or are destroyed by psychopaths like Al-Hakim, who was to bring down the Fatimid Dynasty in his twenty-five-year reign in Cairo ending in 1021. Rulers come along who overreach their capabilities and resources and in turn produce unified counterforces in place of formerly fragmented opponents. In the tenth century, Al-Mansur, an egomaniac who had emerged from various intrigues as the caliph of Cordoba, expanded south below the Atlas Mountains in North Africa for gold and slaves and soldiers. He then undertook more than fifty jihads into Christian areas of northern Spain to pillage and eventually expand Muslim rule to all of present-day Spain. In 997, he called for the destruction of the Church of St. James in Leon, a very important pilgrimage site because James, who was revered as the brother of Jesus, was thought buried in the tomb. The tomb was about all that was left undisturbed. The doors and bells of the cathedral and slaves were taken back to expand the mosque in Cordoba. Al-Mansur left Cordoba in weaker condition, and Muslim rule in Spain became more fragmented after 1000. Such excesses are not the preserve of Muslim rulers. Phillip II was do the same for Spain five-hundred-plus years later.

The First Crusade

Pilgrimages to Jerusalem and other sites had been common for Christians before the Crusades, with large groups going to the holy land in 1070. On these treks, pilgrims were prohibited from bearing arms. The reforms of the Cluniacs, who stressed Jesus as the Prince of Peace, also became influential in the eleventh century, attracting popes, including Urban II, who saw in their monastic and celibate life a model for Christian behavior. Many were attracted to the Cluniac reforms, and new monasteries and churches were established, often on the borders between Christian and Muslim territories.

This new tradition of peace and service in parts of Christian Europe ran counter to knightly tradition and actions in defending Europe against Magyars, Muslims, and other invading groups. Knights, who were retained to wage war and kill, were not generally associated with pilgrimages. Attitudes begin to change dramatically in the decades leading up to the First Crusade. One explanation is that there were large numbers of wars between minor principalities within Europe, and the church leadership decided it would be better to harness these energies in directions useful to the Latin Church. This tension between the violent battles of knights and the Cluniac reforms became a part of the traditions and mythologies of the various crusader military orders.

A related issue was Spain. The Church in Rome and other Christians to the north envied the prosperity of southern Spain. Even before the excesses of Al-Mansur, the infidel Moor became the symbol to unify opposition. Driving the Moors from Europe became an objective supported by Rome, leading to many campaigns to reconquer Spain in the eleventh century centering in Aragon and Castile. In retrospect, these campaigns were precursors to the Crusades, combining pilgrimage and arms, and eventually led to the worst excesses of the Inquisition.

Pope Urban II's call at the Council of Clermont in 1095 to save the Eastern Church and regain the Holy Land in what became known as the First Crusade was extraordinarily successful, mobilizing well over one hundred thousand in an eastward pilgrimage cum holy war. Some important demographic and economic factors were also at play. Mayer (1988) points out that the number of local famines was increasing in the tenth and eleventh centuries, associated with increases in population and aggravated by the practice of splitting up land inheritances between all male heirs. In response, primogeniture was introduced in northern France, forcing younger male siblings to fend for themselves. These population pressures were reinforced by other changes in the family structure that were brought about by the Catholic Church after 500 and that will be discussed further below. In southern France and Italy, the practice grew of common ownership, so that some members of the family could travel for raiding or other adventures and still retain their rights in the family land. Earlier, the Normans and other Scandinavian and Germanic tribes had moved into parts of Europe and settled rather than returning to their homelands. All of these factors helped contribute to a situation in 1000 where there was an ample supply of mercenaries and an increasing number of wars between local lords. Edmund Burke characterized employment in the British East India Company as a form of outdoor relief for middle-class families in England; in the same way, the Crusades were a way for Europe to export adventurers and potential troublemakers, at least temporarily. And settlement plus mortality from war and disease ensured a smaller return flow.

Almost from the start, the First Crusade became a series of unintended consequences, mostly negative. Byzantium was concerned about the advances into its territories of central Asians, the Seljuks, and what it wanted when it sought Rome's assistance was mercenaries it could deploy in its defense. Instead, it got a number of independent crusading groups embracing pilgrims, adventurers, knights (with some finance from their usual employers), and many camp followers with meager, if any, resources. The majority of the crusader groups needed supplies and raided villages along the way, Christian or not. Mortality was high from diseases like malaria and typhoid that were more severe when accompanied by malnourishment, poor water, and crowded conditions. And brutality was infamously memorable, including the cannibalism of the unfortunate local population of Maʿara in December 1098, an event kept alive in Arabic chronicles. Pope Urban II certainly was motivated to issue his call to increase the power of Rome and the Latin Church versus the Eastern Church of Byzantium. It is doubtful he foresaw likely consequences of the fervor generated by his call or the lethal results of sanctioning pilgrimages cum arms. And once started, there was no controlling the several sequences of crusading groups and their leaders.

Why did the crusaders undertake such a risky venture? Mortality was high at home, so an unknown probability of death may not have loomed large against the possible gains. For some, these gains were material, such as the promise that loot could be kept on their return. Some had visions of the Middle East as a land of milk and honey, which, compared to home, it probably was. Many were paid to participate by their local rulers. Others were promised that outstanding debt or crimes would be written off. And the general offer was indulgences for sins and, by implication, those sins committed along the pilgrimage route. Most crusaders would return home, but many of the leaders sought an economic base and were inclined to attack centers like Antioch, even if that went against the interests of Byzantium. While Latin Christians maintained a presence in the Eastern Mediterranean into the 1300s, the loss of Jerusalem in 1187 to Saladin at the battle of Hattin was the beginning of the end for the crusader kingdoms.

Some consequences of the Crusades

Steven Runciman, in volume 3 of *History of the Crusades* (1954), concludes that not only were the Crusades a failure for Europe in regaining the Holy Land but that instead of containing Islam, the Crusades encouraged its expansion by motivating the faithful and destroying the Eastern Church. Saunders (1962) sees the destruction of the power of Eastern Christianity as particularly significant. The Fourth Crusade that was to attack Muslim Cairo instead, through intrigues by Venice among others, culminated in the sack of Christian Byzantium, paving the way for its eventual demise. These events opened the door for the Mongols to move in, resulting in the destruction of monuments and libraries in parts of the Middle East. The successor Central Asian dynasties were principally Sunni Muslim, and under their administration, there was a relative decline of interest in the sciences and learning in general.

Another consequence is that the Crusades remain stronger in the collective memory of Muslims than of Christians and Jews. Yet Jewish villages were systematically subjected to pillage and slaughter in Europe as the crusaders passed through them along the way, the slaying of one infidel being as good as another in the quest for indulgences from the inexhaustible "treasury of merits" that Jesus had earned from God. One explanation of this seeming paradox is that Jews have experienced so many subsequent persecutions from Christians that the Crusades do not rank that high. One reason that the Crusades do not loom as important for the West is that in the end, Rome and Europe lost the battle but were to win the war of economic dominance in the subsequent centuries. So the cost of a failed expansion was not a brake on the future and was in fact a stimulus to the subsequent explorations of the Portuguese and Spanish.

The Crusades remain an important symbol for the Muslim world but especially for Arabs. The brutality of the First Crusade, including the slaughter of Eastern Christians as well as Jews and Muslims in Jerusalem, is only one factor. This carnage was in total contrast to the Muslim conquest of Jerusalem of Umar in 638 or reconquest by Saladin in 1187. Umar permitted Christians and Jews to live in Jerusalem, while Byzantium had restricted Jews and the crusaders were to ban Jews and Muslims. Saladin returned to the more restrictive practices of Umar's successors, which was still an improvement over Christian rule. The crusaders did not integrate well, living in castles and learning little of local language or culture, except for those that became *oriental*, a term of derision as used by most Franks (the contemporary term of reference for Europeans). Several ironies surround Saladin, one being that he was a Kurd and another that he was not celebrated in the Muslim world until the 1800s, though he was a romantic and honorable opponent of the knights in Western literature much earlier (Hillenbrand 1999).[3] Saladin established what was to become the Mamaluk Empire in Egypt, which survived until it was absorbed by the Ottomans in 1521.

The argument advanced here is that the Crusades are especially symbolic for Arab Muslims in the Middle East because they signaled the beginning of a major shift in the relationship between Europe and the Middle East. Muslim perceptions of the Franks, as of most barbarians, was quite negative; they were considered sexually lax and of course unclean because of their aversion to bathing (Hillenbrand 1999). Moreover, crusader kingdoms in the Middle East became symbolic in the region as Europe's first colonies (Maalouf 1984). For Arabs, the collective memory is stronger because by the end of the Crusades, their position in the Muslim world had substantially declined, as Turkish and Central Asian empires became the secular centers of Islam. Most Muslims in India and East Asia were converts in the sixteenth and seventeenth centuries, partly as a reaction to Dutch and Portuguese treatment of coastal rulers and Asian shipping in their attempts to control seagoing commerce. South and East Asian Muslims will have grown up with many unfavorable memories of European expansion, but not of the Crusades, which is not the case with Arabs. Maalouf (1984, 266) concludes his study of *The Crusades through Arab Eyes* by saying, "And there can be no doubt that the schism between these two worlds dates from the Crusades, deeply felt by the Arabs, even today, as an act of rape."

[T]he Crusades are especially symbolic for Arab Muslims in the Middle East because they signaled the beginning of a major shift in the relationship between Europe and the Middle East.

But the ability of the Franks in war was acknowledged, and after the first twenty years, their rule was probably less onerous than that of Muslim rulers. Maalouf (1984) cites the chronicler, Usamah Ibn Munquid, to the effect that the Franks treated all peasants equally and by a given set of rules, whatever their religion, exacting the same taxes and leaving their property and land unmolested. The Franks had transplanted a type of feudalism to their new lands in which relationships of knights and peasants were not subject to arbitrary decisions from kings. Maalouf argues further that a failure of most Muslim empires was that institutions were not developed to provide continuity in economic life when succession battles led to discontinuities at the top. Maalouf makes an important point, but the argument here is that this is a feature of most regimes that are not built on some consensus of interest groups and is no monopoly of Muslim empires.

The Inquisition was one of many unintended consequences of the First Crusade and the need for a scapegoat to explain the subsequent loss of Jerusalem and failures of subsequent crusades to secure a permanent presence of the Latin Church. The open schism between the Latin and Eastern Christians in 1054 was an important motivation for Pope Urban II's call for a crusade to the Holy Land, as he hoped to heal the rift and emerge as the leader of all Christians. But one strand of the belief brought back by the early crusaders from Bulgaria was that of the Cathars, which attracted many followers in Europe but especially in Languedoc in southern France. Cathars were hard to identify because their catharsis of purification came typically at the end of their lives. However, the Cathars were critical of the materialist orientation of the Catholic Church in Europe, leading to the Inquisition beginning in 1209, which became the special responsibility of Dominicans after 1233 and Franciscans in 1246.

The infamous Spanish form of the Inquisition followed the capture of Cordoba in 1236. The victors built a church to partially replace the mosque, a common enough practice though a major loss to architectural history. Muslims and Jews, if they had not fled, were to convert or die. Many did convert and still were the victims of torture to confess their heresy, as all *conversos* were regarded with suspicion. Another reaction to Muslim rule in Spain was to regard bathing as sacrilegious, and baths were destroyed, as was done later at Aztec sites. The rejection of Muslim rule, at least at the leadership level, was complete by the fall of Granada in 1492, and Ferdinand and Isabella issued an edict expelling all Jews. As a result, there was migration of large numbers of Muslims, Jews, and *conversos*, representing a great loss of human capital. While not as fanatical as the Taliban in Afghanistan, there were many aspects of the *reconquista* of Spain that set back the cause of learning. And the intolerance continued to flower throughout the Counter Reformation in the sixteenth century, the refugees taking their knowledge to Northern Europe. The last execution for heresy in Spain took place in 1826, and the Inquisition was officially suppressed in 1834.

Another unintended consequence of the Crusades was the formation of military orders of knights that not only generated the whole chivalric tradition but in fact had economic functions. Two major military orders formed the army of the crusaders in defense of Christian conquests.[4] Initially, the orders took vows of chastity and service and were viewed as exemplary in behavior as well as effective soldiers. The Knights Hospitallers began as the operatives in hospices in Jerusalem to help with the survivors of the siege of Jerusalem, but they were to add a military wing in black in response to the rise of the Templars. The Knights Templar devoted themselves to escorting pilgrims between crusader centers as well as from Europe to Jerusalem. The Hospitallers and Templars received large contributions from Europe, which they were able to augment by conquests.

In addition, the Templars became rich as they controlled a series of castles stretching from Europe to Syria that permitted the safe transfer of funds by debits and credits without transport of precious metals. In short, they became an army, a landowner, and a bank, rivaling the power and arousing the jealousy of Rome. As a consequence, they eventually became victims of the Inquisition in 1312, though by rumor they still survive symbolically today as a part of Masonic ritual.

A second consequence of the Crusades was the increased competition between Venice, Genoa, and Pisa for trade with the Eastern Mediterranean. Initially, Venice did not want to disrupt its trade with Muslims and did not support the First Crusade, while Pisa and Genoa transported crusaders and supplies. But by 1099, when Jerusalem had been secured, the calculating Venetians agreed to send supplies and support, which led to clashes with Pisa and attempts to monopolize this commerce for Venice. In a series of extortionate agreements over the next century, Venice was to acquire control of Tripoli and trading privileges at other crusader ports and a share of the loot from their capture led attacks on Hungarian Christians as well as Byzantium in the Fourth Crusade. In short, Venice, which was basically a militarily oriented city-state whose prosperity was based on trade, became a major beneficiary of the Crusades. Genoa, which was essentially a city run by merchants, was never able to obtain a foothold in the Eastern Mediterranean and to trade with Asia. As a consequence, Genoa sought to outflank Venice, in part, by helping to finance the voyages of Columbus. Columbus himself was to refer to his great adventure as a crusade, a tradition kept alive in name by the Knights of Columbus.

Perspectives on Europe's Economic Ascendance

Social scientists have not been reluctant to assign religion a role in stimulating or retarding economic growth. Weber ([1905] 1958) extolled the *Protestant Ethic* and suggested the retarding effect of otherworldliness and the caste system on the economic performance in India. Tawney (1948) elaborated the position that there was a connection between the Protestant Reformation and the growth of capitalism in Europe with the implication that the Catholic Church had a retarding influence. These explanations neglected the very capitalistic institutions of the Italian city-states (as well as the Templars), not to mention the economic acumen displayed by Parsis (Zoroastrians) in India, Jews in many settings, the Samurai in Japan, and traditional Hindu and Muslim business communities. So examination of the role of religion from an economic perspective is not a new activity, and I have done so in the context of the sacred cow controversy in India (Heston 1971). That exploration argued that the usual economic explanations would only take one so far and that religious motivations clearly played a role in explaining the gender composition of the cattle population in India. However, there is a tendency for economists to attribute the influence of religion as affecting tastes and demand, as, for example, the prohibitions on eating pork in Islam and Judaism. And as I have shown in discussing the incentives of crusaders, there are many nonmonetary exchanges that influence human welfare and, hence, behavior.

It is in a similar vein that this section examines some secular and religious explanations for the economic differentials that developed after 1600. An interpretation accepted in much of the world is that European gains were at the expense of the rest of the world, for which some evidence can certainly be provided. But in the realm of exploitation, perceptions are often more important than reality. In the context of religion, it is common to translate perceived economic grievances into an attack on the beliefs of the exploited by the alleged exploiters, a point to which I return below. In this section, I first examine the economic role attributed to institutions, science and technology, or simply to the chance of the draw.

The role of institutions

In *Rise of the Western World*, North and Thomas (1973) argue that a crucial element in allowing Europe to grow rapidly was the development of institutions permitting a more efficient allocation of economic resources. When productive resources become scarce, it is important to develop rights in property and productive capital to achieve an efficient allocation of resources and to generate investment. Individual merchants will not want to commit resources to long-run projects if the physical capital could be arbitrarily expropriated by rulers or robbers. Also important in the North and Thomas framework is the need to provide a system where individuals can capture the rents from developing and applying technology in new ways. This is especially true in the case of new ideas that become public goods (patents most easily protect innovations embodied in commodities) for which the innovator cannot charge. A classic case was the need for navigators to calculate the longitudinal position of their vessels. Once a method to calculate longitude was found, there was no way to prevent it from becoming public knowledge, and no charge could be levied to allow recovery of resources invested by the discoverer. One solution was a prize, such as Prince Henry the Navigator of Portugal offered in the fifteenth century, for which in fact there were many entrants but no successful claimants. A similar system financed by an international consortium of industrial countries has been proposed to stimulate drug companies to fund research to find inexpensive treatments for HIV, malaria, and the like, which firms would not normally do because the market would not permit recovery of investments in drug development.

North and Thomas (1973) argue that these institutions developed in Northern Europe as they broke away from systems that they had held in common with Southern Europe. This break was accompanied by bargaining between different constituents of Northern European countries, the lords and landowners and the merchants and artisans. These institutions were exported to North America, while South America mainly received the Southern European version. North and de Soto (1993) have argued that this has been to the detriment of the economic development in Latin America, a theme to be explored later.

Mancur Olson (1982) has taken a similar viewpoint in his analysis of the predatory state and of the role of countervailing interest groups. Two other elaborations of the institutional view that have been developed, namely, *transactions costs* and *ideology*, deserve mention. The first is that that economic efficiency is improved when transactions costs are reduced. The most obvious illustration is transport, where reductions in costs permit specialization and economies of scale in production, raising global output. Williamson (1981) and others have applied the notion of transactions costs to organizations and other potential impediments to the efficient use of resources, like taxes and tolls, administrative permits, and the like. In the religious realm, prohibitions of interest and usury laws impose transactions costs on credit markets. A major transactions cost to doing business at a distance is loss due to theft on land and sea routes. Maintenance of relatively safe internal travel was a major role of land-based empires that was often financed by tolls; the quality of protection tended to decline with disruptive changes in rule. But another major transactions cost is imposed when rights to resources are ambiguous and therefore subject to administrative decisions. For example, capital becomes dead, in de Soto's (2000) terminology, if it is not free to move to different uses because title is unclear, another point to which we will return in the conclusion.

The second elaboration is ideology, or what is often termed *social norms*. The economic role of social sanctions is important and fluid. Social norms and possible sanctions appear to have allowed markets to operate by involving future delivery of goods where no enforcement mechanism by a third party, like government, existed. For example, at annual medieval fairs, often transactions involved promises to deliver goods the following year based upon an advance payment or other agreement. No government existed to enforce such contracts. A frequent mechanism was the collective guarantee to deliver on the contract by the guild of which the individual artisan accepting an advance was a member. The penalty to a guild member who did not deliver was to be ostracized, a high cost if social mobility is low. These informal enforcement mechanisms of contracts are widespread throughout the world and underpin many forms of rotating credit. However, informal enforcement is less effective in impersonal settings such as large cities.

In this institutional view of economic history, the ability of societies to use resources and provide incentives for long-term investment evolved from authoritarian rule to a shared power structure. Rulers and forms of governance were to develop from simply selling protection to citizens for a share of their labor days and/or output to a money rent basis and some sharing of power. One of the criticisms of this line of explanation is that technological improvements are always there and simply need the right set of incentives to be applied. An alternative framework is discussed below.

North and Thomas (1973) see Northern Europe as the place where these developments in competition between different economic interests and the ruler first took firm roots. By contrast, the stagnation of Spain and many earlier empires that had achieved economic levels far above those of Northern Europe in the fifteenth century could be attributed to these institutions' only being well formed in recent times, if at all. Why these institutions had not developed in other parts of the world is not really part of the North and Thomas story. Landes (1998), in his contemporary version of Adam Smith's *The Wealth of Nations*, sees culture playing a key role in fostering institutions allowing systematic development of new technologies. The evidence that Landes gives to support a cultural explanation seems largely anecdotal, but his treatment of technology and science is important and is treated below.

Where tribal organization was typical, resources were often held in common, and in this framework, it is a major social adjustment to move to a system of private rights in property. While many areas with large Muslim populations were tribal in origin, so was Northern Europe. Furthermore, settled agriculture was common throughout China, India, and the Middle East as well as in Europe, so a general explanation of why all this happened in Northern Europe and not elsewhere, based on early social organization, does not seem well founded. Jack Goody (2000) argues that family structure in Eurasia and other areas of settled agriculture shared many more similarities with each other than differences until at least 1000.

North and Thomas (1973) do see demographics as one major stimulus to change. As noted earlier, faster population growth in Europe in the eleventh century was seen as an impetus for the crusades. In particular, they argue that the plague or Black Death of the fourteenth century was a demographic shock that put pressures on the feudal lords because their labor force was suddenly sharply reduced, as was the surplus they could command. The consequence in Western Europe was the breakup of the system of feudal dues and traditional obligations, which was replaced by a more market-oriented system of money rents and wage labor. This leaves us with the puzzle of why Eastern Europe and Russia should go a different path, with those controlling large tracts of land able to strengthen their hold over serfs, an opportune time to turn to the role of technology.

Science and technology

There are many other explanations of what allowed Europe to move ahead in the millennium after 800 and impose its calendar, rather than the Islamic, Indian, or Chinese calendars, on the world. One type of explanation focuses on what prevented these other civilizations from maintaining their advantage in human capital and knowledge, while others focus on the question of why Europe was able to overtake the rest. Landes (1998) believes that most of the factors that North and Thomas (1973) emphasize, like property rights, are important but were well defined in Europe much earlier. His explanation stresses the role of science and technological advance that had its origins in a series of gradual changes from about 1000 that become much more evident after 1500.

Landes (1998, 201) cites three crucial factors: "(1) the growing autonomy of intellectual inquiry; (2) . . . the creation of a language of proof recognized, used, and understood across national and cultural boundaries; and (3) the invention of invention, that is the *routinization* of research and its diffusion." These characteristics of the European Enlightenment were presumably absent from or had been forgotten by other societies.

Justin Lin (1995) has offered an explanation of the Needham puzzle, namely, Why did China lose the substantial lead in science and technology that it had achieved by 1200? His model is one where the technological improvements in the early stages are primarily due to farmers' and artisans' experimenting with improved ways of doing things. If the probability of success from tinkering increases with the number of experiments, then civilizations with larger populations will undertake more experiments and have more successes. For Lin, this describes the situation in China during the high point of China's technical advances in the 1000 to 1200 period; this was a time when China had a very large population and experienced no substantial natural catastrophes or invasions. However, Lin also argues that after initial technological successes in a productive sector, it gets harder and harder to make further advances without building on records of previous advances and attempts to establish principles. In Lin's view, China would have had to systematically record results to have maintained its momentum, but the Mandarin bureaucracy did not provide resources or encouragement for this type of intellectual activity.

What Lin (1995) sees as different in Europe is that in the sixteenth and seventeenth centuries, advances in technology and science came to be systematically recorded. This may have been facilitated by the development of medieval universities in Oxford, Paris, and elsewhere. Lin also argues that competition between various European states may have promoted advances, as compared to China, where the unified bureaucracy tended to stifle new developments. Lin's story is, then, quite consistent with the ideas of Landes (1998) and Maddison (2002) and offers a theory of why the advances did not happen in other civilizations. A similar story could probably be told for India.

In the European case, the competition was heightened by the Reformation and Counter-Reformation and the reaction of Northern Europe to the stifling effect of the Papacy on types of scientific inquiry, like that of Galileo in 1632. Associated with the rise of scientific and technical advances in Northern Europe was a corresponding shift in economic and political power from Spain. Europe, as opposed to the crusaders themselves, did absorb as much knowledge as it could from the Muslim world. The Council of Vienna in 1312 was to establish centers for the study of Arabic, Greek, Hebrew, and Syriac. There was little interest shown in the languages of Europe by the Muslim world during the Crusades or subsequently. Obviously Europe had more to learn from the Muslim world than vice versa, but the establishment of institutions for studying others was a part of an impetus to systematically record information on which future generations could build, and this the Catholic Church fostered, and universities and other institutions in Northern Europe advanced.

After the Crusades and the disruptions of 1100 to 1300, secular leadership of the Muslim world shifted away from Arab leaders. The three great Muslim empires of the sixteenth and seventeenth centuries, the Ottoman, Safavid, and Mughal, far surpassed Europe economically. However, the Sunni rule of the Ottomans, Shi'a rule of Persia, and mixed rule of the Mughals made cooperation as difficult as between the Eastern and Latin churches a few centuries earlier or between Catholic and Protestant Europe in the sixteenth century. Each of these Muslim empires excelled in art, architecture, military technology, and administrative practice, but their interest in fostering improvements in productive technology or systematically recording recent additions to scientific knowledge, outside of armaments, was limited.

There were a number of reasons for this. These were land-based empires that could obtain substantial surpluses for their leadership from the taxation of agriculture and expanding their empires, while in Europe, there was more population pressure and a need to diversify from agriculture to industry and trade. Some believe that the intellectual openness of the first centuries of Islam lost steam after 1300 and that adherents of the Sunni and Shi'a traditions tended to theological discourse rather than scientific inquiry. Perhaps the intellectual rigidity of Spain during the Inquisition and Counter-Reformation is a parallel.

Indeed, it is a seeming paradox that Portugal and Spain, which fostered the European expansion to the west and east, should have turned so inward after the Reformation. Portugal led many of the advances in navigation in the fifteenth century, but a century later, the crown looked upon royal voyages to Asia as only a source of rents, not of scientific or intellectual interest. In fact, it was the Northern Europeans who more systematically studied practices in India from the vantage point of Portuguese Goa than the Portuguese themselves. As political and economic historians have noted, the situation of Spain is seemingly paradoxical, with the acquisition of apparently unlimited supplies of precious metals leading only to military expansion, political and intellectual suppression, and subsequent economic decline. The following digression on Spain and factors affecting empires, Muslim and other, is more speculative.

The Dutch Disease phenomenon

Another approach to the sixteenth and seventeenth centuries is to put some of the changes in the world of Spain; Portugal; and the Ottoman, Safavid, and Mughal Empires in a modern political-economic perspective. What has been discovered in the past fifty years is that the blessings of natural resources can be a curse in disguise. A standard description uses the experience of the Dutch in the 1970s, when the economy was blessed by the discovery of North Sea oil and gas. The government took most of the rental income from these supplies and used them to expand social benefits, higher education, and other programs. The value of exports of the Netherlands expanded rapidly, leading to a large supply of foreign exchange that had the effect of raising the value of the guilder in terms of foreign currencies. As a result, it became expensive to buy the traditional Dutch exports of agricultural and manufactured goods. So while total exports expanded, traditional industries suffered and workers were laid off, but the expanded government revenues provided a very comfortable safety net. When the oil and natural gas revenues declined, so did government resources to finance the expanded programs. And Dutch Disease now set in with a vengeance as the declining industries could not quickly recover when the guilder devalued, and the population dependent on the government saw their entitlements dwindle.

The analogy with sixteenth-century Spain is clear on two fronts. Spain's oil and gas were the silver and gold of Mexico and Peru. This had the effect of making precious metals the best export for Spain, to the detriment of traditional industries like woolens and the wine. It is true that in the twentieth-century Netherlands, the decision of the government to expand services was carried out within a parliamentary democracy, which sixteenth-century Spain was not. But like the Dutch, Spain overspent its revenues, the Spanish crown seeking to expand the influence of Rome to its own glory. Contemporaries sought explanations for the decline of traditional industries in terms of the loss of work ethic among the shepherds, the lax morals of society, and a variety of social evils. But the root of the problems of twentieth-century Holland and sixteenth-century Spain was a large increase in resources available to the leadership that was independent of taxation efforts or of productive activities of the population. The leadership, the parliament in the Netherlands and the crown in Spain, did not need to seek support from other elements in society to obtain more than ample resources for what they saw as priority uses.

One can see the parallels of the Dutch with most oil economies around the world. When leaders can acquire large revenues without trade-offs from other parts of a society, and democratic institutions are not strong or are nonexistent, then the quality of leadership and outcomes is very much a matter of chance. In recent years, a form of Dutch Disease has persisted in Venezuela, Nigeria, Zambia, Iran, Iraq, Saudi Arabia, and probably other countries. Several oil economies have been able to sterilize their foreign exchange earnings and avoid some of the worst economic consequences of Dutch Disease. However, factors generating large surpluses for rulers, whether they are natural resources or exploitation of newly acquired territories, do not seem to be good for long-run development of institutions.

Pushing this line of thought further, when a regime can obtain ample revenues without the need to build a coalition of support for its policies, then it does not usually establish strong institutions. In recent times, quasi-monopoly positions in oil and other natural resources and even crops like cocoa through marketing boards have provided a basis for unfettered rule by any who could claim control. In earlier times, regimes could achieve an analogous position to Spain by continued conquest of new territories. It was not easy for empires to continue expansion or even to maintain surpluses, in part because their revenue base was typically from the land and payments could be withheld. One conclusion of this digression is that like most regimes in the world, the empires of Muslim and non-Muslim rulers were sensitive to the particular individuals in power. Some rulers were highly competent, establishing conditions where both ruler and ruled prospered while others were arbitrary, short-sighted, and ruled by fear. In some cases, strong ideologies supported the divine nature of the rulers and in turn provided some constraints on the behavior of the rulers. But in few cases were institutions created that allowed continuity of administration and intellectual advancement.

Unintended consequences

Joseph Schumpeter is said to have illustrated the concept of *unintended consequences* by observing that "good brakes make cars go faster." This is an essential element of the story that Deepak Lal (1998) puts forward to explain what allowed Europe to get ahead. He stresses the introduction of elements of a codified legal system and, following Goody (2000), the consequences of a changed family system. Lal argues that as the Latin Church took on both religious and civil roles in society as it filled the void left by the fall of the Roman Empire, it began under Gregory VII to place itself above local leaders. One way to do this was to establish a legal framework for civil activities, and so contract laws began to be written in 1075. Such laws were to provide a framework for expanded commerce but also led to an unintended reaction against the Church and in favor of separating civil and religious transactions.

Lal (1998) accepts the argument of Goody (2000) that the Catholic Church was successful in spreading a very different family system in Christian areas of Europe than had existed in settled areas of Eurasia before, say, 400. As settled communities were established in the Bronze Age in Eurasia, the family had evolved in similar patterns as a collective economic and social unit, frequently based on clan identification and organized around male patrimony. Marriages were made and conventions adopted of acceptable partnerships in ways to keep resources within the larger family. This was a common pattern in all of Asia; in Classical Greece and Rome; and in Judaism, Islam, and early Christianity.

While the press points out the growing numbers of Muslims, the fastest-growing religion is probably the Pentecostal tradition of Christianity.

But when Christianity was accepted by Roman leadership in the fourth century, the Church began to advocate changes in family structure, beginning with a ban in 314 of *levirate* (the widow marrying a brother of the deceased husband) and its less common mirror image, *sororate* (a widower marrying a sister of the deceased). In 597, Pope Gregory I introduced a number of marriage reforms that were gradually to become social norms in much of Europe (Goody 2000, chap. 3). One change prohibited marriages of *affines*, like cross-cousin marriages that are common in many societies to keep capital within the family or clan. And incest was defined in a much narrower way than in Eurasian families, where, for example, marriage of half-siblings was permitted. The stricture against divorce was already there. No secondary marriage unions within the family were permitted, such as levirate, discussed above. The institution of godparents was created to keep orphans, and their assets, if any, in the church.

Like the Virgin Mary, women had a special place in the Catholic Church. Women were always a larger share of the followers of Christianity and frequently became attached to particular priests or monasteries. While widow remarriage was not, as in some Hindu practice, prohibited, it was strongly discouraged. Rather, it was taught that the widow should dedicate her love and devotion to the Church. Some teachings of the Catholic Church being formulated may seem paradoxical with regard to sexual relationships. On one hand, original sin and the view that sexual intercourse was only for procreation generated a great deal of guilt and reinforced celibate behavior while discouraging remarriage. And the Catholic Church on one hand was restricting the number of approved marriage unions while at the same time it was encouraging large families within approved unions.

The Church also encouraged marriage on the basis of the choice of the man and woman rather than of parents. This clearly served the purpose of making it likely that the larger family lost control of dowry of the woman and dower of the man, as both could inherit under church doctrine. Such love marriages introduced a new element into family formation in Europe and differentiated Europe from the rest of Eurasia while at the same time introducing a great deal of guilt related to sex. This did not stop royalty from making strategic marriages or from seeking divorce and in other ways crossing church doctrine, all elements supporting the Reformation.

The Church also sought control of potential wealth through the priesthood and children of concubines or other out-of-wedlock relationships. Abraham bred off-spring of his wife's handmaid, and priest concubinage was common in the early Church. Later, the move to celibacy vows for priests added to the probability that the inheritance of his family would go to the Church.

Another reform of the Church was to prohibit adoptions that transferred rights of inheritance in the case of the childless. This may account for two other offsetting institutions, namely, orphanages and homes for the elderly or abandoned. Goody (2000) argues that the net effect of these reforms, combined with premodern mortality levels, meant that 40 percent of marriages would produce no heirs. In terms of family structure, there were fewer families, with perhaps more children of the union per family. The Catholic Church did accumulate large amounts of land, much to the envy of the royalty in France, England, and elsewhere. An unintended consequence was the increasing conflicts between church and state and the reactions in Northern Europe leading to the Reformation.

After 400, the Catholic Church gradually took on dual roles, one secular, engaging in disputes ranging from civil to military conflict and generating a codified legal framework for business transactions, inheritance, and the like; and the other religious, often involving property matters, land administration, and social services, as well as fostering learning. Lal (1998) believes changes in the family were critical to the development of individualism in Europe, which he regards as unique. The link here is that young men in the reformed European family were not necessarily guaranteed an inheritance and were raised in an environment in which many social responsibilities of family were assumed outside the home. Lal sees individualism as a characteristic of Europe arising as the Christian family system gradually underwent a transformation that was not characteristic of other parts of Eurasia or other traditions like Hinduism, Islam, or Judaism. He views this individualism and the development of a legal framework of commerce as key factors in allowing Europe to move ahead economically compared to other areas of Eurasia.

Lal's (1998) story is suggestive but is only one interpretation of the possible effects of Europe's changed family structure that Goody (2000) documents. Another possible consequence is what Crosby (1986) terms the "biological expansion of Europe." Crosby sees Europe expanding between 900 and 1700 to settle in three continents and to settle or colonize the remainder. Another interpretation of the Goody evidence is that demographic pressures in Europe were the main force of expansion. With more property within the church and fewer extended families, there was great pressure on young males to find a source of livelihood. This undoubtedly contributed to individualism, but it would also be a reason for young men to seek adventure. The first overseas expansion of Portugal and Spain is clearly in response to their geographic position and control of the Western Mediterranean, and the direct experience with Moorish rule, not necessarily demographic pressures. However, in the case of Portugal, crews were recruited for their ships from all over, including many from Northern Europe. The major difference between the European experience and other expansive societies including Arabs during the first century after the death of Mohammed, or the Golden Horde of Central Asia, is that the extent of European settlement was much larger, especially in the Americas, Australia, and New Zealand.

In addition to demographic pressures, Lin (1995) argues that Europe's terrain was such that it was difficult to unify, leading to competition. While we are not far along in a theory of the physical limitations of empire, it is quite clear that more difficult geographical terrain, other things equal, makes it more difficult to expand the size of domain. The terrain of Northern Europe in the sixteenth century did not favor large states to the extent of present-day areas of Eastern China, India, Iran, or Turkey. As military technology improves, including armed ships, regimes can command a larger land area or make previous regimes untenable. The Italian city-states sought surpluses from expanding trade, influence, and strategic ports, not from expanding their land domains. As with Portugal, naval power could compensate to some extent for land area.

Unintended consequences should have more weight in explanations of Europe's economic expansion than is usually given. A number of policies of the Catholic Church and the rapid demographic recovery from the plague of the fourteenth century appear to have unleashed an outward movement of Europeans. Some elements of chance, namely, the topography of Europe, left it hard for any one power to reach political ascendance and seem to have encouraged competition not only on the battlefield but in industry, technology, and science. The failed Crusades led to a reaction in the Catholic Church, leading it to an inward battle against heretics in the Inquisition that, in turn, probably encouraged the Reformation that articulated some "heresies" into a coherent theology. The Crusades also spelled the end to the flowering of medicine, science, and scholarship in Islam that had been fostered in Alexandria and Baghdad. The Fourth Crusade in effect ended the power of Byzantium, opening up the Middle East to a new set of Muslim rulers from Central Asia. The Catholic Church had some positive influences in fostering higher education and introducing a legal framework for commerce. But some of the reforms of family structure, aimed at enhancing the flow of wealth to the Church, induced conflicts that helped reinforce the Reformation. Continuity of institutions and rulers was weak throughout Eurasia after 1000 unless there were pressures to form support groups or an accepted ideology to constrain despotic rule.

Fundamentalism

David Brooks (2003) has reminded those of us brought up in a secular tradition that religion is not fading as a force in societies around the world. While the press points out the growing numbers of Muslims, the fastest-growing religion is probably the Pentecostal tradition of Christianity: with the inroads it has made among Catholics in Latin America and its rapid growth in Africa, it now numbers close to 400 million around the world. What is the relationship of fundamentalist views to this growth in religious affiliation in many parts of the world?

The interpretation of Marty and Appleby (1992) is that for Christianity, at least, the relationship is complex but weak. In the United States, Marty and Appleby see a tendency for the media to group Pentecostals and Evangelicals with fundamentalist groups. But because fundamentalist groups tend to literal interpretations of the Bible, have taken antievolution efforts as a major political project, and tend to be antimodern, they do not mix well with the others. Pentecostals deal with miracles, healings, and speaking in tongues, so their practices are not congenial to fundamentalists. Evangelicals, like Billy Graham, are too ecumenical, embracing Catholics and reaching out to make conversions in all parts of the world. Fundamentalism across religions offers a specific reading of certain texts or of the history of their religion and peoples. Marty and Appleby sum up their findings as follows:

> We have seen that fundamentalists today in various religious traditions, sensing and studiously reflecting upon the evocative and defining power of the sacred, attempt to harness this power for what, upon close scrutiny, turns out to be an almost bewildering variety of political, social and religious ends. United only by a common conviction that the sacred is under sustained attack by the forces of secularization, fundamentalists seek to reconsecrate the world. (P. 192)

While some associate fundamentalism with resistance to the secular and the modern world, spokesmen and terrorists in the name of fundamentalist causes have embraced the latest in information technology and secular advances in technology in their organization and communications. Fundamentalist appeals frequently focus on sacred space that provides a concrete focus. This is true of Hindus, who continue to appeal to followers to right the wrongs in Ayodya, where Muslims built a mosque on the site thought to be the birthplace of the god Ram. And Jerusalem is the sacred space for Christians, Jews, and Muslims and continues to provide a fundamentalist appeal. Combined with visions of a second coming shared by small groups of Christians and Jews, it provides in some cases a strange marriage of interest of two fundamentalist traditions. There is no question of the strong appeal of these traditions and the amazing degree of political influence they have been able to generate, particularly in the case of Israel and indirectly in the United States, where Christian fundamentalists typically support Israel. Wahabis in Saudi Arabia have been able to similarly obtain great political leverage on the regime far beyond their numbers. For present purposes, we accept the view of

Marty and Appleby (1992) that without denying the fervor of true believers, fundamentalism is used for a wide variety of political aims by many leaders who claim to be adherents.

The growth of organized religions around the world, with the exception of Europe, does not appear to be directly connected to politics. However, in many instances, such as the growing number of Evangelical Christians in Brazil and other Latin American countries, it can be viewed as a reaction to the failures of governments and other institutions to address concerns of major population groups. One of those institutions in Latin America is of course the Catholic Church, which has been a hierarchy heavily identified with governments and one that does not provide direct access to God in the way that Evangelical worship provides.

In terms of what is often termed social capital, I would argue that the Evangelical traditions of Christianity and the mosques and temples of Muslims and Hindus in countries of immigration are important. Frequently, they perform an educational function, are intermediaries to government, and are a network of communication and information. The number of mosques that are alleged to foster terrorism, or temples and organizations financing separatist movements in India, Ireland, or Turkey, are probably small compared to those providing religious education and social identification for their members.

Conclusion

This article began with a discussion of crusades and jihads and their symbolic importance in the past thousand years. An examination of the period of the Crusades suggested that they marked a number of important changes: the decline of the influence of Arabs, the decline in importance of Byzantium, the rise of Muslim empires ruled by Central Asian groups, the increasingly inward orientation of the Catholic Church as exemplified by the various Inquisitions, and a gradual hardening of lines between Sunni and Shi'a Islam. The winners from the Crusades were the new Turkish Islamic groups and the Italian city-states. The losers were many, including Jews and especially Arabs, whose collective memory still resonates with the barbaric nature of the Crusades.

Scholars like Maalouf (1984) ask the obvious question of why the Arab world has not been able to put such injustices behind it. One reason that has been discussed is that Europe was able to get on with the ultimate failure of the Crusades in retaining the Holy Land because of their later successes. European average incomes and levels of technology and learning were to substantially surpass the levels that the Arab world once achieved relative to Europe. A second reason is that Europe (sometimes with the United States) has done nothing but rub salt in the wounds with its colonial conquests, disrupting partitions so well described by Kitchens (2003), and its policies with respect to oil and the establishment and maintenance of Israel. And the whole European approach to the "other" involved in the Orientalist scholarship of colonial administration and power relationships has done little to improve understanding.

In reviewing a number of explanations of the economic success of Europe, most of the factors that scholars suggested differentiated the "West and the Rest" have little to do with anything intrinsic to the Muslim world. The eventual scientific and technological leadership of Europe beginning in the seventeenth century is clear. Lin (1995) argues that China failed to follow up its advantages in part because it was a homogeneous empire dominated by a set of administrators who were focused on maintaining tradition and past glory. In Europe, on the other hand, there was competition between small Northern European states and later between Protestant and Catholic areas. This competition was reinforced by the pressures on individuals to seek success independent of their family fortunes, resulting from the less inclusive family structure produced by Catholic marriage reforms. Goody (2000) sees this as a major change compared to the more inclusive family structures that had characterized Europe and the rest of Eurasia and, though modified by urbanization, remains strong in Eurasia and in the Islamic and Jewish traditions. The aggressive colonization and settlement patterns in Europe also seem related to this changed family structure as well as the political-economic structure of those states surrounding the Mediterranean.

Unintended consequences are a part of any account of Northern European ascent as well as descent in empires like Spain or Moghul India. When succession is unclear and there are few brakes on the behavior and decisions of rulers, mobilization of opposition is likely to bring down poorly performing regimes. Whether successors can pick up the pieces will depend on whether there is continuity of institutions and of stakeholders.

Is there anything special about the Muslim world? In the Middle East, it has been noted that democracies are scarce, but many examples of dictatorships, like Iraq, involve secular, not Islamic, governments. A simpler explanation is that when leaders can obtain control of resources without building up a consensus, as is possible in petroleum-based regimes, it is very conducive to autocratic government. There is one feature of European and North American success that North and Thomas (1973) emphasize, and that is security of property from arbitrary decisions by governments.

A central theme of de Soto (2000) is that in much of Latin America, Africa, Asia, and Eastern Europe, there are major restrictions on the mobility of capital because ownership and transfer are restricted. Such restrictions are very strong in Egypt, for example, where to obtain title to desert land requires from eight to fourteen years with eventual approval coming not automatically but through bureaucratic discretion—that is, rarely without a payment. Such stories can be repeated in India, the Philippines, and in many parts of Latin America. The bottom line is that savings efforts by individuals are not easily expanded because of the bureaucratic obstacles to obtaining title. This in turn leads to a great deal of dead capital, by which de Soto means resources that cannot be moved to more efficient uses without recourse to administrators where the decision rules are not transparent. These kinds of restrictions on use of capital are prevalent in the Middle East and elsewhere, and these higher transactions costs have the effect of retarding economic growth. Hong Kong and Singapore are clear exceptions, as are the special economic zones in China, but for the mainland, the ownership and control of capital in China is still shrouded in ambiguity.

In short, there are many explanations of the political and economic structure of Muslim countries that have not reached their growth potential that have nothing to do with Islam, just as success stories like Malaysia have less to do with Islam than with substantial investments in human capital of both genders. The heritage of autocratic decision making appears a common feature of many countries whose economic performance has been disappointing.[5] The suggestion of North and Thomas (1973) and of Justin Lin (1995) that this may have grown out of the competition between interest groups within the states of Europe and reinforced by the competition between the numerous states remains a plausible explanation.

The relative economic deprivation of peoples can be a powerful motivating factor in behavior leading to civil war or protracted protest. In the present state of hostility and misunderstanding between much of the Muslim world and the United States, it is easy to take inherent religious or societal differences as the source, creating still larger apparent gaps that the politically expedient can exploit. In this article, the theme is that a large source of difference has an economic base with roots going back to the period of the Christian Crusades and that this continues to exert an influence in the Arab consciousness.

Notes

1. Quoted in the *New York Times*, 15 February 2003, p. A11. An intellectual and theological rationale of this quotation is provided by Paul Berman (2003) in an article that appeared as this piece was going to press. Berman's fuller exposition will appear in book form and is titled *Terror and Liberalism* (Norton).

2. Kindleberger (1996) in *World Economic Primacy* offers a cyclical version of primacy of civilizations and regards the ascendancy of the West as a temporary bubble. The key mechanism, he argues, is that civilizations cannot continue to maintain any technological advantage against newcomers. Mancur Olson (1982) in the *Rise and Decline of Nations* offers an explanation that is complementary to the institutional position discussed in the text.

3. The fact that Saladin was a Kurd did not prevent Saddam Hussein in 1991 from appealing for Muslim support claiming that he, like Saladin, was battling the crusaders.

4. There were other orders such as the Teutonic. As the name implies, the Teutonic Knights were German in origin and were eventually to play a role in the formation of Prussia as a state.

5. China might seem a major exception to this statement, but this is partly an illusion since decision making does involve a great deal of bargaining between regional and other power groups. Shirk (1994) has referred to the internal bargaining within the Communist Party of China as a process of "playing to the provinces," something at which most leaders in China are quite skilled.

References

Ali, Tariq. 2002. *The clash of fundamentalisms: Crusades, jihads and modernity*. New York: Verso.
Armstrong, Karen. 1991. *Holy war*. New York: Doubleday.
Berman, Paul. 2003. The philosopher of Islamic terror. *New York Times Magazine*, 11 March.
Brooks, David. 2003. Kicking the secularist habit. *Atlantic Monthly*, March, 26-28.
Crosby, Alfred W. 1986. *Ecological imperialism: The biological expansion of Europe, 900-1900*. New York: Cambridge University Press.

de Soto, Hernando. 2000. *The mystery of capital: Why capitalism triumphs in the West and fails everywhere else*. New York: Basic Books.

Goody, Jack. 2000. *The European family: An historico-anthropological essay*. New York: Blackwell.

Heston, Alan. 1971. An approach to the sacred cow of India. *Current Anthropology* 12:191-205.

Hillenbrand, Carole. 1999. *The Crusades: Islamic perspectives*. Chicago: Fitzroy Dearborn.

Huntington, Samuel P. 1996. *The clash of civilizations and the remaking of world order*. New York: Simon & Schuster.

Kindleberger, Charles. 1996. *World economic primacy, 1500-1990*. New York: Oxford University Press.

Kitchens, Christopher. 2003. The perils of partition. *Atlantic Monthly*, March, 99-107.

Lal, Deepak. 1998. *Unintended consequences*. Cambridge, MA: MIT Press.

Landes, David. 1998. *The wealth and poverty of nations*. New York: Norton.

Lin, Justin Yifu. 1995. The Needham puzzle: Why the Industrial Revolution did not originate in China. *Economic Development and Cultural Change*, vol. 43.

Maalouf, Amin. 1984. *The Crusades through Arab eyes*, translated by Jon Rothschild. New York: Schocken Books.

Maddison, Angus. 2002. *The world economy: A millenial perspective*. Paris: Development Centre of the OECD.

Man, John. 1999. *Atlas of the year 1000*. Cambridge, MA: Harvard University Press.

Marty, Martin E., and R. Scott Appleby. 1992. *The glory and the power: The fundamentalist challenge to the modern world*. Boston: Beacon.

Mayer, Hans Eberhard. 1988. *The Crusades*. Oxford: Oxford University Press.

North, Douglas C., and Robert Thomas. 1973. *The rise of the Western world: A new economic history*. New York: Cambridge University Press.

Olson, Mancur. 1982. *The rise and decline of nations*. New Haven, CT: Yale University Press.

Peters, Edward. 1988. *The Inquisition*. New York: Free Press.

Runciman, Steven. 1954. *The history of the Crusades*, vol. 3. Cambridge: Cambridge University Press.

Said, Edward. 1978. *Orientalism*. New York: Random House.

Saunders, J. J. 1962. *Aspects of the Crusades*. Christchurch, New Zealand: University of Canterbury Press.

Shirk, Susan. 1994. *How China opened its door*. Washington, DC: Brookings Institution.

Tawney, R. H. 1948. *Religion and the rise of capitalism: A historical study*. London: Murray.

Weber, Max. [1905] 1958. *The Protestant ethic; and the spirit of capitalism*, translated by Talcott Parsons. New York: Scribner.

Williamson, Oliver E. 1981. *The economics of organization: The transactions cost approach*. Philadelphia: University of Pennsylvania Press.

Travelers' Tales in the Tablighi Jama'at

By
BARBARA METCALF

The extensive Islamic missionary movement of Tablighi Jama'at, which originated in colonial India but is now worldwide, encourages participants to go out on small group tours to invite others, primarily nominal Muslims, to return to faithful adherence to Islamic teachings, above all the canonical prayer. At the conclusion of a tour, participants should report back, orally or in writing, their experiences to the mosque-based group (local, regional, or national) from which they set out. A sample of these reports, called *karguzari*, are the basis of this article. The reports reflect two discourses: one of *jihad*, in the sense of the nonmilitant "greater jihad" focused on self-discipline; and one of Sufism, embedded in the efforts of the charismatic group rather than in institutional *tasawwuf*.

Keywords: Tablighi Jama'at; Islamic missionaries; *karguzari*

The colonial period in South Asia witnessed far-reaching changes in religious thought and organization as well as in the domains of life that increasingly came to be signified as "religious." No change was more momentous than the emergence of politicized religious communities in public life. This was true for all the Indian religious traditions. Two further changes, again ones that ran across religious traditions, were also significant. One represented efforts to measure current behavior and doctrine against textual norms. The effort to line up behavior with what were imagined to be pristine divine teachings was a major theme of what might be called "an improvement ethic" characteristic of socioreligious movements of the last century of colonial rule. Second, again across traditions,

Barbara Metcalf is a professor of history at the University of California, Davis.

NOTE: A version of this article was originally presented at a two-part panel, "Piety and Politics in South Asian Islam," held at the University of Wisconsin Annual Conference on South Asia, 2001. I am grateful to Peter Bertocci, the organizer; Shelly Feldman, discussant; and other members of the panel and audience on that occasion for their helpful comments.

DOI: 10.1177/0002716203253213

there was an extension in the range of those deemed authoritative in religious matters to what might be called "lay" participants outside the traditions of learning or birth that had previously determined who could claim to speak and act for fellow adherents. Both of these changes are evident in the Muslim movement popularly known as Tablighi Jamaʿat, the "preaching" or "inviting" society. This movement is notable, however, in that it stands apart from explicit concerns about public life and competition to secure communal interests in the larger society. It is what could be called a movement of encapsulation.

The Tablighi Jamaʿat traces its origins to north India in the 1920s. At that point, even though its rhetoric focused wholly on Muslim failure and the need to draw nominal Muslims to fidelity, it was in fact one of many Muslim movements stimulated to action by aggressive Hindu attempts to "reconvert" what were seen as nominal Muslims to Hinduism. The movement took on new energy after the partition of the subcontinent in 1947, most importantly in Mewat, the location of the movement's origins, where Hindus had engaged in ruthless "ethnic cleansing." Tablighi Jamaʿat began a worldwide program, particularly from the 1960s, with the spread of immigrant populations to America and Europe and beyond. It now engages non–Indo-Pakistani populations as well.

It is conventional today to point to either of the annual international three-day congregations held in Raiwind in Pakistan or Tungi in Bangladesh and describe the turnout at each—of some 2 million—as the largest annual congregations of Muslims outside those who gather each year to perform the *hajj* at Mecca. Even in India, where there has been a preference for regional meetings rather than a single national meeting, a congregation held in Bhopal in December 2002 apparently drew about a million people.

Those who began this movement were themselves *ʿulama* linked to the reformist seminary at Deoband. Typical of the Deobandi ʿulama, they were also part of Sufi networks, devoted to their sheikhs from whom they received initiation and charismatic blessing, engaged in sufi disciplines and inner purification, cherishing the genealogy of holy men whose links passed back to the Prophet Muhammad himself. The Deobandis emerged in the brutal context of post–1857 Mutiny repression, which fell particularly hard on north Indian Muslims. They turned inward to disseminate what we might call cultural renewal through devotion to correct Islamic interpretation and practice coupled with devotion to the Prophet Muhammad. The key figures in this movement were widening circles of ʿulama trained in newly formalized *madrasas*, supported by the outpouring of publications permitted by newly available printing presses—pamphlets, polemical literature, summaries of correct practices, advisory opinions given to individual questioners, biographies, and collections of anecdotes about the holy and learned. Religious leaders, long dependent on patronage of the wealthy and pious endowments, came to depend on popular support.[1]

The Deobandis were only one of several Sunni Muslim reformist groups that had emerged at the turn of the century. One, popularly called "Barelvi," while also giving a new popular role to the holy and learned ʿulama, were more catholic in their acceptance of customary practices associated with veneration of *saiyyids*, holy men, saints, and the Prophet (Sanyal 1996). Another, the Ahl-i Hadith, in contrast, was like the Arabian Wahhabis (who traced their origin to an iconoclastic late-eighteenth-century reform movement and who found renewed vigor in internal competition within Arabia in the 1920s). They broke with the use of the historic schools of legal interpretation (for the Deobandis and Barelvis and other north Indians, the Hanafi school) in favor of direct recourse to the Qur'an and the prophetic *hadith*. They opposed Sufi customs, and they discouraged pilgrimage to the Prophet's grave in Madina. Theirs was a minority position. These orientations are salient today, describing not only jurisprudential positions but also categorizing mosques, voluntary organizations, and, in some contexts, political parties as well.

[T]he Tabligh movement stands in dramatic contrast to...the Afghan Taliban, which sought to use state institutions to achieve morality rather than depend on invitation and persuasion directed toward individuals.

As they emerged in the late nineteenth century, these competing groups debated to some extent with reformist Hindus, such as the Arya Samajis, who were increasingly concerned to "reconvert," as they saw it, non-Hindus within India, and with Christian missionaries. But even in those contexts, the primary audience was other Muslims. In other words, a reason to debate Arya Samajis or Christians was less to influence them than to show oneself as the spokesman or defender of "Islam" in public life to one's fellow Muslims. This was a new understanding of Islam, as a corporate identity in competition with others, and it created a new role for both religious and political leaders.

A scion of several generations of ʿulama associated with Deoband, Maulana Muhammad Ilyas (d. 1944) is taken to be the founder of Tablighi Jamaʿat (Sikand 2002).[2] The context for his program was the period of intense Hindu-Muslim tension that followed the dashed expectations of the First World War and the Khilafat movement when north India in particular was rent by riots and particularly intense missionary activities by the Arya Samajis. His response was not to move into new arenas that were emerging for the ʿulama, like politics, but to intensify the original Deobandi program of inner-looking grassroots reform of individual lives as a solution to the same problem of defending Islam.

Maulana Ilyas argued that what had been seen as the responsibility (*farzu'l kifaya*) of the 'ulama, namely, teaching fidelity to correct behavior, was in fact the obligation of all Muslims (*farzu'l 'ain*), a radical example of the move to "lay" leadership. The key to his program was to get Muslims to move out of their normal, everyday enmeshments and pressures to go out in small groups to call other Muslims to this correct practice. He felt that schools were not the way to reach people. Lived experience was. The combination of the group interactions while on a mission coupled with the powerful impact on the teacher himself or herself of teaching others was the key to his program (Metcalf 1994).

Here is a description of the current center of Tabligh work in Pakistan in a recent autobiography of a person who began his involvement in Tablighi Jama'at in the 1940s:

> Almighty Allah is most merciful. A great task of revival of the *ummah* is going on at Raiwind, where there is a totally different atmosphere. People remain busy with *Taleem* [teaching], *Zikr* [repetition of sacred phrases], *Tilawat* [Qur'anic recitation] and briefing for the *Tabligh* missions. They are helpful and loving, leading simple austere lives, only concerned with *Akhirat* [the world to come] and aloof from petty selfish concerns. . . . They arrange *ijtimas* [convocations], go out to different countries for a year or seven months and remain busy in the local mosques inviting people to participate in the missionary work among Muslims, who have become Muslims in name only and abandoned all religious practices. I went frequently on Fridays to Raiwind and attended the briefing and *du'a* by Haji Abdul Wahab. Maulana Ihsan led the Friday prayers. I would enjoy the company of Masihuz Zaman Sahib and Bhai Matloob and also visit the enclosure for foreigners from Arab countries, Europe, Africa and Far East. . . . Jamaats would go on foot to the remotest areas of Pakistan and suffer hardships to win the pleasure of Allah *subhanahu Taala*. . . . A majority of our people do not understand the meaning of *Kalama* [the attestation of faith]; prayers do not regulate our lives; and we fail to discharge our duties. Our rich do not pay *zakat* [obligatory alms] and accumulate wealth in safe deposits. [Others emphasize] education, . . . industrial development, . . . economic prosperity. These are really offshoots; the root lies in our spiritual and moral development. Without faith and submission to the will of Allah we cannot succeed. *Tabligh* is a world reform movement. . . . It is mass moral education for drawing people closer and reforming their habits. . . . We have been warned. . . . Our faith is not complete unless we take up the task of *da'wah* [mission, "inviting"] in right earnest. (Inam-ul-Haq 1999a)

Several themes are clear in this brief, insider's overview of the movement. A central theme is the absolute focus on individual moral behavior in contrast to social and economic programs. Indeed, a major complaint of opponents is precisely this failure to engage with what are seen as pressing social, economic, and political needs of the day. In this regard, the Tabligh movement stands in dramatic contrast to the ideology of a second Deobandi-related movement, in this case one that called itself Deobandi (as Tablighis do not), namely, the Afghan Taliban, which sought to use state institutions to achieve morality rather than depend on invitation and persuasion directed toward individuals (Metcalf 2002b). A second theme of the Tablighis is the priority of teaching other Muslims on the grounds that however many Muslims there may be in name, *almost none* are properly Muslim. It is up to a faithful few, like the first lonely Muslims of Mecca, to achieve a veritable revolution in mass behavior. Finally, the call to Tabligh is one of high seriousness. Tabligh may be inward looking in the sense of not having a political program. But it insists that the individual *must be effective in the world*. It is not enough to study, pray, and engage in Sufi disciplines oneself. The obligation to mission is not negotiable: on fulfilling it hinges nothing less than one's own ultimate fate at the Day of Judgment.

Tabligh [insist] that preaching must be done face to face, that intellectuality and argument are irrelevant to influencing lives, and that what counts is a meeting of hearts.

All of these themes are evident in firsthand accounts of Tabligh tours, examples of which I briefly describe in the remainder of this article. The writing up or oral recounting of one's experiences as part of a preaching tour is part of the discipline of participation in Tabligh activities and would serve, through recollection and self-examination, as part of the self-fashioning and self-education the movement ideally fosters. Accounts of tours are known by a term that is not indicative of a genre but of what it is that they communicate, namely, *kaarguzaari*. *Kaar* is simply "work," "action," "profession," or "matter." A person who is *kaarguzaar* is someone skilled or expeditious or accomplished in his or her work. *Kaarguzaari* denotes the discharge of one's duty or business, or "good service" (Platts [1884] 1977, 799). Hence, *"Eek tabliighi jama'at kii kaarguzaari"* might be simply translated as "the service of a tablighi jama'at."

There is no formal bureaucratic structure to this highly decentralized, voluntary movement; there are no offices and no archives; and even if there were, they presumably would not be open to outsiders. Hence the accounts, which I feel fortunate to have seen at all, are simply a chance collection. According to a full-time Tabligh worker who resides in Raiwind, accounts once read are not kept.[3] In contrast, Yoginder Sikand, author of a well-researched history of Tablighi Jama'at, was assured that accounts are kept in the Delhi headquarters, although he was not able to see them.[4]

Some accounts have recently been posted on the Web. At one point, al-Madina included a link called variously "Kar Guzari" or "karguzari," in one frame further specified as "true stories in the path of Allah" (www.al-madina.com, links: karguzari; elderspeech; DawaLinks; 1999, 2000, 2001).[5] Three printed sources, to which I will now turn, include an account of a mission conducted immediately after partition (Anonymous n.d.), accounts that appear in a collection of letters sent to the center in New Delhi in the 1960s (Muhammad Sani Hasani n.d.), and finally, an account of a four-month tour undertaken to China in the 1980s by a group from Maharashtra (Muhammad Hanif 1997).

From Delhi to East Punjab, 1950

The earliest account I have seen (Anonymous n.d.) has presumably been pre-served and informally reprinted because it is such a powerful and dramatic account of Tabligh at a time of considerable danger and difficulty. It is readily available, whether as a copy available for a few pennies, lithographed on eight folded sheets with no publication information, at an outdoor book table, as I first found it, or reprinted in more conventional pamphlet format. In 1947, the account argues, many Muslims in India apostatized to save their lives. The *amir* in Delhi asked Tablighis at the center in New Delhi to be willing to give their lives to bring them back to the fold of Islam. Two jama'ats set out, seen off with tears and prayers. Their extraordinary account is organized in terms of a dynamic: four successive severe tests, each met with divine aid, each followed by new resolve and ultimately success.

Other Muslims were apparently often too fearful for their own safety to offer help, but gradually the jama'ats dispersed and began to find their way to the former Muslims. A group was set on by police, beaten to unconsciousness, and jailed with no provision made for food and drink. They were forced to undertake the latrine detail for the prison. After three days, help from beyond, as they understood it, arrived in an unlikely form. A Hindu officer was jolted into memories of earlier years in Multan. Thus, he was not only a Hindu but a refugee from what had become Pakistan and, hence, a person who might have been expected to be partic-ularly hostile toward any Muslims, let alone Muslims on a proselytizing mission. The officer, however, is reported to have said to the prisoners, "When our children had any difficulty, we would take them to Muslims who were like you. We called them 'Tablighi Jamat people' and you seem to be some of them. . . . They were very good people and I loved them." This was the jama'ats' first experience of "help from beyond." The subsequent weeks in jail brought improved conditions and, in fact, afforded an opportunity to engage in Tabligh toward some 250 Muslim prisoners.

The second test came when refugee Sikhs arrived on the scene. They, in contrast to the Hindu officer, came "with guns and rifles ready to kill." The Tablighis besought them for permission to pray. Their cries and prayers for help were answered, although not before "the floor was red with blood." The guns of the Sikhs had simply jammed. The Tablighis, of course, saw this again as divine aid. The Sikhs on their part were reportedly so frightened by this event that in the end they brought a doctor who nursed the Tablighis' wounds. One Sikh, they continued, even tried to learn their teaching and helped guide them on the next stage of their journey.

Again the Tablighis set out, and again they were imprisoned, this time when they settled at a mosque being used by the government for border control. They were put into an old *haveli* where the well still reeked from the bodies of Muslims killed during partition. Their captors provided them with neither food nor water. A week later, the police returned, expecting to find them dead. Finding them instead alive, they ordered the Tablighis to the mountains, where yet again the Tablighis were arrested. They were beaten, robbed, and thrown into the Ganges in flood. Divine aid this time came in the form of the roots of a tree, which saved them.

Finally a huge wave came, washing them up on shore. This was truly divine aid since had they continued down the river, the local people, as they later learned, would have followed police orders to let them drown. The final miracle was that one person still had his clothes in a bag around his waist. His turban and *kurta*, torn into pieces, sufficed to cover everyone's private parts. Again a non-Muslim, a Sikh police inspector, was forced to recognize the extraordinary power, *zabardast taaqat*, of those on such a mission. This exemplary tale illustrates in extreme form the seriousness and importance Tablighis give to their work, coupled with the divine blessing they confidently expect for doing it. Moreover, in particularly dramatic form, it conveys the sense that the larger world is one antagonistic to the faith of true Muslims.

Letters from Europe and America to the Center, 1960s

A chapter of the biography of Maulana Muhammad Yusuf (d. 1965), the second overall amir of Tablighi Jama'at at the center at Nizamu'd-din, New Delhi, is composed of accounts of the experience of the first generations of Tablighis who spread beyond the subcontinent, primarily to places (including, in fact, Japan) where migration and work took subcontinental Muslims beginning in the 1960s. The chapter includes extracts from letters written to "Hazratji" Maulana Yusuf. Again, the difficulty of the enterprise is underlined, not now because of *physical* danger but because of the *moral* danger posed by what are caricatured as the values of America and Europe. These values are recognized as profoundly alluring. In Maulana Yusuf's own words,

> For those going to do the work of preaching religion in the materialist-worshipping countries of Europe and America, there is need of those men of God who have purpose and conviction; who, when they see the glittering and alluring life and society of those countries, will not let their mouths water, but instead, at the sight of life contrary to Islam and practices contrary to those brought by the Prophet, on whom God's blessing and peace, will rather, weep. (Muhammad Sani Hasani n.d., 517)

A line of poetry opens the chapter: "O believer, come! Let us show you/A visit of the Divine, within the house of idols" (ibid., 516).

The letters again confirm the priority to be given to lapsed Muslims, not to the non-Muslim population. Yet the letters also express high hopes for what a mere handful, if truly faithful like the Prophet's embattled followers in Mecca, can accomplish. Indeed, as a 1961 letter writes, the improvement once Tabligh is launched is virtually "without effort" (Muhammad Sani Hasani n.d., 524). Others look ahead to a larger dream:

> May Allah make us the means and cause of turning this capital of infidelity and ingratitude [London] into a center of peace and faith. (Ibid., 521)

Presumably, a time would come when Muslims would not only seek out fellow Muslims.

For the most part, however, at this point the letters reflect more the dangers posed by non-Muslims than the opportunity for converting them. This marks a change from the early days of the movement, which had emphasized *internal* Muslim failures. Either Muslims were neglectful of their religious life completely or they followed deviations in the form of false customs described not as Hindu or Western but as the influence of Sufism or of Shi'ism. At this point, however, Tablighis in America and Europe devoted considerable energy to setting true Islam against a world of "materialism, self-absorption, and lack of modesty, kindness, and courtesy" (Muhammad Sani Hasani 1967, 516). A Pakistani in New York wrote back to the Center that "people stay out half the night. They work all day, then amuse themselves, men and women, wasting what they earn and oblivious of the End" (ibid., 534). A Tablighi in Detroit wrote that adolescents (*sayana qaum*) there were "worse than animals" (ibid., 543).

From Maligaon to China, 1986

In the mid-1980s a jama'at set out from Maligaon, a town in the state of Maharashtra of late known as one of severe communal tensions, for China. The detailed, book-length account of this four-month jama'at to China is compelling because of the close view it provides of the daily activities on tour. A particularly important dimension of this tour is that it describes interactions between peoples who shared no common language (aside from a precious scattering of contacts who knew some Arabic).[6] The account thus provides a striking example of Tabligh insistence that preaching must be done face to face, that intellectuality and argument are irrelevant to influencing lives, and that what counts is a meeting of hearts.

The account also serves to nuance the meaning of Tabligh apoliticism. As the accounts already cited have made clear, Tabligh draws two boundaries, one between Muslims and an alien cultural world of non-Muslims and a second between the faithful and the vast majority of Muslims who, however pious they may think themselves, are Muslims only in name. Certainly the latter demarcation is important in this account. The Maharashtrians encountered what were to them shocking local practices, for example, several that reflect on ritual cleanliness. They found the Chinese Muslims using toilets with no modesty or concern for the direction of the *qibla* direction of Mecca; they also used toilet paper; they ate with the left hand or even with chopsticks; they were wholly oblivious of the Prophetic practice of using the *miswak* twig for teeth cleaning. The Tablighis found what seemed to them to be women dressed like men. Men and women, moreover, mixed freely in public life. Muslims allowed photography. They wasted their time in "boxing." These failures, as they were seen, were interestingly attributed to the Chinese Muslims' being "in the grip of the West" (Muhammad Hanif 1997, 38).

But however much they had gone astray, the Chinese Muslims were also seen as victims in a way that could only intensify opposition to the Chinese state, a critique perhaps easier for Muslim Indians than for Pakistanis, for example, given the alliances of their respective states. Muhammad Hanif (1997) attributed the failure of local imams to cooperate with the Tablighis to their fear of Chinese government reprisals. He recounted stories of outright persecution on the part of the state and dedicated his book "to the oppressed Chinese Muslims."

In Conclusion

The stories Tablighis tell about themselves can only be understood in the light of the stories they tell about the Prophet Muhammad, the Companions of the Prophet, and those who have followed them. The stories assert that the high standard set in the *hadith* is gone and that it is again the time of *jahiliyya*, a time of ignorance classically understood as the pre-Muhammad age in Arabia. In this, Tabligh thinking espouses the same interpretation of the current day as do many twentieth-century Islamist thinkers, notably the Egyptian Sayyid Qutb (1906-66), who place jahiliyya not in the distant past but in the present.[7] There is, thus, a particular urgency to Muslims seeking to follow prophetic example today.

The locus classicus for interpreting the early years of Tabligh work in India in a context of jahiliyya was written by Maulana Abu'l-ala Maududi (1903-79). Maududi would later become a critic of Tablighi Jama‘at because, like Qutb, he favored political Islam. Indeed, he would emerge as one of the premier Islamist thinkers of the century. Nonetheless, in 1939 he was filled with admiration when he saw Tablighi activities firsthand in Mewat, the area southwest of Delhi where the movement first flourished. His story, published in a leading Urdu journal, told of the unlettered but sturdy Mewatis as the mirror of the Arab Bedouins of the pre-Islamic jahiliyya whose lives were transformed through Islam. Maududi's description of the Mewatis, with their Hindu names, their ignorance of prayer (so that they would gape at someone praying and worry that he had a stomachache), their idols and tufts of hair, has been absorbed into Tabligh legend. "It seemed as if that very spirit, with which at the beginning of Islam the Arab Bedouin rose up for the *tabligh* of the straight path, now had been born in these people." If this were the time of *jahiliyya*, there had to be Bedouins (Abu'l-ala Maududi [1939] 1979, 25).

If Tablighi ideology, despite its fundamentally different program, shares certain assumptions and symbols with political Islam, it also draws on a second language, evident in the accounts as in much Tabligh language. This is a Sufi idiom. Tablighis believe themselves able to receive, through divine blessings granted on account of their work, the high spiritual state and charisma accorded to Sufis. The Sufis gain their blessings through lives devoted to disciplines, meditation, and moral purification coupled with the powerful charisma of succession transmitted through the elder to whom they pledge allegiance. These states can now to be gained by participation in the charismatic community of the jamaʿat. Thus, the participant gains through his experiential states in this life the assurance that what he is doing is receiving divine blessing.

[S]ome Tablighis, in fact, will emphasize Muslim failure to live morally as a cause of recent Muslim suffering today.

Muhammad Hanif (1997), for example, used such terms as *lutf* (joy, grace), *kaif* (exhilaration), and *sukun-i qalb* (peace of heart) to describe the spiritual experience of his jamaʿat. The 1950 account spoke of being granted the light of insight (*nur-i basiirat*) and of the gnosis (*maʿarifat*) and revelations (*inkishaaf*) accorded those who participated. Story after story, like those described above, illustrate how a jamaʿat becomes a vehicle for what are essentially the *karamat*, or miracles, gained in classic Sufi accounts by a particular holy man who enjoys God's favor.

The second, and more formative, discourse is the one alluded to above in relation to jahiliyya, the essentially military vocabulary that this "greater jihad" shares with the "lesser jihad" of warfare against the *kuffaar*. Both, for starts, are *jihad*, quoting a tradition invoked by one of the leading Deobandi intellectuals, Hazrat Maulana Mufti Muhammad Shafiiʿ that "the meaning of jihad is those who remove obstacles to religion; one is with the *kuffaar* and one is with the self and Satan" (Anonymous n.d., 5). The shared idiom of jihad gives shape to the jamaʿat, which, like a political undertaking, is led by an amir (including an amir of each group going out) and guided by consultation *(shura)*. Tablighi preaching tours are described as *gasht/jaula*, patrols, and *khuruj*, sorties. Anyone who is "lucky" enough, as described in a 1960s letter (Muhammad Sani Hasani n.d., 538), to die in the course of a Tabligh tour is a *shahiid* as much as someone is who dies in a militant jihad. Tablighis' efforts, like those of an armed *mujahid*, are understood to be *fi sabiliʾllah*, in the path of God. There is also the assertion that as in the lesser jihad, the participant will receive exponentially increased reward for all acts performed in the course of Tabligh so that the canonical prayer during a tour merits the equivalent of twenty *lakh* prayers of one at home; one rupee spent in the work of jihad is worth a *karoor* of rupees, and so forth (Anonymous n.d., 2-3). In both forms of jihad, the believer is enjoined to effective action in a world that needs to be changed. The 1950 account opens with a couplet that begins "from *actions* [which includes calling others to those actions] life is made" (Anonymous n.d., 1).

Among the *karguzari* on the Web site noted above are travels for preaching tours all over the earth—to Turkey, Palestine, Denmark, Singapore, the Solomon Islands, Bangladesh, Central Asia, Brazil. But also listed as *karguzari*, discharging a duty, is a *karguzari* of the armed fighting in Chechnya dated April 2000. The posting describes it as "jihad for the sake of Allah"; it is "an obligatory worship of Allah that we are performing." "The Russian bear," as it is called, is an immoral regime. The account calls attention to attacks on civilian targets carried out by Putin "trying to tarnish the image of the Mujahideen in Chechnya." "We have no quarrel with the innocent Russian people," the account continues, "our argument is with the Russian government and army, not the women, children and elderly citizens of Russia."[8]

Some observers assume that participation in the peaceful jihad of Tablighi Jamaʿat is a first stage toward militant jihad or at least toward more active political forms of organization. That assumption, like the more extreme assumption that the Tablighi Jihad serves as a cover for terrorists,[9] remains to be demonstrated. It is, however, clear that for millions of participants, the injunction to disseminating individual moral reform is the movement's only mission. If pressed to talk about political issues, some Tablighis, in fact, will emphasize Muslim failure to live morally as a cause of recent Muslim suffering today, particularly in the swathe of land that swings from Chechnya through Kashmir, to Afghanistan, Iraq, Bosnia, and—most important—Palestine, in contrast to those more public figures who explicitly condemn Christian, Zionist, and other oppression. One of the foundational texts of the movement, from 1945, uses in its English translation "Muslim Degeneracy" to target its primary concern.

Yet for all this crucial difference, as the accounts show, Tablighis share fundamental attitudes with the militants, not least their belief that Islam must be defended. They also are shaped by a commitment to individual action as effective in shaping the larger world, and they share the conviction that that the faithful few, who act "in the way of Allah," can achieve far-reaching transformations. They also cultivate a cultural encapsulation that divides them starkly from a larger, evil, and threatening world.[10]

Notes

1. For the early history of Deoband, and brief discussion of other movements of the time, see Metcalf (2002a, 2002b).

2. This book serves as an excellent source for the movement, and its extensive bibliography offers a guide to further resources concerning the movement. See also Masud (2000).

3. Personal communication, Islamabad, December 1998.

4. Sikand, personal communication, June 2002.

5. There is no official Web site of the organization. www.al-madina.com, however, reproduces such material as the texts meant to guide participants' actions, sometimes known as "The Tabligh Curriculum" or "The Blessings/Virtues of Actions." See, however, Note 7, below.

6. The book-length form of this account reflects perhaps both the fact that the author is someone with many varied previous books to his credit as well as the need for such a pioneer effort to be well documented.

7. For Sayyid Qutb, see the unpublished dissertation of John Calvert (1994). See also his "The World Is an Undutiful Boy: Sayyid Qutb's American Experience" (2000).

8. www.al-madinah.com/Karguzari/Chechnya/chechnya.htm, accessed from 1999 to 2001, no longer existed in January 2003, although the home page of "al-madina" was available, and the *karguzari* were located at www.webonthenet.com/Karguzari.

9. See, for example, B. Raman, "Moscow's Muddled Objectives," available 4 January 2003 at www.atimes.com. Questions have also been raised in the United States since the "American Taliban," John Walker Lindh, and members of two alleged "sleeper cells" arrested near Buffalo, New York, and Portland, Oregon, in 2002 all were understood to have interacted with or participated in tablighi activities.

10. For the peaceful Inam-ul-Haq, whose evocation of the loving, simple, austere, generous lives at Raiwind I quoted early in the article and whose own commitment was to "the greater jihad," in poems published shortly before his recent death, that line increasingly became "the West." He wrote movingly in "August 1998" of arrogant Americans seeking to frighten and subdue the weak, "whose hostility is dangerous but friendship fatal." In "The Second Coming," he identified Jews as the driving force behind Christians and looked forward to their slaughter at the Last Day: "And there will be an end to villainy/The righteous alone will inherit/The Kingdom of the earth" (Inam-ul-Haq 1999b, 21-22, 96).

References

Abuʾl-ala Maududi. [1939] 1979. *Ihya-i din ki jad o jahad ka sahih tariqa aur ek qabil taqlid namuna* (A right way of the struggle for revival of religion and an example worthy of imitation). Reprinted in *Tablighi Jamaʿat, Jamaʿat-i Islami and Barelvi Hazrat*, edited by Maulana Muhammad Manzur Nuʾmani, 19-37, Lucknow, India: Al Furqan Buk Dipo.

Anonymous. N.d. [1950?]. Eek tabliighi jamaʿat kii kaarguzaari (The service of a tablighi jamaʿat). (No publication information. 64 pp. Rs. 8 available at outdoor stand, Jami Masjid, Delhi, 1999)

Calvert, John. 1994. Discourse, community and power: Sayyid Qutb and the Islamist movement in Egypt. Unpublished dissertation, McGill University, Montreal, Quebec, Canada.

———. 2000. The world is an undutiful boy: Sayyid Qutb's American experience. *Islam and Christian Muslim Relations* 11 (1): 87-103.

Inam-ul-Haq. 1999a. *Memoirs of insignificance*. Lahore, Pakistan: Dar ut-Tazkeer.

———. 1999b. *Sighs and satisfactions*. Lahore, Pakistan: Sang-e Meel Publications.

Masud, Muhammad Khalid, ed. 2000. *Travellers In faith: Studies of the Tablighi Jamaʿat as a transnational Islamic movement for faith renewal*. Leiden, the Netherlands: Brill.

Metcalf, Barbara. 1993. Living hadith in the Tablighi Jamaʿat. *Journal of Asian Studies* 52 (3): 584-608.

———. 1994. Remaking ourselves: Islamic self-fashioning in a global movement of spiritual renewal. In *Accounting for fundamentalisms: The dynamic character of movements*, edited by Martin E. Marty and R. Scott Appleby, 706-25. Chicago: University of Chicago Press.

———. 2002a. *Islamic revival in British India: Deoband, 1860-1900*. 2d ed. Delhi: Oxford University Press.

———. 2002b. "Traditionalist" Islamic activism: Deoband, Tablighis, and Talibs. In *Understanding September 11*, edited by Craig Calhoun, Paul Price, and Ashley Timmer, 53-66. New York: New Press.

Muhammad Hanif Millii, Maulaanaa. 1997. *Nuquush-i chiin: mulk chiin main chaar mahiine ke liʾe bhejii gaʾii ek tabliighii jamaʿat kii kaarguzaarii—mushaahidaat, mahsusaat, jaʾizee* (Impressions of China: The service of a tablighi jamaʿat sent for four months in the country of China—Testimony, feelings, survey). Jalaalpur, Uttar Pradesh, India: Paigham Bok Dipo.

Muhammad Sani Hasani, Maulana. N.d. [1967?]. *Sawanih hazrat maulana muhammad yusuf kandhalawi* (The life of Hazrat Maulana Muhammad Yusuf Kandhalawi). Lucknow, India: Majlis-i sohafat wa nashriyat, Daru'l-ʿulum Nadwatu'l-ʿulama.

Platts, John T. [1884] 1977. *A dictionary of Urdu, classical Hindi and English.* New Delhi: Oriental Books Reprint Corporation.

Sanyal Usha. 1996. *Devotional Islam and politics in British India: Ahmad Riza Khan Barelwi and his movement, 1870-1920.* Delhi: Oxford University Press.

Sikand, Yoginder. 2002. *The origins and development of the Tablighi-Jamaʿat (1920-2000): A cross-country comparative study.* New Delhi: Orient Longman.

Southeast Asia is the most populous Islamic region in the world yet has gained only limited attention. This survey article tries to explain what are the specific characteristics of Islam in this world region. After a historical overview of the spread of Islam in insular Southeast Asia, its contemporary political contexts in Indonesia, Malaysia, South Thailand, and the Philippines are scrutinized. Finally, a number of contentious issues in Southeast Asian Islam are discussed, such as the nature of Islamic revivalism, current outbreaks of ethno-religious conflict, and the possible threat of extremism.

Keywords: Southeast Asia; Islam; history; revivalism; cultural transmission; diffusion, adaptation; mysticism

Southeast Asia and Islam

By
VINCENT J. H. HOUBEN

Islam as "the unconditional surrender to the will of Allah" constitutes one of the most remarkable developments in world history. Its ideas and thoughts, rendered through the prophet Mohammed and the holy Qur'an, have been adopted in wide parts of the world. In contrast to Christianity, Islam is much more than a religion; it is a "way of life" that encompasses all areas of human activity, private and public, ranging from the theological to the political. In the course of time, within Islam several different traditions have emerged that, on one hand, retain the unity of the believers but, on the other hand, led to much diversity. This diversity has become even more complex as the Islamic religion was engraved upon existing local traditions

Vincent J. H. Houben studied history and Indonesian languages at Leiden University, the Netherlands, where his doctoral dissertation examined the system of indirect rule in the principalities of central Java in the middle of the nineteenth century. From 1986 until 1997, the author worked as lecturer of Indonesian history at Leiden University. In 1997, he became a full professor of Southeast Asian studies at the University of Passau, Germany. He became a professor of Southeast Asian history and society at the Humboldt University, Berlin, in 2001. Over the past twenty years, Professor Houben has published on a wide range of Southeast Asian topics ranging from aspects of colonialism to political discourse after the Asian crisis.

DOI: 10.1177/0002716203255394

in a different manner in various world regions. Therefore, an attempt to analyze the relationship between Southeast Asia, a highly heterogeneous region in itself, and the development of Islam within the scope of one article cannot be more than incomplete and of a generalizing nature. It is striking that although Southeast Asia is the most populous Islamic region in the world, within Islamic studies the region has been perceived as "periphery" and therefore has gained only limited attention.

In contrast to this, within modern Southeast Asian studies since the 1950s, Islam has played a prominent role. The fact that more Muslims are living in Indonesia than in any other country of the world constitutes an obvious reason. The emergence of independent nation-states in insular Southeast Asia after the end of the Second World War, the modernization of its societies, and the occurrence of religious-ethnic or regional-religious conflicts in which the relationship between Islam and other beliefs was and still is one of the core issues have attracted the attention of many regional scholars from various disciplines. This attention is not new, however. Already the colonial governments of the nineteenth and early twentieth centuries were acutely aware of the potential force of Islam that could threaten European supremacy. Therefore, Islam, as it existed in their colonial domains, was watched intensively in an attempt to seek accommodation or to reach some form of domestication.[1] Since the so-called war on terrorism started, Islam is again seen by many Western governments with suspicion, just like in the colonial era. To infer from the present-day crisis a "clash of cultures" seems more to render a service to fundamentalism on all sides than to help to gain a productive insight into the meaning of Islam in our current world.

Scholarly literature on Islam in Southeast Asia covers a wide field. Until the 1950s, the field was largely dominated by philologists studying literary traditions and students of religion who were interested in the theological dimensions of Islam in the Southeast Asian region. The field studies undertaken by the anthropologist Clifford Geertz in Indonesia marked the beginning of studying Islam as a phenomenon in local society. His book *Religion in Java* (1960) is still considered to be very illuminating for understanding what position Islam occupied in the socioreligious world of that island. Before him, Harry J. Benda (1958) wrote a path-breaking study on Indonesian Islam during the Japanese occupation from 1942 until 1945. It was the first political history of Indonesian Islam to appear. Since then, a huge corpus of literature on Islam in Malaysia, Indonesia, and the Philippines has emerged that covers almost all aspects of human life in these countries. One of the latest trends is to scrutinize the relationship between Islam and the emergence of civil society in the region (Nakamura, Siddique, et al. 2001). Most contributions to date possess a rather strict thematic and/or country focus, whereas the number of works covering Southeast Asia as a whole remain the exception.[2]

It needs to be highlighted forthwith that most literature on Islam in Southeast Asia is produced within the region itself, written in non-Western languages, and aimed at a local audience. These often little-known books, articles, pamphlets, and the like have the major benefit of representing a perspective "from within" and contain a wealth of detailed information. On the other hand, the authors of these writings are involved in internal debates on issues of local importance and often miss the detachedness and generalization of outside observers. In reverse, foreign scholars of Islam often reflect the academic discipline they come from, which on one hand offers an exogenous point of view but at the same time, consciously or not, underlines the inequality between them and their object of study (see Heryanto 2002). Some Western authors write on Islam on the basis of extensive fieldwork, whereas others continue to work from behind their desks at home.

For the sake of an overview, several strands or approaches in Southeast Asian studies on Islam can be distinguished. First, there is the philological tradition. The advent and further deepening of Islam in Southeast Asia was accompanied by cultural transfer from the Middle East, Persia, and India. This process happened, amongst other ways, through transfer by translation and adaptation of an Islamic literary canon. Any collection of Malay manuscripts contains poetry, legends, histo-

To infer from the present-day crisis a "clash of cultures" seems more to render a service to fundamentalism on all sides than to help to gain a productive insight into the meaning of Islam in our current world.

ries, and theological and legal treatises that originate from the Arabic Peninsula. These were mostly rendered in nonvocalized Malay in Arabic script. Likewise, a large Javanese written corpus exists that contains Javanese-Islamic mysticism and Islamic religious instruction but also the Menak Amir Hamza cycle and other literary works.[3] Recently, Peter Riddell (2001) produced a survey of theological writings produced by Malay-Indonesian scholars from the sixteenth century on. It bears witness to the process of transmission of Islam to the Malay world and the appearance of a "distinctive" theology in this region.

A second category of studies on Southeast Asian Islam has adopted the perspective of religious and legal studies. Islam as a system of ideas started in the Middle East with Arabic as a medium. What type of Islam spread to Southeast Asia, and how it was modified and further developed locally, lies at the heart of this approach. In Southeast Asia, Sunnite Islam is practiced and a strong tendency toward Sufi mysticism exists. At the same time, especially through the *Haj*, links with new orthodox streams in the Arabic world have developed as well. A representative of the Islamic studies approach is Mark Woodward (1989), writing on the relationship between Muslim law and mystical doctrine in Central Java.[4] In Western academia, the religious studies perspective has now partly become integrated into the wider field of cultural studies.

A third strand in Islamic studies on the Southeast Asian region takes up the anthropological-sociological angle. The region possesses complex societies and different ethnic groups who have developed their own way of practicing the religion, which is an amalgam of pre-Islamic patterns and those introduced by Islam. At present, Islam can be found in highly modern urban settings but at the same time in still largely traditional rural surroundings. The Islamic "revivalism" that has occurred in Southeast Asia since the 1970s belong to this category. An example of the social studies approach is the 1986 study of Taufik Abdullah and Sharon Siddique on Islam and society in Southeast Asia.

Finally, a fourth group of Islamic studies is concerned with the political economy of Southeast Asia. Especially over the past few decades, Islam as a political factor has grown markedly, which has forced governments to try to accommodate Islam within the political nation. The development of political Islam or, more broadly, the relationship between state and Islam in Southeast Asia, has gained increasing attention. The 1997 book by Hefner and Horvatich is one example; a volume edited by C. van Dijk and A. H. de Groot (1995) is another. Also belonging to this category are studies on Islamic entrepreneurs and commercial elites in Southeast Asia.

The distinction between the four different approaches is of course arbitrary, and in reality there are many overlaps. This article attempts to portray some major issues concerning Islam as a regional phenomenon from an area studies and interdisciplinary point of view. The basic question underlying it is, Are there analogies between developments in Malaysia, Indonesia, and the South Philippines stressing current developments but also looking at the long-term historical context? First, it is asked what the typical characteristics of Islam in the Southeast Asian region are. Second, current developments in the Islamic countries are highlighted, looking also at those where Muslims constitute a minority. Finally, issues of debate and conflict on contemporary Southeast Asian Islam are raised.

Southeast Asia as an "Islamic" Region

Southeast Asian Islam has certain distinct qualities, which are the result of the way in which the religion came to the region and how it developed under colonialism and thereafter. Although the region is generally perceived as lying at the outskirts of the Islamic world, today substantial numbers of Muslims live here. Almost 90 percent of the more than 230 million inhabitants of Indonesia are Muslim, whereas 58 percent of the inhabitants in Malaysia are Malays and therefore Muslim. Also, the Sultanate of Brunei has a majority of 67 percent Muslim. In all other Southeast Asian countries, Muslims are present but constitute a minority within the population (Singapore, 14 percent; elsewhere, about 5 percent). Even in countries where the overall majority is non-Muslim, provincial majorities of Muslims can be found, such as in the southern Philippines, south Thailand, and west Myanmar. Of the total Southeast Asian population of 550 million in 2002, more than 230 million and therefore slightly more than 40 percent are registered as Muslim, of which more than 200 million are in Indonesia alone.

Since the seventh century A.D., Muslim traders from India, Persia, and south Arabia frequented the harbors of insular Southeast Asia. When they settled in greater numbers, they brought their own religious experts (mullahs), erected houses of prayer in their own town quarters, and performed all other obligations expected of them. The crucial turning point was when a local ruler became converted to Islam. Having accepted this religion, the ruler could command a new, more universal kind of legitimacy that transcended his own group and therefore allowed for the rise of greater polities, whereas both ruler and subjects could draw on the global solidarity of the *ummat*. Of particular importance was the concept of *daulat* (Arab. *dawlah*), which was an expression of sovereignty or legitimacy through the power of God. The solidarity between ruler and subjects was regulated through *adat* (Arab. *Ada*) or customary usage (Schumann 1999). Southeast Asian rulers produced genealogies in which they claimed to be direct descendants of the Prophet through Saiyid or Sharif (descendents of Mohammad's grandsons). Malay political concepts that emerged, such as *kuasa, kewibawaan*, and *derhaka*, were developed on the basis of Islamic models.

Islam spread throughout insular Southeast Asia like a slow, giant wave, starting from northern Sumatra as early as the thirteenth century and reaching Borneo and the southern Philippines in the sixteenth century A.D. In 1300, the kingdom of Pasai at the northeastern tip of Sumatra had become Muslim; the first Muslim graveyards in East Java date to the same period. In 1500, Islamic polities could be found throughout Sumatra, Java, Sulawesi, and the Moluccas. Later, the coastal areas of Kalimantan and the islands of Sulu, Mindanao, and Palawan joined the Islamic world. On mainland Southeast Asia, certain ethnic groups, like for instance the Cham in Cambodia and Arakanese in Myanmar, converted to Islam as well.

Several eyewitness reports on early Islamic societies in Southeast Asia, such as that of the Venetian merchant Marco Polo, who visited northeast Sumatra at the end of the thirteenth century, confirmed that the petty kingdoms of Perlak and Pedir were Islamic. The Morrocan world traveler Ibn Battuta came to the same area during the mid-fourteenth century. A Chinese Muslim called Ma Huan called at Java in 1433. The Portuguese traveler Tome Pires reported on the situation in Java in 1515, and after that both Western accounts and indigenous testimonies became more numerous and detailed.

Islam seems to have spread from Pasai, a small kingdom on the coast of north Sumatra. Indigenous sources make a connection to south India, stating that the "apostle" of Islam came from Ma'bar, a place at the Coromandel coast. As there existed a long tradition of trading connections between south India and insular Southeast Asia, this historical representation makes sense. Islam came to north India later than to south India. South Indian Islam was connected to the Hadhramaut in current Yemen. It is therefore no coincidence that the Shafi'i's legal school started in this area and is still followed both in south India and Indonesia

(Robson 1981). To trace back Southeast Asian Islam to Bengal seems less likely, despite similarities between the biography of the Javanese mystic Siti Jenar and the Satya Pir cult in Bengal. A theory of A. H. Johns (1961, 1995) on the role of traders from Gujarat in the diffusion of knowledge from the Persian mystic Al Hallaj, who lived in the second half of the ninth century, has been rejected recently by Micheal Feener (1998).

In modern academic histories, the advent of Islam is connected with a period of expansion of maritime trade. Small Muslim trading communities, consisting of Arabs, Indians, but also converted local traders, were present in the archipelago from the first century of the Hijrah. These gained prominence only much later. In the sixteenth century along Java's north coast, a string of port polities came to the fore that developed into junctions of international trade. There an Islamic "middle class" settled, mixed with the local population, and eventually took over the local administration. The mosque of Demak was apparently already built in the last quarter of the fifteenth century (Pigeaud and de Graaf 1976). Javanese historical chronicles present a different story that links the coming of Islam to the activities of nine apostles *(wali sanga)*, who, under the leadership of Sunan Kalijaga of the town of Demak, spread Islam in Java. As a turning point in the history of the island, the alleged conquest of the Hindu kingdom of Mojopahit in 1527 is portrayed. Recent studies have shown, however, that at the Mojopahit court, Islamic consultants had been present for a long time and that the kingdom went through a period of decline rather than being conquered by a coalition of Islamic towns.

Earlier, in the fourteenth century, Malacca on the Malay Peninsula developed into the central staple of the Malacca Straits, a vital passage in the maritime trading network between the Indian Ocean and the China Sea. In indigenous chronicles, most importantly the Malay Annals *(Sejarah Melayu)*, the conversion of the ruler and his adoption of the title of sultan is described as crucial historical event. At the moment, it is still undecided what school of Islam was predominant in Malacca, but the adoption of Islam brought clear advantages, since it attracted large numbers of Indian cloth merchants, stressing the individual worth of all men and offering legal security under Islamic law (Andaya and Andaya 1982, 52-54).

The expansion of Islam was largely a peaceful process, and conversion was no great obstacle to the ordinary people. The continuation of local pre-Islamic ritual practices was accepted, and the act of conversion, through the profession of faith (Arab. *Shahadah*), did not presuppose knowledge of the Qur'an. The five duties were only performed in a haphazard way. Shari'ah or the legal modalities based on the revelation of the Prophet were subordinated to mystical practice, which had been there for a long time. But the "road" toward religion, which is the other meaning of shari'ah, started with outward practice and was followed by an inward deepening conviction. Likewise, Islam spread geographically from the coastal areas toward the interior through the brokerage of Islamic teachers. These so-called *kyai* (Jav.) or *maulana* (Arab.) lived in rural villages, where they set up schools (called *surau* in Malaysia and *pesantren* in Java). There, young males were instructed how to recite texts from the Qur'an and given an introduction in Qur'an interpretations *(tafsir)*, Islamic theology *(kalam)*, and mysticism. Religious teachers and returned pilgrims *(haji)* possessed great social prestige in the countryside and often acted as spokesmen for the local communities toward higher authority.

The colonial era made a great impact on the development of Islam in Southeast Asia. Europeans had been present in the region since the sixteenth century. Until the beginning of the nineteenth century, they occupied major coastal centers and altered the existing maritime trading system to fit their own needs. A major event was the Portuguese sack of Malacca in 1511, which led to a shift in the political configuration of the Malay world. It was only in the nineteenth century that European colonialism turned from the coasts to the hinterlands and subjected the majority of

---

Numerous Western authors have reiterated that Southeast Asian Islam has been more moderate than Islam in the Middle East since it laid only a thin veneer upon an indigenous traditional culture of animism and Indian influence.

---

the population. Not only did colonial states expand horizontally, erecting new international boundaries that did not exist beforehand, but also vertically, altering indigenous social and political structures. On the whole, Muslim regional and local elites lost out in the process, which explains why much of the anti-Western resistance movements were led by representatives of these groups (see, for instance, Adas 1979).

In most areas of Indonesia, the Dutch pushed Muslim local rulers and elites aside, trying to base their power on customary law *(adatrecht)* and the brokerage of chiefs with a high social prestige in the community. Christian missionary activity was avoided in strongly Islamized areas but promoted in the central Moluccas, Nord Sulawesi, central Kalimantan, Flores, and central Sumatra. The establishment of Dutch power was accompanied by a number of military expeditions, which in the case of Aceh in north Sumatra took the form of prolonged battle. On the Acehnese side, the conflict was styled as a holy war *(jihad)* against the infidels, but eventually the area was conquered. The Dutch Islamologist C. Snouck Hurgronje had provided the Dutch colonial officials with strategic information on internal differences in this part of Sumatra.

In contrast, the British in Malaysia introduced indirect rule and maintained the sultans as formal heads in their provinces. The sultans had to follow the advice of an English resident in all matters of government except custom and Islam. In this way, a union of interests was established that resulted in great stability and much less resistance to Western hegemony. The position of official Islam was strengthened by the power-sharing arrangement between Sultans and colonizers.[5]

In the late nineteenth century, several Western developments took place that altered the way in which Islam functioned. The introduction of steam shipping allowed for a massive pilgrimage to Mecca, which in turn made ties between the Arab Peninsula and Southeast Asia much closer (Jonge and Kaptein 2002). The introduction of printing in the vernacular language facilitated the spread of new, Islamic ideas to a general reading public, thereby reducing regional disparities in Islamic thinking. The pan-Islamic movement that swept across the Islamic world in the early decades of the twentieth century also influenced the development of Southeast Asian Islam. Pan-Islamism can, on one hand, be seen as an effort to purify the religion from too many compromises with local cultures; on the other hand, it was a modernizing response to European dominance and therefore not at all "conservative." The new, Wahhabi consciousness of *Darul Islam* (Arab. *Dar al-Islam*, or territory of Islam) emerged through oral contacts, pilgrimage, and study in Cairo but also through the emergence of a local Islamic press (Evans 1987). A more direct transmission of ideas was done through Meccan fatwas intended for Muslims in Indonesia, for example (Kaptein 1997).

A special role in Southeast Asia was played by Singapore, a hub in the movement of people and cultural-religious ideas. The itinerary of most hajis went via Singapore, where Hadhramauti controlled the route to Jeddah. In Singapore, magazines such *Al Imam* and *Al Munir* tried to educate their readers and offered them translations of articles from the Middle East (Roff 1994, chap. 2). In Indonesia and Malaya, it came to social conflict between the Islamic religious establishment (*kaum tua*, or the old group) against the *kaum muda* (the young group of reform-minded Muslims).

Nationalism in Southeast Asia also contained an important Islamic strand. The first supraregional nationalist movement in Indonesia was the Sarekat Islam, founded in central Java 1912. It rejected the association between Indonesians and the West, since an acceptance of Western culture would lead to a retreat of Islam. However, the movement went into decline quite rapidly because it did not pursue any concrete long-term goals and a part of the leadership became social revolutionaries. Another, more stable movement was the modernist Muhammadiyah, founded by Haji Ahmad Dahlan (1868-1923) of the kauman in Yogyakarta, who had studied in Mecca. It aimed at raising living and educational standards among Muslims through modern schools, hospitals, and so on (Alfian 1989). In Malaya in the 1920s, the kaum muda became increasingly politicized, although it was not able to reach the stage of political nationalism with mass support. The periodical *Seruan Azhar*, published between 1925 and 1928 by Malayan and Indonesian student at the al-Azhar university in Cairo, discussed not only pan-Islamism but also pan-Malayanism (uniting Malaya and Indonesia) and anticolonial nationalism. In the 1930s, a pen friend initiative by the Islamic reformist newspaper *Saudara* developed into the first pan-Malayan nationalist movement, avoiding anything political out of fear for repressing and therefore stressing its social and cultural aims (Roff 1994, 87-89, 212-18).

What made Southeast Asian Islam distinct from prevalent forms in India or the Arabian Peninsula? Numerous Western authors have reiterated that Southeast Asian Islam has been more moderate than Islam in the Middle East since it laid only a thin veneer upon an indigenous traditional culture of animism and Indian influence. Comparing Morocco with Indonesia, Clifford Geertz (1968) noted that Islam, with the exception of a few pockets in Sumatra, Kalimantan, and Sulawesi, entered an area of "high culture" centered around the Hindu-Buddhist Javanese state and therefore did not construct a civilization but "appropriated" one. In this way, Islam fits in with a general Southeast Asian pattern of selective borrowing of cultural elements that come from the outside.

The idea of the centrality of the Hindu-Buddhist heritage in Javanese culture and also the centrality of Javanese culture for Indonesia as a whole can be questioned, however.[6] It belongs to a picture that was developed by Orientalist scholars in colonial times, which was prolonged and strengthened particularly during the Suharto era (1965-98). There is no doubt that in Javanese Islam, orthodox thought and practice was and still is mixed with pre-Islamic traditions and therefore "javanized." Also, a majority of the Javanese Muslims have been coined as "abangan," supposedly nominal Muslims who do not follow rules of Islamic conduct. They were contrasted with "santri," or more devout Muslims. The issue is how to define "Islamic." If the definition is broadened beyond orthodoxy and takes in mixed cultural or pluralistic forms, there seems to be nothing special about Javanese Islam. Also, the santri-abangan categorization cannot be considered to be static over time, just like Islamization or deepening of Islamic identity is an ongoing process. In a similar vein, the fact that the greatest number of Indonesian Muslims lives on the island of Java does not mean that Javanese Islam stands for Islam in Indonesia as a whole.

A second special characteristic of Southeast Asian Islam is portrayed through its mysticism. This point is connected to the first one in the sense that mysticism facilitates the fusion of Islamic with pre-Islamic cultural forms. The mystical character of Southeast Asian Islam originated in Sufism. Islamic traders and teachers joined in mystical brotherhoods (tarekat) that performed common religious exercise in the form of dzikir, which consists of repetition of the name of Allah and religious formulae to reach a state of trance, which in its turn allows one to come nearer to the Almighty. According to Feener, the dominant Sufi school of doctrine in the Southeast Asian region comprised two roots, first an elaboration of the Neoplatonic ideas of Ibn al-Arabi (a twelfth-century mystic born in Spain) and second the Sufism formulated by al-Ghazahli (1058-1111). Other authors and encyclopedic texts covering a wide spectrum and different origins were studied alongside these two, all part of a highly complex cultural transfer into local manuscripts. Similarly, Malay authors, like Hamzah Fansuri in the sixteenth century and Nur al-Din al-Raniri in the seventeenth century, acted as transporters of Islamic mystic ideas (Feener 1998, 584).

Contemporary Political Contexts: Majority and Minority Islam

The development of Islam since the end of the colonial period was strongly influenced by state policies. There is a large difference between countries where the majority of the population is Muslim and those areas where Islam exists among minorities.[7]

Indonesia

During the Second World War, the Japanese tried to mobilize rural Islam for their own purposes. This led to an increased Islamic awareness when the country was declared independent on 17 August 1945. After lengthy discussions among nationalist leaders, amongst whom were also Islamic representatives, it was decided that, despite representing the overall majority of the population, Islam would not become the official state religion. Even the Jakarta Charter, which envisaged the requirement for all Muslims to follow the prescriptions of their religion, was not applied. The state philosophy of Pancasila did however prohibit atheism and compelled every citizen to adhere to an officially recognized religion.

During the years of parliamentary democracy (1950-57), Islamic parties acquired an important place in the political spectrum but no dominance. The elections of 1955 produced a stalemate between the secular nationalist, the communist, Masyumi (modernist Islamic), and Nahdatul Ulama (conservative Islamic) parties. Tensions between the central government led by Sukarno and the provinces, however, led to a series of regional revolts in which partly Islamic radicalism played a role. In 1948 in West Java, the independence of Darul Islam (House of Islam) was proclaimed. Later, South Sulawesi and Aceh joined this separatist movement, but in 1958 the central government was able to restore unity through military intervention. Since Masyumi had been implicated, it was banned from parliament. Sukarno associated himself increasingly with the Communist Party, which in the end led to a coup and the end of his power.

Under the rule of Suharto in the 1970s and 1980s, the social and political role of Islam was repressed. The party system was simplified, and all Islamic parties were forced to fuse into the PPP (Partai Persatuan Pembangunan). Several laws—on marriage, on the equalization of state and Islamic courts—restricted Islam further. In 1984, the Nahdatul Ulama left the PPP and in this way emancipated itself from state dominance. Around 1990, a turnaround in state policy occurred, and against the opposition from army circles, Suharto began to court Islam to strengthen his own power base. In 1990, ICMI (Ikatan Cendekiawan Muslimin Indonesia) was founded, a modernist organization led by state officials. Islamic religious, financial, and educational institutions were financially supported by the government and in official contexts Muslim rules of behavior were respected. Yet Suharto's policy to domesticate Islam for his own political ambitions failed. The Nahdatul Ulama, led by Abdurrahman Wahid, remained aloof. Besides a tiny minority of fundamentalists, who wanted to establish a theocratic state, the major groups belonged to either the modernists or the neomodernists. The latter are more positive toward influence from the West, concentrate less on political issues, and are more interested in furthering the social and economic advancement of the community of Muslims. The modernist approach seeks a compromise between traditional Islam, the universality of the ummah, and the model of the nation-state (Schwarz 1994, chap. 7).

The fall of Suharto in 1998 provoked a proliferation of Islamic parties and organizations. More than nine Islamic parties participated in the elections of 1999, but as in 1955, these could not attain more than one-third of the popular vote. Nevertheless, a coalition of traditionalist and modernist Islamic parties, the so-called middle axis, ensured that not the PDI-P (Partai Demokrasi Indonesia-Perjvanganr, Indonesian Party of Struggle) leader and daughter of Sukarno Megawati was elected president but Suharto's main foe, Abdurrahman Wahid. He encouraged pluralism and openness but overrepresented his own traditional party in his cabinet and collided with army circles, which led to his removal from office in July 2001. Since then, Indonesia has been led by President Megawati, a woman acceptable to both secular nationalist and nonorthodox Muslim, middle- and lower-class groups.[8]

Malaysia

The connection between state and Islam that was assigned to the sultans under British rule was continued after independence in 1957, particularly after the creation of the Malaysian Federation in 1963. The aim was to maintain racial harmony on one hand and uphold the privileged position of the Muslim Malays on the other. In contrast to Indonesia, Islam became the official religion, although at the same time religious freedom was guaranteed. Malay interests were articulated through the secular government party UMNO (United Malays National Organization), although already in 1951, a radical Islamic opposition party, PAS (Parti Islam Se-Malaysia), was established. In 1969, major racial riots broke out, which forced the government to reconsider its policies. A more active pro-Malay policy was pursued, through the New Economic Policy that aimed to raise to level of Malay participation in the modern economy. Also steps were undertaken to "Islamize" society through the creation of new institutions, for instance, in education, but also through the introduction of Islamic banking.

Since 1981, Malaysia has been ruled by Mahathir, who has striven for technological progress in combination with the advancement of the Malays and Islamic values. A state-led Islamization was pursued through the establishment of institutions for Islamic studies, a strengthening of clerical traditions, and participation in international Islamic discussion. Also, the interpretation of law was gradually Islamized. Key institutions like the Pusat Islam and the Yayasan Dakwah that coordinate official missionary activity are directly subordinate to the premier's office for religious affairs. The ultimate aim is to maintain the dominance of the secular state by balancing the various streams in Malaysian Islam and creating a common value system to be able to mobilize the Malays (Stauth 1999, 279-84; Stark 1999, 46).

State patronage of modernist Islam in Malaysia has been partly successful but has also provoked opposition, in particular from the PAS and Darul Arqam. PAS was created early and was more Malay-nationalistic than the pluralist UMNO. Between 1974 and 1978, it joined the government coalition, but afterwards it became more radical, especially since the establishment of the Majlis Syura as decision-making body strengthened the influence of the ulama. The establishment of the shari'ah state was adopted as the official goal of the organization. Taking the Iranian revolution as an example provoked a debate on the danger of an upsurge of "Shiite Ayatollah" in a country where the majority of Muslims belonged to the Shafi'i school of Sunni Islam. Since then, the conflict between UMNO and PAS on "true Islam" has escalated. PAS has a strong backing in the northeastern states of Kelantan and Trengganu. Dissatisfaction with government policies has led to electoral gains in recent years.

Darul Arqam was a fundamentalist movement with more than ten thousand followers that split off from PAS when it joined the government coalition in the 1970s. It was strongly focused on its leader, Ashari Muhammad, and represented, despite its Sunni origin, also Shiite and millenarian characteristics. Members lived in closed-off communes. It established its own business empire, originally based on trade in halal products. The council of Islamic Affairs in Kuala Lumpur considered it to be a deviation of Islamic religion, and the government saw it as a threat to Malay unity. In 1994, the national fatwa committee prohibited the organization, and Ashari was captured in Thailand and distanced himself on television from his own doctrines (Stark 1999, 29-31, 64-74).

Islam in South Thailand and the Southern Philippines

In several countries of Southeast Asia, Islam is the religion of a minority only. When colonial boundaries were drawn, these in part crosscut existing polities and societies. Like that of almost any minority, the position of Muslims living at the fringes of national territories has been problematic. Neighboring countries that have a Muslim majority and international Muslim organizations, like the Muslim World League and the Organization of the Islamic Conference, have put pressure on countries with Muslim minorities to treat these properly and have financially supported them.

Thailand

In South Thailand, in particular the provinces of Narathiwat, Yala, Patani, and Sarun, the majority of the population consists of some Thai-speaking but largely Malay-speaking Muslim groups. This area belonged formerly to the realm of Patani, of which the ruler belonged to the Malay world but at the same time acknowledged the suzerainty of the Thai king. In 1909, the border between British

Malaya and Siam was drawn, in which the latter relinquished its rights over Kelantan, Trengganu, and other northern Malay states. Since then, the Thai government has been active to assimilate the "Thai Muslims" to turn them into real Thai citizens. At first, the Muslim Malays decided to ignore the Thai state but to honor the king. Premier Phibun pursued a strongly nationalist policy in the years between 1938 and 1944, which resulted in the annexation of the northern Malay states. The substitution of Islamic law for Siamese law and the compulsory attendance of state schools provoked strong resistance from the Muslim population. Haji Sulong, president of the Islamic Religious Council, submitted a petition in which full autonomy was demanded, but he was arrested. In 1948, a large-scale revolt was put down by government forces, which marked the beginning of decades of conflict. Immigration from the north and encroachment on Muslim education and the Malay language led to widespread resistance. In the 1970s, rural resistance groups emerged, among them PULO (Patani United Liberation Organization) and PNLF (Patani National Liberation Front). In the 1980s, peace-making efforts were undertaken and a more accommodative official attitude toward Islam was adopted, as a result of which separatism lost support under the local population. However, since 2001, new violence has erupted.[9]

From time to time, the relationship between Bangkok and Kuala Lumpur has been strained over the issue of the Muslims in South Thailand. Cross-border contacts existed with the PAS in Kelantan, and a silent migration toward this Malaysian province was more or less condoned from the Malaysian side. In 1981, tensions erupted when more than one thousand Muslims fled to Kedah and Perak and Kuala Lumpur refused to send them back. The Thai were convinced that many of these belonged to the PULO and were apparently secretly supported by the Malaysian army (Nair 1997, 173-82). More important for local Muslims is the financial support of Islamic education from the Middle East and the rising cultural awareness through the strengthening of the religious element in everyday life. Whether Muslim minority struggle can be equated with an emerging civil society can be questioned, just like the contention that the recruitment of talented Muslims to high state office reflects equal opportunity for Muslims and non-Muslims (Horstmann 2001).[10]

Philippines

Moros is the name for a dozen different ethnic groups of Muslims, currently numbering around 4 million people, who live in the southern Philippines. Since the ninth century, Islamic traders on the route to China visited this area, which became part of the Malay-Muslim world in the fourteenth century, encompassing the lands adjacent to the Sulu and Celebes seas. On the island of Mindanao, various sultanates existed, whereas the islands toward North Borneo were dominated by the Sultanate of Sulu, with its capital on Jolo. Until the nineteenth century, attempts by the Spaniards to conquer this part of the Philippines failed, with the exception of an enclave at Zamboanga and the acceptance of Spanish sovereignty by the sultan of Sulu. After the Americans colonized the Philippines, there was again an effort made to control the area. The Bates agreement of 1899, in which the authority of the sultan of Sulu was acknowledged, was undermined when a single Moro-province was established, migration from the north started, and the Muslim local heads (orang besar) lost power. A program of national integration through "colonial democracy" failed.

After independence in 1946, state-induced migration toward the south continued, local resources were taken, and the Moros were increasingly marginalized. After a 1968 massacre of young Moros in Jabidah (the so-called Corregidor Incident), Nur Misuari founded the Moro National Liberation Front (MNLF). Soon afterwards, major fighting between the Moros and the Philippine army broke out, which produced severe losses of life and triggered the flight of many Moros to Sabah in north Malaysia. In 1976, a peace settlement was agreed upon in Tripolis, which anticipated the establishment of autonomous status for the south. Since then, there have occurred splits in the ranks of the Moro leaders over the degree of cooperation with the national government.

In 1977, the Moro Islamic Liberation Front (MILF) came into existence, out of which in 1991 the Abu Sayyaf faction was formed. These two groups aim at the establishment of an independent Islamic state by way of armed struggle. In contrast to combat between radical groups and Philippine army forces, there have been attempts to find a political solution. One was the establishment in 1990 of the Autonomous Region of Muslim Mindanao (ARMM), to be followed in 1996 by installation of a Southern Philippine Council for Peace and Development (SPCPD) and the installation of Nur Misuari as regional governor. Since 2000, an all-out war against the MILF was started; in 2001, president Arroyo resumed peace talks, but recently new violence has broken out. A basic issue is access to the region's rich natural resources, which is handed out by the national government to northern and foreign firms. Land disputes erupt between immigrant settlers, now constituting a large majority of the population in the south, and local Muslim tribal groups, who are discriminated against and marginalized.[11]

Current Issues in Southeast Asian Islam

The revivalism debate

A major theme in almost any study on contemporary Southeast Asian Islam is the revivalist movement that since the 1970s has led to an increasing Islamic consciousness. In its most simple form, it is thought that the increasing modernization of Southeast Asian societies has led to social change and an erosion of traditional values, which in turn led to an Islamic response to become more pious. The label of "revivalism" is, however, as problematic as any other label that has been applied to Southeast Asian Islam since it presupposes unity where pluralism exists.[12] In current discussion, besides "revivalism," several other terms circulate such as "renewal," "resurgence," "revitalization," and the like. All these suggest that Islamic consciousness has been on the decline but has revived since the 1970s. There is hardly any reason to suggest that Islam was on the retreat before it reemerged or that the process of rising Islamic awareness in Southeast Asia ended in the 1980s. What changed is that Islam became more publicly visible and articulate as the societies of Southeast Asia went through an era of rapid modernization.

A more proper term would be "Islamization" to describe a bottom-up process of growing religious identification and piety by people of all generations and backgrounds. In this vein, the Malays talk about *kebangkitan Islam*, which indicates a "rise" or a rising "consciousness" of the religion. Jomo and Cheek (1992, 79) have defined it as the sum of various cultural responses, to the times Muslims live in, of

---

Within the Southeast Asian region, the fate of Muslim minorities adds to the general feeling of Islam being under attack and so creates an additional vehicle for rising Islamic consciousness.

---

which the political dimension is crucial in many but not all cases. The common element is that Islam is seen as *the* key for understanding the state, politics, law, and society (Milne and Mauzy 1999, 82). However, cause and effect are less clear-cut than it seems at first sight, and the characterization of rising Islamic consciousness as primarily a reaction seems to be rather one sided. A long-term, self-sustained dynamism toward further Islamization can be observed as well.

For Malaysia, there has been an academic discussion on the causes of rising Islam in which Malay ethnic consciousness and the rise of a Malay urban middle class are seen as decisive factors. However, causality has been much more complex, as Hussin Mutalib (1993) has already argued. One could distinguish between various phases of rising consciousness and should also point to the diversity of the movement and internal dissent. There exists also an interaction between local and global contexts, which in turn influences the content of the process of Islamization. Since the 1960s, the international world has been confronted with a number of wars (between Israel and its neighbors, in Afghanistan by the Soviet Union and the United States, in the Balkans, in Iraq) that have left the impression that the Muslim world is under attack. Simultaneously, from the Indian subcontinent and the Middle East, a new wave of reformism, which urged Muslims everywhere to develop a new order based on Qur'an and Sunnah, spread out. One of its intellectual architects was Maududi (1903-1979). The perceived external threat and internal reformism has led to a closer identification with Islam among the Muslims in general. As a third strand of causality, the situation in individual countries and localities needs to be added also.

Both in Indonesia and Malaysia, local developments have strengthened the general trend toward a deeper identification with Islam but in a distinct manner. In Malaysia, the post-1969 search for a common ground of progressive Malay statehood (in contrast to Chinese and Indian identities) was found in Islam. It started among students at the University of Malaya in the late 1970s and developed through nonparty organizations like ABIM (Angkatan Belia Islam Malaysia, or the Malaysian Islamic Youth Movement), led by the later Vice Premier Anwar Ibrahim. Increased access of rural Malays to urban institutes of higher education, through the New Education Policy, widened the basis for the *dakwah* (call to faith) missionary movement. Mahathir was quick to capitalize on this and strengthened the government's Islamic bias through co-option and institution building. It managed to politically institutionalize a social-cultural movement of central importance to the Muslim-Malays and in this manner legitimize UMNO rule. At the end of the 1990s, this power arrangement was challenged by PAS and by the Keadilan Movement of Anwar Ibrahim, but the government has not been toppled.

Only in the 1990s did the Suharto government in Indonesia start to patronize and at the same time circumscribe Islam. Also here, Islamic consciousness had been on the rise since the late 1970s. The expansion of formal education, the desire for an arena for public association and debate in an atmosphere of tightening political repression, and economic advancement were all factors that contributed to an increased rallying around Islam. State policies led to a decline of institutions of abangan or nonorthodox Islam and thus, willingly or not, strengthened santri streams in society. The largely oppositional character of Islamization in Indonesia has led some observers to believe that democratic and pluralist forms rather than conservative Islam will carry the day (Hefner 2000, 17-19). This may be a foregone conclusion, but since the fall of Suharto in 1998 Indonesia still experiences much instability and strife, and although political Islam has gained a higher profile, it is internally divided. Deepening Islamic consciousness has become part of the current struggle between centralism and regionalism that has not been resolved so far.

In settings where Muslims constitute an oppressed minority, such as south Thailand and the southern Philippines, the relationship between Islamization and the struggle for self-determination is an obvious one. Drawing on international networks of Muslim solidarity and strengthening Islamic identity are effective instruments of mobilizing local populations against deprivation. Peaceful solutions of resource sharing and regional autonomy can be expected to be more productive than repression, but the stakes involved often conduce state governments to do otherwise. Within the Southeast Asian region, the fate of Muslim minorities adds to the general feeling of Islam being under attack and so creates an additional vehicle for rising Islamic consciousness.

Islam between ethnicity and statehood

Contemporary Islam in Southeast Asia cannot be disentangled from its relationship to the state nor from its "groundedness" in the primordial loyalties of local descent. In fact, the triangle of religion-nation-ethnicity is loaded with tension in this world region that displays so much diversity. Malaysia is a clear example of a multiethnic country where the core of the nation is constructed around Malayness, which implies automatically its inclusion in Islam. This might explain why Malaysia, in contrast to Indonesia, has been relatively stable. The Chinese and Indian minorities have not been inclined to challenge the existing ethnic-religious arrangement, as long as economic progress is guaranteed. Both minorities support the UMNO government and have not joined the Malay opposition, partly while they fear further restrictions under the possible establishment of a true Islamic state. Seen from the perspective of Islam, the situation in the Philippines is diametrically opposed to that of Malaysia. There the nation is solidly based on Catholicism and Filipino majority rule, which puts the Moro Islamic ethnic groups at the margins. The same holds true for Thailand, where the Thai Buddhist nation has over a long period marginalized the Muslim ethnic minority population in the South. Here the "mapping" of the nation has been markedly centric, which is easier when the country consists of one landmass as opposed to nations, like Indonesia and the Philippines, which consist of thousands of islands (Winichakul 1994).

Indonesia represents another format altogether. Although the large majority of the population is Muslim, the format of the unitary nation-state is contested and ethnicity extremely pluralist. Islam in the Outer Islands has been more orthodox than on Java, where the Muslim Javanese add up to about half of the country's population. Javanese dominance was particularly strong during the rule of Suharto, but now this has been challenged. Since 1998, Indonesia has faced large-scale violent ethno-religious conflict. In the Moluccas, Christian and Muslim groups have fought bitterly, the latter being supported by Laskar Jihad, a militia fighting a "holy war" against the Christian community and led by Ja'far Umar Thalib, who is of Arab-Madurese descent and an ex-mujahideen in Afghanistan (Noorhaidi 2002). Also, in central Sulawesi, east Java, and west Kalimantan, representatives of various ethnicities with different religious background are engaged in violent confrontations (Wessel and Wimhöfer 2001). The causes of these waves of conflict are complex and differ from other long-standing regional conflicts, for instance, between the Indonesian central government and the GAM (Geraken Aceh Merdeku, Independent Aceh Movement) in Aceh. To categorize them as "religious" and thus implicate Islam as the decisive driving force would be highly misleading.

An extremist threat?

Since 11 September 2001, and particularly since the Bali bombings of 12 October 2002, Southeast Asia has become, in American terminology, the second front in the worldwide battle against terrorism. Southeast Asian governments have been compelled to join the so-called antiterrorist coalition. ASEAN (Association of South-East Asian Nations) concluded an antiterrorist pact that includes the Philippines, Malaysia, Indonesia, Thailand, and Cambodia. Security experts who are close to the Pentagon distinguish between level one and level two antiterrorist coalitions, in which level one indicates bilateral cooperation with Washington and the employment of military force against suspected terrorist groups and level two indicates those countries that are unwilling or unable to employ force in coordination with the United States or one of its allies. Consequently, in Southeast Asia, the Philippines, Singapore, and Malaysia are classified as level one partners, whereas Thailand and Indonesia belong to level two. The Philippines have permitted American soldiers on its soil to battle against the Abu Sayyaf in the south. Singapore has cracked down several times on Jema'ah Islamiyah members who are suspected to have links with al-Qaeda. Malaysia has committed itself domestically and detained suspected Islamic militants but has taken a low profile internationally. Despite recent bomb explosions in south Thailand, premier Thaksin has claimed that there are no terrorists within the country. The attitude of Indonesia has been extremely cautious to avoid provoking Muslim groups within its borders. Those responsible for the Bali bombing seem to have been captured. The internment of Abu Bakar Ba'asyir, the leader of Jema'ah Islamiyah, was only forthcoming after considerable external pressure.

In the present climate of Western opinion, simplified projections of a general Muslim extremist threat abound, which in turn may produce overacting. There certainly exist networks of extremists, which make it possible to take local conflict to a global level. Yet the large majority of Muslims in Southeast Asia are moderate and peaceful citizens of their countries. The global war on terrorism is perceived by Muslims in Southeast Asia as an instrument to strengthen American hegemony in the region. Islamic rhetorics are used to express mass discontent but do not signal the desire for an all-out holy war against the West.

Fundamentalist Islam can be found in several corners, but its potential threat must be judged against contextual factors along the lines presented above. Separatism and ethno-religious conflicts have sprung up in the region regularly, and the effects of the Asian economic crisis of 1997-98 have exposed even more clearly the political and economic roots of these confrontations. PULO in south Thailand and the MILF in Mindanao are trying to establish their own state but are now classified by the national governments of Thailand and the Philippines as "terrorist." Links with al-Queda have not been proven, however. Jema'ah Islamiyah, trying to create a daulah Islamiyah in Indonesia, the Philippines, Malaysia, and Singapore and Abu Sayyaf or the disbanded Laskar Jihad seem to be different. But these groups can hardly be considered to represent Southeast Asian Islam. Rather, they fit into a new kind of warfare, in this case led by Afghan veterans linked up to international terror networks that are using fundamentalist Islam as ideological foundation.

Concluding Remarks

This article has attempted to survey the specific characteristics of Islam in Southeast Asia. It has shown that the development of the religion in this region has to be seen in the context of processes that influenced the community of Muslims as a whole but also those that were specific to Southeast Asia itself. Islam in Southeast Asia is pluralist, has been modified by local cultures, but cannot be considered to be peripheral, even when one looks beyond sheer numbers of believers.

Islam has been a substantive part of the region's history since the thirteenth century. In the course of time, a number of fundamental processes of accommodation took place. The first was that between state and Islam, be it in its precolonial, colonial, or present-day format. Nowadays, different modes of political Islam are in place in Malaysia, Indonesia, Thailand, and the Philippines, ranging from co-option to outright repression. The second process of accommodation is connected to the link between the Middle East and Southeast Asia and concerns reformism. Both at the end of the nineteenth century and since the 1970s, an attempt was made to reinstate orthodox Islam as the center of human thinking and acting, both individually and social-politically. Whether the term "revivalism" accurately captures the essence of these processes should be questioned. A third strand of accommodation between religion and region concerns the relationship between ethnicity and Islam, which, particularly in the past few years, has been embedded in conflict.

In the context of current world politics, the Western official view of Islam seems to have narrowed to that of a terrorist threat. Although some terror groups that use fundamentalist Islam as an instrument to gain support are based in Southeast Asia, these are not representative of Southeast Asian Islam. The relationship between Southeast Asia and Islam can only be understood on its own terms, looking both at its historical development and contemporary contexts.

Notes

1. I do not agree with a comment by Hefner that within Southeast Asian studies, Islam has been neglected out of political opportunism. See Hefner and Horvatich (1997, 8-11) on a dual marginalization.

2. Exceptions are a series of essays published in 1983 and reprinted in Hooker (1988); a compilation of essays compiled by Ahmad Ibrahim, Sharon Siddique, and Yasmin Hussain (1985); a collection of articles on social issues edited by Taufik Abdullah and Sharon Siddique (1986); and Martin van Bruinessen's state-of-the-art essay (1987). More numerous are popular works, such as the one of Volker Stahr (1997), but these are aimed at the general public and do not contain new information.

3. The University Library of Leiden contains one of the world's biggest collection of Malay and Javanese manuscripts. Recently, a new catalogue of Malay works was produced. See Wieringa and de Lijster-Streef (1998). Javanese manuscripts were listed in Th. Pigeaud (1967-80); in Malaysia and Indonesia also, large collections are held that have been inventoried in recent years by Nancy Florida, Timothy Behrend, Jennifer Lindsay, Allen Feinstein, and others.

4. The legal approach is exemplified by Lev (1972) and Peletz (2002).

5. For a recent survey of colonialism in Southeast Asia, see Kratoska (2001).

6. For a recent study on Javanese Islam, see Beatty (1999).

7. An earlier overview of this kind was made by Deliar Noer (1988).

8. The best survey history of Indonesia is Ricklefs (2001).

9. Fragments of the history of the Patani region can be found in standard Thai histories like Wyatt (1984). For an interesting comparative study on South Thailand and the southern Philippines, see Syed Serajul Islam (1998).

10. On civil society in South Thailand, see Chaiwat Satha-anand (2001); on equal opportunity, Preeda Prapertchob (2001).

11. There exists a large literature on the Moro conflict. See for instance Man (1990), Turner et al. (1992), McKenna (1998), and Federspiel (1998).

12. Roy Ellen remarked that labels such as "syncretist," "scripturalist," "fundamentalist," and "millenialist" are not separable and do not take into account for personal, local, and temporal differences. See Ellen (1988, 63).

References

Abdullah, Taufik, and Sharon Siddique, eds. 1986. *Islam and society in Southeast Asia*. Singapore: ISEAS.

Adas, Michael. 1979. *Prophets of rebellion. Millenarian protest movements against the European colonial order*. Chapel Hill: University of North Carolina Press.

Alfian, Muhammadiyah. 1989. *The political behavior of a Muslim modernist organization under Dutch colonialism*. Yogyakarta, Indonesia: Gadjah Mada University Press.

Andaya, Barbara Watson, and Leonard Y. Andaya. 1982. *A history of Malaysia*. Houndmills, Basingstoke, UK: Macmillan.

Beatty, Andrew. 1999. *Varieties of Javanese religion. An anthropological account*. Cambridge: Cambridge University Press.

Benda, Harry J. 1958. *The crescent and the rising sun. Indonesian Islam under the Japanese occupation 1942-1945*. The Hague, the Netherlands: Van Hoeve.

Bruinessen, Martin van. 1987. New perspectives on Southeast Asian Islam? *Bijdragen tot de Taal-, Land- en Volkenkunde* 143 (4): 519-38.

Dijk, Cees van, and A. H. de Groot. 1995. *State and Islam*. Leiden, the Netherlands: CNWS.

Ellen, Roy F. 1988. Practical Islam in South-East Asia. In *Islam in South-East Asia*, edited by M. B. Hooker. Leiden, the Netherlands: Brill.

Evans, D. H. 1987. The "meanings" of pan-Islamism: The growth of international consciousness among the Muslims of India and Indonesia in the late nineteenth and early twentieth century. *Itinerario* 11 (1): 15-34.

Federspiel, Howard. 1998. Islam and Muslims in the southern territories of the Philippine islands during the American colonial period (1898 to 1946). *Journal of Southeast Asian Studies* 29 (2): 340-56.

Feener, Michael. 1998. A re-examination of the place of al-Hallaj in the development of Southeast Asian Islam. *Bijdragen tot de Taal-, Land- en Volkenkunde* 154 (4): 571-92.

Geertz, Clifford. 1960. *Religion of Java*. Glencoe, IL: Free Press.

———. 1968. *Islam observed. Religious development in Morocco and Indonesia*. New Haven, CT: Yale University Press.

Hefner, Robert W. 2000. *Civil Islam. Muslims and democratisation in Indonesia*. Princeton, NJ: Princeton University Press.

Hefner, Robert W., and Patricia Horvatich, eds. 1997. *Islam in an era of nation-states. Politics and religious renewal in Muslim Southeast Asia*. Honolulu: University of Hawaii Press.

Heryanto, Ariel. 2002. Can there be Southeast Asians in Southeast Asian studies? *Moussons* 5:3-30.

Hooker, M. B., ed. 1988. *Islam in South-East Asia. Second impression*. Leiden, the Netherlands: Brill.

Horstmann, Alexander. 2001. Wertschätzung und Ächtung: Moral and Politik in Südthailand. *Internationales Asienforum* 32 (3-4): 337-60.

Ibrahim, Ahmad, Sharon Siddique, and Yasmin Hussain, eds. 1985. *Readings on Islam in Southeast Asia*. Singapore: ISEAS.

Islam, Syed Serajul. 1998. The Islamic independence movements in Patani of Thailand and Mindanao of the Philippines. *Asian Survey* 38 (5): 441-56.

Johns, A. H. 1961. Sufism as a category in Indonesian literature and history. *Journal of Southeast Asian History* 2:10-23

———. 1995. Sufism in Southeast Asia: Reflections and reconsiderations. *Journal of Southeast Asian Studies* 26 (1): 169-83.

Jomo, K. S., and Ahmad Shabery Cheek. 1992. Malaysia's Islamic movements. In *Fragmented vision: Culture and politics in contemporary Malaysia*, edited by Joel S. Kahn and Francis Loh Kok Wah, 79-106. Sydney: Allen & Unwin.

Jonge, Huub de, and Nico Kaptein, eds. 2002. *Transcending borders. Arabs, politics, trade and Islam in Southeast Asia*. Leiden, the Netherlands: KITLV Press.

Kaptein, Nico, ed. 1997. *The Muhimmât al-Nafâ'is. A bilingual Meccan fatwa collection for Indonesian Muslims from the end of the nineteenth century*. Jakarta, Indonesia: INIS.

Kratoska, Paul, ed. 2001. *South East Asia: Colonial history*. 6 vols. London: Routledge.

Lev, Daniel S. 1972. *Islamic courts in Indoensia. A study in the political bases of legal institutions*. Berkeley: University of California Press.

Man, W. K. Che. 1990. *Muslim separatism: The Moros of southern Philippines and the Malays of southern Thailand*. Oxford: Oxford University Press.

Milne, R. S., and Diane K. Mauzy. 1999. *Malaysian politics under Mahathir*. London: Routledge.

Mutalib, Hussin. 1993. *Islam in Malaysia. From revivalism to Islamic state*. Singapore: Singapore University Press.

Nair, Shanti. 1997. *Islam in Malaysian foreign policy*. London: Routledge.

Nakamura, Mitsuo, Sharon Siddique, et al., eds. 2001. *Islam and civil society in Southeast Asia*. Singapore: ISEAS.

Noer, Deliar. 1988. Contemporary political dimensions if Islam. *Islam in South-East Asia*, edited by M. B. Hooker, 183-215. Leiden, the Netherlands: Brill.

Noorhaidi, Hasan. 2002. Faith and politics: The rise of the Laskar Jihad in the era of transition in Indonesia. *Indonesia* 73 (April): 145-69.

Peletz, Michael G. 2002. *Islamic modern. Religious courts and cultural politics in Malaysia*. Princeton, NJ: Princeton University Press.

Pigeaud, Th. 1967-80. *Literature of Java: Catalogue Raisonné of Javanese manuscripts in the Library of the University of Leiden and other public collections in the Netherlands*. 4 vols. The Hague, the Netherlands: Nijhoff.

Pigeaud, Th., and H. J. de Graaf. 1976. *Islamic states in Java 1500-1700*. The Hague, the Netherlands: Nijhoff.

Prapertchob, Preeda. 2001. Islam and civil society in Thailand. The role of NGOs. In *Islam and civil society in Southeast Asia*, edited by Mitsuo Nakamura, Sharon Siddique, et al., 104-16. Singapore: ISEAS.

Ricklefs, M. C. 2001. *A history of modern Indonesia since c. 1200*. 3d ed. Houndmills, UK: Palgrave.

Riddell, Peter. 2001. *Islam and the Malay-Indonesian world. Transmissions and responses*. Singapore: Horizon.

Robson, S. O. 1981. Java at the crossroads. *Bijdragen tot de Indische Taal-, Land- en Volkenkunde* 137 (2/3): 259-92.

Roff, William R. 1994. *The origins of Malay nationalism*. 2d ed. Oxford: Oxford University Press.

Satha-anand, Chaiwat. 2001. Defending community, strengthening civil society. A Muslim minority's contribution to Thai civil society. In *Islam and civil society in Southeast Asia*, edited by Mitsuo Nakamura, Sharon Siddique, et al., 91-103. Singapore: ISEAS.

Schumann, Olaf. 1999. Der Islam. In *Südostasien-Handbuch*, edited by Bernhard Dahm and Roderich Ptak, 434-53. München, Germany: Beck.

Schwarz, Adam. 1994. *A nation in waiting. Indonesia in the 1990s*. Boulder, CO: Westview.

Stahr, Volker. 1997. *Südostasien und der Islam. Kulturraum zwischen Kommerz und Koran*. Darmstadt, Germany: Primus.

Stark, Jan. 1999. *Kebangkitan Islam. Islamische Entwicklungsprozesse in Malaysia*. Hamburg, Germany: Abera.

Stauth, Georg. 1999. Malaysia. In *Südostasien Handbuch*, edited by Bernhard Dahm and Roderich Ptak, 271-84. Munich, Germany: Beck.

Turner, Mark, R. J. May and Lulu Respall, eds. 1992. *Mindano: Land of unfulfulled promise*. Quezon: New Day.

Wessel, Ingrid, and Georgia Wimhöfer, eds. 2001. *Violence in Indonesia*. Hamburg, Germany: Abera.

Wieringa, E. P., and Joan de Lijster-Streef, eds. 1998. *Catalogue of Malay and Minangkabau manuscripts in the Library of Leiden University and other collections in the Netherlands*. Leiden, the Netherlands: Legatum Warnerianum.

Winichakul, Thongchai. 1994. *Siam mapped. A history of the geo-body of a nation*. Chiang Mai, Thailand: Silkworm.

Woodward, Mark. 1989. *Islam in Java. Normative piety and mysticism in the Sultanate of Yogyakarta*. Tuscon: University of Arizona Press.

Wyatt, David. 1984. *Thailand. A short history*. New Haven, CT: Yale University Press.

Reel Bad Arabs: How Hollywood Vilifies a People

By
JACK G. SHAHEEN

Live images on big screen and television go beyond a thousand words in perpetuating stereotypes and clichés. This article surveys more than a century of Hollywood's projection of negative images of the Arabs and Muslims. Based on the study of more than 900 films, it shows how moviegoers are led to believe that all Arabs are Muslims and all Muslims are Arabs. The moviemakers' distorted lenses have shown Arabs as heartless, brutal, uncivilized, religious fanatics through common depictions of Arabs kidnapping or raping a fair maiden; expressing hatred against the Jews and Christians; and demonstrating a love for wealth and power. The article compares the stereotype of the hook-nosed Arab with a similar depiction of Jews in Nazi propaganda materials. Only five percent of Arab film roles depict normal, human characters.

Keywords: Arabs; Hollywood; film industry; stereotypes; xenophobia; movie reviews

Introduction

Al tikrar biallem il hmar (By repetition even the donkey learns).

This Arab proverb encapsulates how effective repetition can be when it comes to education: how we learn by repeating an exercise over and over again until we can respond almost

Jack G. Shaheen is a professor emeritus of mass communications at Southern Illinois University. Dr. Shaheen is the world's foremost authority on media images of Arabs and Muslims. He regularly appears on national programs such as Nightline, Good Morning America, 48 Hours, *and* The Today Show. *He is the author of* Arab and Muslim Stereotyping in American Popular Culture, Nuclear War Films, *and the award-winning* TV Arab. *Los Angeles Times TV critic Howard Rosenberg calls* Reel Bad Arabs: How Hollywood Vilifies a People *"a groundbreaking book that dissects a slanderous history dating from cinema's earliest days to contemporary Hollywood blockbusters that feature machine-gun wielding and bomb-blowing 'evil' Arabs."*

NOTE: "Reel Bad Arabs" by Jack G. Shaheen was first published in *Reel Bad Arabs: How Hollywood Vilifies a People*, published by Olive Branch Press, an imprint of Interlink Publishing Group, Inc. Text copyright © Jack G. Shaheen 2001. Reprinted with permission.

DOI: 10.1177/0002716203255400

reflexively. A small child uses repetition to master numbers and letters of the alphabet. Older students use repetition to memorize historical dates and algebraic formulas.

For more than a century Hollywood, too, has used repetition as a teaching tool, tutoring movie audiences by repeating over and over, in film after film, insidious images of the Arab people. I ask the reader to study in these pages the persistence of this defamation, from earlier times to the present day, and to consider how these slanderous stereotypes have affected honest discourse and public policy.

Genesis

In [my book *Reel Bad Arabs*], I document and discuss virtually every feature that Hollywood has ever made—more than 900 films, the vast majority of which portray Arabs by distorting at every turn what most Arab men, women, and children are really like. In gathering the evidence for this book, I was driven by the need to expose an injustice: cinema's systematic, pervasive, and unapologetic degradation and dehumanization of a people.

When colleagues ask whether today's reel Arabs are more stereotypical than yesteryear's, I can't say the celluloid Arab has changed. That is the problem. He is what he has always been—the cultural "other." Seen through Hollywood's distorted lenses, Arabs look different and threatening. Projected along racial and religious lines, the stereotypes are deeply ingrained in American cinema. From 1896 until today, filmmakers have collectively indicted all Arabs as Public Enemy #1—brutal, heartless, uncivilized religious fanatics and money-mad cultural "others" bent on terrorizing civilized Westerners, especially Christians and Jews. Much has happened since 1896—women's suffrage, the Great Depression, the civil rights movement, two world wars, the Korean, Vietnam, and Gulf wars, and the collapse of the Soviet Union. Throughout it all, Hollywood's caricature of the Arab has prowled the silver screen. He is there to this day—repulsive and unrepresentative as ever.

What is an Arab? In countless films, Hollywood alleges the answer: Arabs are brute murderers, sleazy rapists, religious fanatics, oil-rich dimwits, and abusers of women. "They [the Arabs] all look alike to me," quips the American heroine in the movie *The Sheik Steps Out* (1937). "All Arabs look alike to me," admits the protagonist in *Commando* (1968). Decades later, nothing had changed. Quips the U.S. Ambassador in *Hostage* (1986), "I can't tell one [Arab] from another. Wrapped in those bed sheets they all look the same to me." In Hollywood's films, they certainly do.

Pause and visualize the reel Arab. What do you see? Black beard, headdress, dark sunglasses. In the background—a limousine, harem maidens, oil wells, camels. Or perhaps he is brandishing an automatic weapon, crazy hate in his eyes and Allah on his lips. Can you see him?

Think about it. When was the last time you saw a movie depicting an Arab or an American of Arab heritage as a regular guy? Perhaps a man who works ten hours a day, comes home to a loving wife and family, plays soccer with his kids, and prays

H00786

CALL: 800-818-7243   FAX: 800-583-2665   E-MAIL: order@sagepub.com   WEBSITE: sagepub.com

THE ANNALS OF THE AMERICAN ACADEMY OF POLITICAL AND SOCIAL SCIENCE – PAPERBOUND   *Frequency: 6 Times/Year*

☐ Please start my subscription to The ANNALS of the American Academy of Political and Social Science – Paperbound (J295)
ISSN: 0002-7162

Prices	U.S.A.	Int'l / Canada*
Individuals	☐ $71	☐ $95
Institutions	☐ $454	☐ $478

PAYMENT

☐ Check enclosed. (Payable to SAGE)   ☐ Bill me.

☐ Charge my: ☐ MasterCard ☐ VISA ☐ AmEx ☐ Discover   (Phone number required) _____

_____ Expiration Date

Card # _____

Signature _____

Name _____

Address _____

City/State/Zip Code/Country _____

Phone _____ E-mail _____

☐ Sign me up for SAGE CONTENTS ALERT (please include your e-mail address).

NO POSTAGE
NECESSARY
IF MAILED
IN THE
UNITED STATES

BUSINESS REPLY MAIL

FIRST-CLASS MAIL   PERMIT NO. 90   THOUSAND OAKS, CA

POSTAGE WILL BE PAID BY ADDRESSEE

SAGE PUBLICATIONS
PO BOX 5084
THOUSAND OAKS CA 91359-9707

with family members at his respective mosque or church. He's the kind of guy you'd like to have as your next door neighbor, because—well, maybe because he's a bit like you.

But would you want to share your country, much less your street, with any of Hollywood's Arabs? Would you want your kids playing with him and his family, your teenagers dating them? Would you enjoy sharing your neighborhood with fabulously wealthy and vile oil sheikhs with an eye for Western blondes and arms deals and intent on world domination, or with crazed terrorists, airplane hijackers, or camel-riding bedouins?

Real Arabs

Who exactly are the Arabs of the Middle East? When I use the term "Arab," I refer to the 265 million people who reside in, and the many more millions around the world who are from, the 22 Arab states.[1] The Arabs have made many contributions to our civilization. To name a few, Arab and Persian physicians and scientists inspired European thinkers like Leonardo da Vinci. The Arabs invented algebra and the concept of zero. Numerous English words—algebra, chemistry, coffee, and others—have Arab roots. Arab intellectuals made it feasible for Western scholars to develop and practice advanced educational systems.

In astronomy Arabs used astrolabes for navigation, star maps, celestial globes, and the concept of the center of gravity. In geography, they pioneered the use of latitude and longitude. They invented the water clock; their architecture inspired the Gothic style in Europe. In agriculture, they introduced oranges, dates, sugar, and cotton, and pioneered water works and irrigation. And, they developed a tradition of legal learning, of secular literature and scientific and philosophical thought, in which the Jews also played an important part.

There exists a mixed ethnicity in the Arab world—from 5000 BC to the present. The Scots, Greeks, British, French, Romans, English, and others have occupied the area. Not surprisingly, some Arabs have dark hair, dark eyes, and olive complexions. Others boast freckles, red hair, and blue eyes.

Geographically, the Arab world is one-and-a-half times as large as the United States, stretching from the Strait of Hormuz to the Rock of Gibraltar. It's the point where Asia, Europe, and Africa come together. The region gave the world three major religions, a language, and an alphabet.

In most Arab countries today, 70 percent of the population is under age 30. Most share a common language, cultural heritage, history, and religion (Islam). Though the vast majority of them are Muslims, about 15 million Arab Christians (including Chaldean, Coptic, Eastern Orthodox, Episcopalian, Roman Catholic, Melkite, Maronite, and Protestant), reside there as well.

. . . Their dress is traditional and Western. The majority are peaceful, not violent; poor, not rich; most do not dwell in desert tents; none are surrounded by harem maidens; most have never seen an oil well or mounted a camel. Not one travels via "magic carpets." Their lifestyles defy stereotyping.

... Through immigration, conversion, and birth, ... Muslims are America's fastest growing religious group; about 500,000 reside in the greater Los Angeles area. America's six to eight million Muslims frequent more than 2,000 mosques, Islamic centers, and schools. They include immigrants from more than 60 nations, as well as African-Americans. In fact, most of the world's 1.1 billion Muslims are Indonesian, Indian, or Malaysian. Only 12 percent of the world's Muslims are Arab. Yet, moviemakers ignore this reality, depicting Arabs and Muslims as one and the same people. Repeatedly, they falsely project all Arabs as Muslims and all Muslims as Arabs. As a result, viewers, too, tend to link the same attributes to both peoples.

... Hollywood's past omission of "everyday" African-Americans, American Indians, and Latinos unduly affected the lives of these minorities. The same holds true with the industry's near total absence of regular Arab-Americans. Regular Mideast Arabs, too, are invisible on silver screens. Asks Jay Stone, "Where are the movie Arabs and Muslims who are just ordinary people?"[2]

Why is it important for the average American to know and care about the Arab stereotype? It is critical because dislike of "the stranger," which the Greeks knew as xenophobia, forewarns that when one ethnic, racial, or religious group is vilified, innocent people suffer. History reminds us that the cinema's hateful Arab stereotypes are reminiscent of abuses in earlier times. Not so long ago—and sometimes still—Asians, American Indians, blacks, and Jews were vilified.

Ponder the consequences. In February 1942, more than 100,000 Americans of Japanese descent were displaced from their homes and interred in camps; for decades blacks were denied basic civil rights, robbed of their property, and lynched; American Indians, too, were displaced and slaughtered; and in Europe, six million Jews perished in the Holocaust.

This is what happens when people are dehumanized.

Mythology in any society is significant. And, Hollywood's celluloid mythology dominates the culture. No doubt about it, Hollywood's renditions of Arabs frame stereotypes in viewer's minds. The problem is peculiarly American. Because of the vast American cultural reach via television and film—we are the world's leading exporter of screen images—the all-pervasive Arab stereotype has much more of a negative impact on viewers today than it did thirty or forty years ago.

Nowadays, Hollywood's motion pictures reach nearly everyone. Cinematic illusions are created, nurtured, and distributed worldwide, reaching viewers in more than 100 countries, from Iceland to Thailand. Arab images have an effect not only on international audiences, but on international movie makers as well. No sooner do contemporary features leave the movie theaters than they are available in video stores and transmitted onto TV screens. Thanks to technological advances, old silent and sound movies impugning Arabs, some of which were produced before I was born, are repeatedly broadcast on cable television and beamed directly into the home.

Check your local guides and you will see that since the mid-1980s, appearing each week on TV screens, are fifteen to twenty recycled movies projecting Arabs as dehumanized caricatures: *The Sheik* (1921), *The Mummy* (1932), *Cairo* (1942),

The Steel Lady (1953), *Exodus* (1960), *The Black Stallion* (1979), *Protocol* (1984), *The Delta Force* (1986), *Ernest in the Army* (1997), and *Rules of Engagement* (2000). Watching yesteryear's stereotypical Arabs on TV screens is an unnerving experience, especially when pondering the influence celluloid images have on adults and our youth.

. . . Arabs, like Jews, are Semites, so it is perhaps not too surprising that Hollywood's image of hook-nosed, robed Arabs parallels the image of Jews in Nazi-inspired movies such as *Robert and Bertram* (1939), *Die Rothschilds Aktien von Waterloo* (1940), *Der Ewige Jude* (1940), and *Jud Süss* (1940). Once upon a cinematic time, screen Jews boasted exaggerated nostrils and dressed differently—in yarmulkes and dark robes—than the films' protagonists. In the past, Jews were projected as the "other"—depraved and predatory money-grubbers who seek world domination, worship a different God, and kill innocents. Nazi propaganda also presented the lecherous Jew slinking in the shadows, scheming to snare the blonde Aryan virgin.

Seen through Hollywood's distorted lenses, Arabs look different and threatening.

Yesterday's Shylocks resemble today's hook-nosed sheikhs, arousing fear of the "other." Reflects William Greider, "Jews were despised as exemplars of modernism," while today's "Arabs are depicted as carriers of primitivism—[both] threatening to upset our cozy modern world with their strange habits and desires."[3]

. . . Because of Hollywood's heightened cultural awareness, producers try not to demean most racial and ethnic groups. They know it is morally irresponsible to repeatedly bombard viewers with a regular stream of lurid, unyielding, and unrepentant portraits of a people. The relation is one of cause and effect. Powerful collages of hurtful images serve to deepen suspicions and hatreds. Jerry Mander observes, screen images "can cause people to do what they might otherwise never [have] thought to do."[4]

One can certainly make the case that movie land's pernicious Arab images are sometimes reflected in the attitudes and actions of journalists and government officials. Consider the aftermath of the 19 April 1995 bombing of the federal building in Oklahoma City. Though no American of Arab descent was involved, they were instantly targeted as suspects. Speculative reporting, combined with decades of harmful stereotyping, resulted in more than 300 hate crimes against them.[5]

A Basis for Understanding

. . . [I have reviewed] more than 900 feature films displaying Arab characters. Regrettably, in all these I uncovered only a handful of heroic Arabs; they surface in a few 1980s and 1990s scenarios. In *Lion of the Desert* (1981), righteous Arabs bring down invading fascists. Humane Palestinians surface in *Hanna K* (1983) and *The Seventh Coin* (1992). In *Robin Hood, Prince of Thieves* (1991), a devout Muslim who "fights better than twenty English knights," helps Robin Hood get the better of the evil Sheriff of Nottingham. In *The 13th Warrior* (1999), an Arab Muslim scholar befriends Nordic warriors, helping them defeat primitive cavemen. And in *Three Kings* (1999), a movie celebrating our commonalities and differences, we view Arabs as regular folks, with affections and aspirations. This anti-war movie humanizes the Iraqis, a people who for too long have been projected as evil caricatures.

Most of the time I found moviemakers saturating the marketplace with all sorts of Arab villains. Producers collectively impugned Arabs in every type of movie you can imagine, targeting adults in well-known and high-budgeted movies such as *Exodus* (1960), *Black Sunday* (1977), *Ishtar* (1987), and *The Siege* (1998); and reaching out to teenagers with financially successful schlock movies such as *Five Weeks in a Balloon* (1962), *Things Are Tough All Over* (1982), *Sahara* (1983), and *Operation Condor* (1997). One constant factor dominates all the films: Derogatory stereotypes are omnipresent, reaching youngsters, baby boomers, and older folk.

I am not saying an Arab should never be portrayed as the villain. What I am saying is that almost all Hollywood depictions of Arabs are bad ones. This is a grave injustice. Repetitious and negative images of the reel Arab literally sustain adverse portraits across generations. The fact is that for more than a century producers have tarred an entire group of people with the same sinister brush.

Villains

. . . Beginning with *Imar the Servitor* (1914), up to and including *The Mummy Returns* (2001), a synergy of images equates Arabs from Syria to the Sudan with quintessential evil. In hundreds of movies "evil" Arabs stalk the screen. We see them assaulting just about every imaginable foe—Americans, Europeans, Israelis, legionnaires, Africans, fellow Arabs, even—for heaven's sake—Hercules and Samson.

Scores of comedies present Arabs as buffoons, stumbling all over themselves. Some of our best known and most popular stars mock Arabs: Will Rogers in *Business and Pleasure* (1931); Laurel and Hardy in *Beau Hunks* (1931); Bob Hope and Bing Crosby in *Road to Morocco* (1942); the Marx Brothers in *A Night in Casablanca* (1946); Abbott and Costello in *Abbott and Costello in the Foreign Legion* (1950); the Bowery Boys in *Bowery to Bagdad* (1955); Jerry Lewis in *The Sad Sack* (1957); Phil Silvers in *Follow That Camel* (1967); Marty Feldman in *The Last*

Remake of Beau Geste (1977); Harvey Korman in *Americathon* (1979); Bugs Bunny in *1001 Rabbit Tales* (1982); Dustin Hoffman and Warren Beatty in *Ishtar* (1987); Pauly Shore in *In the Army Now* (1994); and Jim Varney in *Ernest in the Army* (1997).

Some protagonists even refer to Arabs as "dogs" and "monkeys." As a result, those viewers laughing at bumbling reel Arabs leave movie theaters with a sense of solidarity, united by their shared distance from these peoples of ridicule.

In dramas, especially, Hollywood's stars contest and vanquish reel Arabs. See Emory Johnson in *The Gift Girl* (1917); Gary Cooper in *Beau Sabreur* (1928); John Wayne in *I Cover the War* (1937); Burt Lancaster in *Ten Tall Men* (1951); Dean Martin in *The Ambushers* (1967); Michael Caine in *Ashanti* (1979); Sean Connery in *Never Say Never Again* (1983); Harrison Ford in *Frantic* (1988); Kurt Russell in *Executive Decision* (1996); and Brendan Frasier in *The Mummy* (1999).

Perhaps in an attempt to further legitimize the stereotype, as well as to attract more viewers, in the mid-1980s studios presented notable African-American actors facing off against, and ultimately destroying, reel Arabs. Among them, Eddie Murphy, Louis Gossett Jr., Robert Guillaume, Samuel Jackson, Denzel Washington, and Shaquille O'Neal.[6]

In the Disney movie *Kazaam* (1996), O'Neal pummels three Arab Muslims who covet "all the money in the world." Four years later, director William Friedkin has actor Samuel Jackson exploiting jingoistic prejudice and religious bigotry in *Rules of Engagement* (2000). The effects of ethnic exploitation are especially obvious in scenes revealing egregious, false images of Yemeni children as assassins and enemies of the United States.

To my knowledge, no Hollywood WWI, WWII, or Korean War movie has ever shown America's fighting forces slaughtering children. Yet, near the conclusion of *Rules of Engagement*, US marines open fire on the Yemenis, shooting 83 men, women, and children. During the scene, viewers rose to their feet, clapped and cheered. Boasts director Friedkin, "I've seen audiences stand up and applaud the film throughout the United States."[7] Some viewers applaud Marines gunning down Arabs in war dramas not necessarily because of cultural insensitivity, but because for more than 100 years Hollywood has singled out the Arab as our enemy. Over a period of time, a steady stream of bigoted images does, in fact, tarnish our judgment of a people and their culture.

Rules of Engagement not only reinforces historically damaging stereotypes, but promotes a dangerously generalized portrayal of Arabs as rabidly anti-American. Equally troubling to this honorably discharged US Army veteran is that *Rules of Engagement*'s credits thank for their assistance the Department of Defense (DOD) and the US Marine Corps. More than fourteen feature films, all of which show Americans killing Arabs, credit the DOD for providing needed equipment, personnel, and technical assistance. Sadly, the Pentagon seems to condone these Arab-bashing ventures, as evidenced in *True Lies* (1994), *Executive Decision* (1996), and *Freedom Strike* (1998).

On November 30, 2000, Hollywood luminaries attended a star-studded dinner hosted by Defense Secretary William Cohen in honor of Motion Picture Association President Jack Valenti, for which the Pentagon paid the bill—$295,000. Called on to explain why the DOD personnel were fraternizing with imagemakers at an elaborate Beverly Hills gathering, spokesman Kenneth Bacon said: "If we can have television shows and movies that show the excitement and importance of military life, they can help generate a favorable atmosphere for recruiting."

The DOD has sometimes shown concern when other peoples have been tarnished on film. For example, in the late 1950s, DOD officials were reluctant to cooperate with moviemakers attempting to advance Japanese stereotypes. When *The Bridge over the River Kwai* (1957) was being filmed, Donald Baruch, head of the DOD's Motion Picture Production Office, cautioned producers not to over-emphasize Japanese terror and torture, advising:

> In our ever-increasing responsibility for maintaining a mutual friendship and respect among the people of foreign lands, the use of disparaging terms to identify ethnic, national or religious groups is inimical to our national interest, particularly in motion pictures sanctioned by Government cooperation.[8]

Arabs are almost always easy targets in war movies. From as early as 1912, decades prior to the 1991 Gulf War, dozens of films presented allied agents and military forces—American, British, French, and more recently Israeli—obliterating Arabs. In the World War I drama *The Lost Patrol* (1934), a brave British sergeant (Victor McLaughlin) guns down "sneaky Arabs, those dirty, filthy swine." An American newsreel cameraman (John Wayne) helps wipe out a "horde of [Arab] tribesmen" in *I Cover the War* (1937).

In *Sirocco* (1951), the first Hollywood feature film projecting Arabs as terrorists, Syrian "fanatics" assail French soldiers and American arms dealer Harry Smith (Humphrey Bogart). *The Lost Command* (1966) shows French Colonel Raspeguy's (Anthony Quinn) soldiers killing Algerians. And, Israelis gun down sneaky bedouins in two made-in-Israel films, *Sinai Guerrillas* (1960) and *Sinai Commandos* (1968).

Arabs trying to rape, kill, or abduct fair-complexioned Western heroines is a common theme, dominating scenarios from *Captured by Bedouins* (1912), to *The Pelican Brief* (1993). In *Brief*, an Arab hit man tries to assassinate the protagonist, played by Julia Roberts. In *Captured*, desert bandits kidnap a fair American maiden, but she is eventually rescued by a British officer. As for her bedouin abductors, they are gunned down by rescuing US Cavalry troops.

Arabs enslave and abuse Africans in about ten films, including *A Daughter of the Congo* (1930), *Drums of Africa* (1963), and *Ashanti* (1979). Noted African-American filmmaker Oscar Micheaux, who made "race movies" from 1919 to 1948, also advanced the Arab-as-abductor theme in his *Daughter of the Congo*. Though Micheaux's movies contested Hollywood's Jim Crow stereotypes of blacks, *A Daughter of the Congo* depicts lecherous Arab slavers abducting and holding hostage a lovely Mulatto woman and her maid. The maiden is eventually rescued by the heroic African-American officers of the 10th US Cavalry.

Anti-Christian Arabs appear in dozens of films. When the US military officer in *Another Dawn* (1937) is asked why Arabs despise Westerners, he barks: "It's a good Moslem hatred of Christians." Islam is also portrayed as a violent faith in *Legion of the Doomed* (1959). Here, an Arab is told, "Kill him before he kills you." Affirms the Arab as he plunges a knife into his foe's gut, "You speak the words of Allah." And, in *The Castilian* (1963), Spanish Christians triumph over Arab Muslim zealots. How? By releasing scores of squealing pigs! Terrified of the pigs, the reel Arabs retreat.

From as early as 1912, . . . dozens of films presented allied agents and military forces . . . obliterating Arabs.

Arabs invade the United States and terrorize innocents in *Golden Hands of Kurigal* (1949), *Terror Squad* (1988), *True Lies* (1994), and *The Siege* (1998). *The Siege* is especially alarming. In it, Arab immigrants methodically lay waste to Manhattan. Assisted by Arab-American auto mechanics, university students, and a college teacher, they blow up the city's FBI building, kill scores of government agents, blast theatergoers, and detonate a bomb in a crowded bus.

. . . Oily Arabs and robed thugs intent on acquiring nuclear weapons surface in roughly ten films. See *Fort Algiers* (1958) and *Frantic* (1988).

At least a dozen made-in-Israel and Golan-Globus movies, such as *Eagles Attack at Dawn* (1970), *Iron Eagle* (1986), and *Chain of Command* (1993), show Americans and/or Israelis crushing evil-minded Arabs, many of whom are portrayed by Israeli actors.

More than 30 French Foreign Legion movies, virtually a sub-genre of boy's-own-adventure films, show civilized legionnaires obliterating backward desert bedouin. These legion formula films cover a span of more than 80 years, from *The Unknown* (1915) to *Legionnaire* (1998). Scenarios display courageous, outnumbered legionnaires battling against, and ultimately overcoming, unruly Arabs. Even Porky Pig as a legionnaire and his camel join in the melee, beating up bedouins in the animated cartoon, *Little Beau Porky* (1936).

. . . Observes William Greider of the Washington Post, "Much of what Westerners 'learned' about Arabs sounds similar to what nineteenth-century Americans 'discovered' about Indians on this continent . . . acceptable villains make our troubles so manageable." In the past, imagemakers punctuated "anti-human qualities in these strange people," American Indians. They projected them as savages, not thinking like us, "not sharing our aspirations." Once one has concluded that Indians thrive on violence, disorder, and stealth, it becomes easier to accept rather than challenge "irrational" portraits. Today, says Greider, "The Arab stereotypes created by British and French colonialism are still very much with us."[9]

Film producers, broadcast journalists, and military leaders echo Greider's Arab-as-Indian analogy. Seeing marauding desert Arabs approach, the American protagonist in the war movie *The Steel Lady* (1953) quips, "This is bandit area, worse than Arizona Apache." In talking up his film *Iron Eagle* (1986), producer Ron Samuels gushed: Showing an American teen hijacking a jet and wiping out scores of Arabs "was just the kind of story I'd been looking for. . . . It reminded me of the old John Wayne westerns."

Sheikhs

The word "sheikh" means, literally, a wise elderly person, the head of the family, but you would not know that from watching any of Hollywood's "sheikh" features, more than 160 scenarios, including the Kinetoscope short *Sheik Hadj Tahar Hadj Cherif* (1894) and the Selig Company's *The Power of the Sultan* (1907)—the first movie to be filmed in Los Angeles. Throughout the Arab world, to show respect, people address Muslim religious leaders as sheikhs.

Moviemakers, however, attach a completely different meaning to the word. As Matthew Sweet points out, "The cinematic Arab has never been an attractive figure . . . in the 1920s he was a swarthy Sheik, wiggling his eyebrows and chasing the [Western] heroine around a tiled courtyard. After the 1973 oil crisis . . . producers revitalized the image of the fabulously wealthy and slothful sheikh, only this time he was getting rich at the expense of red-blooded Americans; he became an inscrutable bully—a Ray-Ban-ed variation of the stereotypes of the Jewish money lender."[10]

Instead of presenting sheikhs as elderly men of wisdom, screenwriters offer romantic melodramas portraying them as stooges-in-sheets, slovenly, hook-nosed potentates intent on capturing pale-faced blondes for their harems. Imitating the stereotypical behavior of their lecherous predecessors—the "bestial" Asian, the black "buck," and the "lascivious" Latino—slovenly Arabs move to swiftly and violently deflower Western maidens. Explains Edward Said, "The perverted sheikh can often be seen snarling at the captured Western hero and blonde girl . . . [and saying] 'My men are going to kill you, but they like to amuse themselves before.' "[11]

Early silent films, such as *The Unfaithful Odalisque* (1903), *The Arab* (1915), and *The Sheik* (1921), all present bearded, robed Arab rulers as one collective stereotypical lecherous cur. In *The Unfaithful Odalisque*, the sheikh not only admonishes his harem maiden, he directs a Nubian slave to lash her with a cat-o'-nine-tails. In *The Sheik* (1921), Sheikh Ahmed (Valentino) glares at Diana, the kidnapped British lovely and boasts: "When an Arab sees a woman he wants, he takes her!"

Flash forward 33 years. Affirms the sheikh in *The Adventures of Hajji Baba* (1954): "Give her to me or I'll take her!"

Moving to kidnap and/or seduce the Western heroine, clumsy moneyed sheikhs fall all over themselves in more than 60 silent and sound movies, ranging from *The Fire and the Sword* (1914) to *Protocol* (1984). Sheikhs disregard Arab women, preferring instead to ravish just one Western woman.

But Hollywood's silent movies did not dare show Western women bedding sheikhs. Why? Because America's movie censors objected to love scenes between Westerners and Arabs. Even producers experiencing desert mirages dared not imagine such unions.

Some viewers perceived Valentino's *The Sheik* (1921) to be an exception to the rule. Not true. Valentino's Sheikh Ahmed, who vanquishes Diana, the Western heroine in the movie, is actually a European, not an Arab. This helps explain why the European lover-boy dressed in Arab garb was viewed so positively by his essentially female audience. Note the dialogue, revealing Ahmed to be a European:

Diana, the heroine: "His [Ahmed's] hand is so large for an Arab."
Ahmed's French friend: "He is not an Arab. His father was an Englishman, his mother a Spaniard."

Other desert scenarios followed suit, allowing the hero and heroine to make love, but only after revealing they were actually Western Christians!

In Europe, it was otherwise. As early as 1922, a few European movies such as *The Sheikh's Wife* (1922) countered fixed themes, showing Western heroines embracing dashing Arab sheikhs.

Both good and evil sheikhs battle each other in about 60 Arabian Nights fantasies, animated and non-animated. A plethora of unsavory characters, wicked viziers, slimy slavers, irreverent magicians, and shady merchants contest courageous princes, princesses, lamp genies, and folk heroes such as Ali Baba, Sinbad, Aladdin and, on occasion, the benevolent caliph. You can see some of them in the four Kismet fantasies (1920, 1930, 1944, 1955), *Prisoners of the Casbah* (1955), and *Aladdin* (1992).

Even animated cartoon characters thump Arabs. My childhood hero, Bugs Bunny, clobbers nasty Arabs in *1001 Rabbit Tales* (1982). Bugs trounces an ugly genie, a dense sheikh, and the ruler's spoiled son. My other cartoon hero, Popeye, also trounces Arabs. In the early 1930s, Fleischer Studios' lengthy Popeye cartoons presented Arab folk heroes as rogues, not as champions. Popeye clobbers, not befriends, Ali Baba and Sinbad in *Popeye the Sailor Meets Ali Baba's Forty Thieves*, and *Popeye the Sailor Meets Sinbad the Sailor*.

Beginning in the mid-1970s, fresh directors also projected Arab leaders through warped prisms. Emulating their predecessors' stereotypes they, too, displayed Western heroines fending off over-sexed desert sheikhs.

Yet, there are dramatic differences in sheikh images. Once-upon-a-time Arabian Nights movies, such as *Ali Baba Goes to Town* (1937) and *Aladdin and His Lamp* (1952), show indolent sheikhs lounging on thrones. But, contemporary films present oily, militant, ostentatious sheikhs reclining in Rolls Royces, aspiring to buy up chunks of America.

Today's films present anti-Christian, anti-Jewish Arab potentates perched atop missile bases, armed with nuclear weapons, plenty of oil, and oodles of cash. Using Islam to justify violence, today's reel mega-rich hedonists pose a much greater threat to the West, to Israel, and to fellow Arabs than did their predecessors. You can catch a few of their kind in *Rollover* (1981), *Wrong Is Right* (1982), *The Jewel of the Nile* (1985), and *American Ninja 4: The Annihilation* (1991).

Scantily clad harem maidens attend sheikhs in more than 30 scenarios. The rulers shrug off some, torture others, and enslave the rest. Enslaving international beauties in the X-rated movie, *Ilsa: Harem Keeper of the Oil Sheikhs* (1976), is a depraved Arab ruler and his cohort—Ilsa, the "She-Wolf of the S.S." Depraved sheikhs also subjugate dwarfs and Africans; see *Utz* (1992) and *Slavers* (1977).

[O]ne of the elements that makes stereotyping so powerful, and so hard to eliminate, is that it is self-perpetuating.

Often, producers falsify geopolitical realities. During WWII many Arab nations actively supported the Allies. Moroccan, Tunisian, and Algerian soldiers, for example, fought alongside French troops in North Africa, Italy, and France. Also, Jordanian and Libyan troops assisted members of the British armed services. And, late in the conflict, Egypt, Saudi Arabia, and Iraq declared war on Germany.[12]

Yet, most movies fail to show Arabs fighting alongside the good guys. Instead, burnoosed pro-Nazi potentates, some belonging to the "Arabian Gestapo," appear in more than ten sheikh movies; see, for example, *A Yank in Libya* (1942), *Action in Arabia* (1944), and *The Steel Lady* (1953). As early as 1943, about fifty years before the Gulf War, *Adventure in Iraq* (1943) depicts the US Air Force bombing the pro-German Iraqi ruler's "devil-worshiper" minions into oblivion.

From the start, protagonists ranging from Samson to 007 have battled burnoosed chieftains. Flashback to the 1900s. Two 1918 films, *Tarzan of the Apes* and *Bound in Morocco*, show Tarzan and Douglas Fairbanks, respectively, trouncing shifty sheikhs.

Cut to the 1940s. Abbott and Costello, Bing Crosby, and Bob Hope follow suit by belittling Arabs in *Lost in a Harem* (1944) and *Road to Morocco* (1942).

Advance to the 1950s. The Bowery Boys and Tab Hunter thrash robed rulers in *Looking for Danger* (1957) and *The Steel Lady* (1953), respectively.

Flash forward to the 1960s and the 1970s. Elvis Presley, Pat Boone, and Jerry Lewis deride Arabs in: *Harum Scarum* (1965), *The Perils of Pauline* (1967), and *Don't Raise the Bridge, Lower the River* (1968). Other stars bashing sheikhs were Ron Ely in *Slavers* (1977), Michael Douglas in *The Jewel of the Nile* (1985), Cheech and Chong in *Things Are Tough All Over* (1982), and Eddie Murphy in *Best Defense* (1984). And I almost forgot—Burt Braverman drubs two of movie land's ugliest sheikhs in *Hollywood Hot Tubs 2: Educating Crystal* (1990).

The movies of the 1980s are especially offensive. They display insolent desert sheikhs with thick accents threatening to rape and/or enslave starlets: Brooke Shields in *Sahara* (1983), Goldie Hawn in *Protocol* (1984), Bo Derek in *Bolero* (1984), and Kim Basinger in *Never Say Never Again* (1986).

Finally, five made-in-Israel films lambast sheikhs. Particularly degrading is Golan and Globus' *Paradise* (1981). A combination of Western teenagers and chimpanzees finish off the "jackal," a Christian-hating bedouin chieftain, and his cohorts.

Maidens

Arab women, meanwhile, are humiliated, demonized, and eroticized in more than 50 feature films.

Half-Arab heroines as well as mute enslaved Arab women appear in about sixteen features, ranging from foreign legion films to Arabian Nights fantasies. "The Arabian Nights never end," writes William Zinsser. It is a place where young slave girls lie about on soft couches, stretching their slender legs, ready to do a good turn for any handsome stranger who stumbles into the room. Amid all this décolletage sits the jolly old Caliph, miraculously cool to the wondrous sights around him, puffing his water pipe. . . . This is history at its best.[13]

Stereotypical idiosyncrasies abound, linking the Arab woman to several regularly repeated "B" images:

1. They appear as bosomy bellydancers leering out from diaphanous veils, or as disposable "knick-knacks," scantily-clad harem maidens with bare midriffs, closeted in the palace's women's quarters.
2. Background shots show them as Beasts of Burden, carrying jugs on their heads. Some are "so fat, no one would touch them."
3. In films such as *The Sheltering Sky* (1990) they appear as shapeless Bundles of Black, a homogeneous sea of covered women trekking silently behind their unshaven mates.
4. Beginning in 1917 with Fox's silent *Cleopatra*, starring Theda Bara, studios labeled Arab women "serpents" and "vampires." Subsequently, the word "vamp," a derivation of that word, was added to English dictionaries. Advancing the vampire image are movies such as

Saadia (1953) and *Beast of Morocco* (1966). Both display Arab women as Black magic vamps, or enchantresses "possessed of devils."

5. In *The Leopard Woman* (1920) and *Nighthawks* (1981) they are Bombers intent on killing Westerners.

When those dark-complexioned femmes fatales move to woo the American/ British hero, they are often disappointed. The majority of movies, such as *Outpost in Morocco* (1949), posit that an Arab woman in love with a Western hero must die.

A few films allow Arab maidens to embrace Western males. In *A Café in Cairo* (1925) and *Arabesque* (1966), actresses Priscilla Dean and Sophia Loren appear as bright and lovely Arab women. Only after the women ridicule and reject Arab suitors, does the scenario allow them to fall into the arms of Western protagonists.

Regrettably, just a handful of movies—*Anna Ascends* (1922), *Princess Tam Tam* (1935), *Bagdad* (1949), *Flame of Araby* (1951), and *Flight from Ashiya* (1964), present brave and compassionate Arab women, genuine heroines. There are also admirable queens and princesses in several Cleopatra films and Arabian fantasy tales.

. . . Taken together, her mute on-screen non-behavior and black-cloaked costume serve to alienate the Arab woman from her international sisters, and vice versa. Not only do the reel Arab women never speak, but they are never in the work place, functioning as doctors, computer specialists, school teachers, print and broadcast journalists, or as successful, well-rounded electric or domestic engineers. Movies don't show charitable Arab women such as those who belong to the Mosaic Foundation, which donates millions to American hospitals. Points out Camelia Anwar Sadat, Syria and Egypt gave women the right to vote as early as Europe did—and much earlier than Switzerland. Today, women make up nearly one-third of the Egyptian parliament. You would never guess from Hollywood's portrayal of Arab women that they are as diverse and talented as any others. Hollywood has not yet imagined a woman as interesting as Ivonne Abdel-Baki, the daughter of Lebanese immigrants and Ecuador's ambassador to Washington. Abdel-Baki, a specialist in conflict resolution, graduated from Harvard University's Kennedy School of Government and is fluent in five languages. Or De' Al-Mohammed, the University of Missouri's blind fencing star.[14] And many, many more.

Egyptians

. . . Egyptian caricatures appear in more than 100 films, from mummy tales to legends of pharaohs and queens to contemporary scenarios. Reel Egyptians routinely descend upon Westerners, Israelis, and fellow Egyptians. Interspersed throughout the movies are souk swindlers as well as begging children scratching for baksheesh. An ever-constant theme shows devious Egyptians moving to defile Western women; see Cecil B. DeMille's *Made for Love* (1926) and *Sphinx* (1981).

Stephen Spielberg's films *Raiders of the Lost Ark* (1981), *Young Sherlock Holmes* (1986), and *Indiana Jones and the Last Crusade* (1989) merit special attention, as do Golan-Globus' 1960s scenarios, made-in-Israel: *Cairo Operation* (1965) and *Trunk to Cairo* (1965). The producers paint Egyptians as nuclear-crazed and pro-Nazi. Their scenarios are particularly objectionable given the real-life heroics of the Arab Brotherhood of Freedom, a group of brave Egyptians who sided with the Allies during World War II.

Imagemakers are not so harsh with Queen Cleopatra. Beginning with Helen Gardner's *Cleopatra* (1912), Hollywood enlisted stars such as Ava Gardner, Theda Bara, Vivian Leigh, Sophia Loren, Claudette Colbert, and Elizabeth Taylor to portray Egypt's seductive queen. Approximately fifteen movies show Egypt's queen, encircled by stereotypical maidens, pining over Roman leaders. Only four movies display Egyptian queens romancing Egyptians. The majority display Egyptian royals feuding with fellow Egyptians as well as Rome's soldiers.

A few movies, such as Cecil B. DeMille's *The Ten Commandments* (1923) and DreamWorks' Jeffrey Katzenberg's *The Prince of Egypt* (1998), feature Egyptian rogues trying to crush heroic Israelites. I found the animated *Prince of Egypt* to be less offensive than DeMille's scenarios. Though Katzenberg's movie displays plenty of Egyptian villains, *Prince of Egypt* offers more humane, balanced portraits than do DeMille's 1923 and 1956 versions of *The Ten Commandments*. DeMille's 1923 film shows Egyptian guards beating "the dogs of Israel" and Pharaoh's ten-year-old son whipping Moses.

---

*No significant element of public opinion
has yet to oppose the stereotype; even scholars
and government officials are mum.*

From the start, moviemakers linked Egypt with the undead. In Georges Méliès's film *The Monster* (1903), the camera reveals a bearded Egyptian magician removing a skeleton from its casket. Presto! He transforms the bony thing into a lovely maiden. But, not for long. The cunning magician changes the woman back into a skeleton.

Say "Egypt" and producers think "Mummies" and "Money." Beginning with Vitagraph's *The Egyptian Mummy* (1914) and *Dust of Egypt* (1915), Hollywood presented about 26 mummy films. In order to spook viewers, cinematographers placed gauze over the camera's lens, creating chilling, dreamlike, and exotic moods. Topping the list is Universal's *The Mummy* (1932). Due to a fine screenplay and Boris Karloff's performance as the mummy Imhotep, this classic stands the test of time as the mummy film. Other popular mummy movies are *The Mummy's Hand* (1940), *The Mummy's Tomb* (1942), and *The Mummy's Revenge* (1973).

Mummy plots are relatively simple: Revived mummies and their caretaker "priests" contest Western archaeologists. In most scenarios, the ambitious grave-diggers ignore tomb curses. So of course they suffer the consequences for daring to reawaken Egypt's sleeping royals. Meanwhile, the Westerners dupe ignorant, superstitious, and two-timing Egyptians.

Once fully revived, the bandages-with-eyes mummy lusts after the archaeologist's fair-skinned daughter. And, the mummy crushes panicked Egyptian workers and all crypt violators—"infidels," "unbelievers," and "heretics." Occasionally, movies like *The Awakening* (1980) pump up the action by offering decomposed horrors; also in this one, a queen's evil spirit so contaminates the Western heroine, she kills her father.

Obviously, there's more to the state of Egypt, the most heavily populated of all Arab countries, than pyramids and curses. Egypt is comprised of a people who take pride in their culture and their long and honorable history. Moving to modernize its economy and to improve the living standards of its population, Egypt now boasts more than fourteen state universities. The likes of scholarly students or noted Egyptian archeologists, men like the celebrated Kamal El Malakh, are absent from movie screens.

Nor do screenwriters present scenarios patterned after Egypt's renowned journalists and authors, like Rose El-Yousef and Nobel Laureate Naguib Mahfouz. Egyptians, like most other Arabs, are deeply religious and are noted for their warm hospitality. In villages and throughout cosmopolitan cities like Cairo and Alexandria, *Ahlan wa Sahlan* (Welcome, this is your home) is spoken as often as "good morning."

Palestinians

. . . Observed Mark Twain, "We are all ignorant, just about different things." When it comes to the Middle East, many Americans are ignorant about the history and plight of the Palestinian people. One reason is that moviegoers may mistakenly believe reel Palestinians, those ugly make-believe film "terrorists," are real Palestinians. Should this be true, then what must viewers think of Palestinians after exiting movie theaters?

To assume viewers acquire some true knowledge of Palestinians after watching the 45 Palestinian fiction films that I discuss here is both dangerous and misleading. It's the same as thinking that you could acquire accurate knowledge of Africans by watching Tarzan movies, or that you would know all about Americans after watching movies about serial killers.

More than half of the Palestinian movies were released in the 1980s and 1990s; nineteen from 1983–1989; nine from 1990–1998. Absent from Hollywood's Israeli-Palestinian movies are human dramas revealing Palestinians as normal folk—computer specialists, domestic engineers, farmers, teachers, and artists. Never do movies present Palestinians as innocent victims and Israelis as brutal oppressors. No movie shows Israeli soldiers and settlers uprooting olive orchards, gunning down Palestinian civilians in Palestinian cities. No movie shows Palestinian families struggling to survive under occupation, living in refugee camps, striving to have their own country and passports stating "Palestine." Disturbingly, only two scenarios present Palestinian families.

. . . One year after the state of Israel was born, the film, *Sword of the Desert* (1949), presented Palestine according to the popular Zionist slogan, as a land without a people—even though the vast majority of people living in Palestine at the time were, in fact, Palestinians. This myth—no-Palestinians-reside-in-Palestine—is also served up in *Cast a Giant Shadow* (1966) and *Judith* (1966).

A decade after *Sword of the Desert* Paul Newman declared war on the Palestinians in *Exodus* (1960). Hollywood's heroes followed suit. In *Prisoner in the Middle* (1974), David Janssen links up with Israeli forces; together they gun down Palestinian nuclear terrorists. Films from the 1980s such as *The Delta Force* (1986) and *Wanted: Dead or Alive* (1987) present Lee Marvin, Chuck Norris, and Rutger Hauer blasting Palestinians in the Mideast and in Los Angeles. In the 1990s, Charlie Sheen and Kurt Russell obliterate Palestinians in Lebanon and aboard a passenger jet, in *Navy SEALs* (1990) and *Executive Decision* (1996).

In *Ministry of Vengeance* (1989) filmmakers dishonor Palestinians and American military chaplains as well. In lieu of presenting the chaplain, a Vietnam veteran, as a devout, non-violent man, the minister exterminates Palestinians. The minister's parishioners approve of the killings, applauding him.

Seven films, including *True Lies* (1994) and *Wanted Dead or Alive* (1987), project the Palestinian as a nerve-gassing nuclear terrorist. In more than eleven movies, including *Half-Moon Street* (1986) *Terror in Beverly Hills* (1988), and *Appointment with Death* (1988), Palestinian evildoers injure and physically threaten Western women and children.

The reader should pay special attention to *Black Sunday* (1977), Hollywood's first major movie showing Palestinians terrorizing and killing Americans on US soil. Telecast annually the week of Super Bowl Sunday, the movie presents Dahlia, a Palestinian terrorist, and her cohort Fasil. They aim to massacre 80,000 Super Bowl spectators, including the American President, a Jimmy Carter look-alike.

Dictating numerous Palestinian-as-terrorist scenarios is the Israeli connection. More than half (28) of the Palestinian movies were filmed in Israel. Nearly all of the made-in-Israel films, especially the seven Cannon movies, display violent, sex-crazed Palestinian "bastards [and] animals" contesting Westerners, Israelis, and fellow Arabs.

I believe Cannon's poisonous scenarios are not accidental, but rather propaganda disguised as entertainment. Even in the early 1900s studio moguls knew that motion pictures could serve propagandists. Following WWI, Adolph Zukor, the head of Paramount Pictures affirmed this film-as-propaganda fact, saying fiction films should no longer be viewed as simply "entertainment and amusement." The war years, he said, "register[ed] indisputably the fact that as an avenue of propaganda, as a channel for conveying thought and opinion, the movies are unequaled by any form of communication."[17]

Why the Stereotype?

. . . Ask a film industry executive, director, or writer whether it is ethical to perpetuate ethnic or racial stereotypes and you can expect a quick negative response. How then, to explain that since 1970, these very same individuals produced, directed, and scripted more than 350 films portraying Arabs as insidious cultural "others"?

Either filmmakers are perpetuating the stereotype unknowingly, and would immediately disassociate themselves from such activities were they to realize the implications of their actions, or they are doing so knowingly and will only stop when sufficient pressure is brought to bear on them.

It is difficult to imagine that screenwriters who draft scenes of fat, lecherous sheikhs ogling Western blondes, or crazed Arab terrorists threatening to blow up America with nuclear weapons, are not precisely aware of what they are doing. But we sometimes forget that one of the elements that makes stereotyping so powerful, and so hard to eliminate, is that it is self-perpetuating. Filmmakers grew up watching Western heroes crush hundreds of reel "bad" Arabs. Some naturally repeat the stereotype without realizing that, in so doing, they are innocently joining the ranks of the stereotypes' creators.

Huge inroads have been made toward the elimination of many racial and ethnic stereotypes from the movie screen, but Hollywood's stereotype of Arabs remains unabated. Over the last three decades stereotypical portraits have actually increased in number and virulence.

The Arab stereotype's extraordinary longevity is the result, I believe, of a collection of factors. For starters, consider print and broadcast "if it bleeds it leads" news reports. Like most Americans, creators of popular culture (including novelists, cartoonists, and filmmakers), form their opinions of a people, in part, based on what they read in print, hear on the radio, and see on television. Like the rest of us, they are inundated and influenced by a continuous flow of "seen one, seen 'em all" headlines and sound bites.

. . . The image began to intensify in the late 1940s when the state of Israel was founded on Palestinian land. From that preemptive point on—through the Arab-Israeli wars of 1948, 1967, and 1973, the hijacking of planes, the disruptive 1973 Arab oil embargo, along with the rise of Libya's Muammar Qaddafi and Iran's Ayatollah Khomeini—shot after shot delivered the relentless drum beat that all Arabs were and are Public Enemy No. 1.

Right through the 1980s, the 1990s, and into the twenty-first century, this "bad people" image prevailed, especially during the Palestinian intifada and the Israeli invasion of Lebanon. In 1980, the rabid followers of Iran's Ayatollah Khomeini held 52 Americans hostage at the US Embassy in Teheran for 444 days. Nightly, TV cameras blazoned across the planet Khomeini's supporters chanting "Death to America!" and calling our country "the Great Satan" as they burned our flag and, in effigy, Uncle Sam himself.

At the height of the Iranian hostage crisis anti-Arab feelings intensified, as 70 percent of Americans wrongly identified Iran as an Arab country. Even today, most Americans think of Iranians as Arabs. In fact, Iranians are Persians, another people altogether.

... It got worse in the 1990s. Two major events, the Iraqi invasion of Kuwait that led to the Gulf War, and the bombing of New York City's World Trade Center, combined to create misguided mindset, leading some Americans to believe all Arabs are terrorists and that Arabs do not value human life as much as we do. As a result, some of us began even perceiving our fellow Americans of Arab descent as clones of Iraq's Saddam Hussein and the terrorist Osama bin Laden. Well, I think you get the picture.

... Not only do these violent news images of extremists reinforce and exacerbate already prevalent stereotypes, but they serve as both a source and excuse for continued Arab-bashing by those filmmakers eager to exploit the issue. In particular, the news programs are used by some producers and directors to deny they are actually engaged in stereotyping. "We're not stereotyping," they object. "Just look at your television set. Those are real Arabs."

... I discovered more than 50 motion pictures
sans Arab villains, five percent of the
total number reviewed here.

Such responses are disingenuous and dishonest. As we know, news reports by their very nature cover extraordinary events. We should not expect reporters to inundate the airwaves with the lives of ordinary Arabs. But filmmakers have a moral obligation not to advance the news media's sins of omission and commission, not to tar an entire group of people on the basis of the crimes and the alleged crimes of a few.

... Why would anyone take part in the denigration of a people knowingly? I think one answer is the Arab-Israeli conflict. Though the majority of moviemakers are fair-minded professionals, there are some who, in the interests of pursuing their own political or personal agenda, are willing to perpetuate hate. These individuals may be expected to continue to indict Arabs on movie screens for as long as unjust images are tolerated.

New York Times columnist Maureen Dowd offers another answer: "[S]tereotypes are not only offensive [but] they are also comforting. They ...

exempt people from any further mental or emotional effort. They wrap life in the arch toastiness of fairy tale and myth. They make complicated understandings unnecessary."[16] Convenient stereotypes make everyone's job easier. Rather than having to pen a good joke, the writer inserts a stumbling, bumbling sheikh. Looking for a villain? Toss in an Arab terrorist—we all know what they look like from watching movies and TV. No thought required. As for the audience? Well, it also makes some of us feel better to see ourselves as superior to someone else. If one is no longer allowed to feel superior to Asians, Jews, Latinos, or blacks, at least we can feel superior to those wretched Arabs.

. . . Certainly, the Department of Defense's rubber-stamping of motion pictures that lambaste Arabs plays a role. The fact is, the government has a history of playing a role in what movies do and don't get made. As early as 1917, the federal government not only acknowledged the power of film to influence political thought, it took on the wrongful role of censor. As soon as the United States declared war on Germany, the government declared that no Hollywood movie could arouse prejudice against friendly nations. The 1917 film *The Spirit of '76* reveals heroic American revolutionaries such as Patrick Henry and Paul Revere. But, some frames show British soldiers committing acts of atrocities. As England was our World War I ally, the government protested; a judge declared producer Robert Goldstein's movie advanced anti-British sentiments. Calling the film "potent German propaganda,"[17] the judge sentenced Goldstein to prison.

Greed, too, is an incentive. Bash-the-Arab movies make money. Thus, some producers exploit the stereotype for profit.

. . . The absence of vibrant film criticism is another cause. A much-needed recourse against harmful Arab images would be more vigorous criticism emanating from industry executives and movie critics. I recall, still, Bosley Crowther's *New York Times* review of *Adventure in Sahara* (1938). Instead of criticizing stereotypes, Crowther advanced them, writing: "We know the desert is no picnic and you can't trust an Arab very far."

Another factor is silence. No significant element of public opinion has yet to oppose the stereotype; even scholars and government officials are mum. New York's Andrew Cuomo, for example, is running for governor of New York, a state where many Americans of Arab heritage reside. Cuomo is "very interested in the topic of discrimination" and stereotyping; he is alert to the fact that there is "a robust hunger for vulgar stereotypes in popular culture." Imagemakers, he says, are "still stereotyping Italian-Americans, Irish-Americans, African-Americans, Indian-Americans and American Jews."[18] Yet, Cuomo fails to mention coarse stereotypes of Arab-Americans. If we are ever to illuminate our common humanity, our nation's leaders must challenge all hateful stereotypes. Teachers need to move forward and incorporate, at long last, discussions of Arab caricatures in schools, colleges, military, and government classrooms.

Ethnic stereotypes do not die off on their own, but are hunted down and terminated by those whom the stereotypes victimize. Other groups, African-Americans, Asian-Americans and Jewish-Americans, have acted aggressively against discriminatory portraits. Arab-Americans as a group, however, have been slow to mobilize and, as a result, their protests are rarely heard in Hollywood and even when heard, are heard too faintly to get the offenders to back off.

Another reason is lack of presence. With the exception of a few movies, *Party Girl* (1995) and *A Perfect Murder* (1998), Arab-Americans are invisible on movie screens. One reason, simply put, is that there are not many Arab-Americans involved in the film industry; not one is a famous Hollywood celebrity.

What does their absence have to do with contesting stereotypes? Well, one answer is that movie stars have clout. Consider how Brad Pitt altered the scenario, *The Devil's Own* (1996). After reading the initial script, Pitt protested, telling the studio the screenplay made him "uneasy" because it was loaded with stereotypes—"full of leprechaun jokes and green beer." The dialogue, he argued, unfairly painted his character as a stereotypical Irish "bad" guy. Explains Pitt, "I had the responsibility to represent somewhat these [Irish] people whose lives have been shattered. It would have been an injustice to Hollywood-ize it." Unless changes were made to humanize the Irish people, especially his character, Pitt "threatened to walk." The studio acquiesced, bringing in another writer to make the necessary changes.

Also, when it comes to studio moguls, not one Arab American belongs to the media elite. The community boasts no communication giants comparable to Disney's Michael Eisner, DreamWorks' Jeffrey Katzenberg, Fox's Rupert Murdoch, or Time-Warner's Ted Turner.

The lack of an Arab-American presence impacts the stereotype in another way. The industry has a dearth of those men and women who would be the most naturally inclined to strive for accurate and balanced portrayals of Arabs. But a number of high-level Arab Americans in the industry over the course of time would rectify the situation. It's difficult to demean people and their heritage when they're standing in front of you, especially if those persons are your bosses.

. . . Regrettably, America's Arabs do not yet have an organized and active lobby in Los Angeles. To bring about fundamental changes in how motion pictures project Arabs, a systematic lobbying effort is needed. Though the Arab-American and Muslim-American presence is steadily growing in number and visibility in the United States, only a few Arab-Americans meet with and discuss the stereotype with filmmakers. When dialogue does occur, some discriminatory portraits are altered. Declares a February 3, 2001, Council on American-Islamic Relations (CAIR) fax: "The villains in Paramount's upcoming film, The Sum of All Fears, were changed to European neo-Nazis." CAIR officials acknowledged Paramount for this important change, as Tom Clancy's book, on which the movie is based, presents Arab Muslims detonating a nuclear device at the Super Bowl in Denver. In a letter to CAIR, the film's director, Phil Alden Robinson, wrote: "I hope you will be reassured that I have no intention of portraying negative images of Arabs or Muslims."

Ongoing informal and formal meetings with movie executives are essential. Such sessions enable community members to more readily explain to producers the negative effects misperceptions of Arabs have on their children as well as on American public opinion and policy. Also, Arab-Americans need to reach out and expand their concerns with well-established ethnic and minority lobbying groups—with Asians, blacks, Jews, Latinos, gays and lesbians, and others.

Positives

To see is to make possible new ways of seeing. . . . I have tried to be uncompromisingly truthful, and to expose the Hollywood stereotype of Arabs for all to see. While it is true that most filmmakers have vilified the Arab, others have not. Some contested harmful stereotypes, displaying positive images—that is, casting an Arab as a regular person.

In memorable well-written movies, ranging from the Arabian nights fantasy *The Thief of Bagdad* (1924), to the World War II drama *Sahara* (1943), producers present Arabs not as a threateningly different people but as "regular" folks, even as heroes. In Sahara, to save his American friends, a courageous Arab soldier sacrifices his life.

Note this father and son exchange from the film *Earthbound* (1980):

Son: "Why do they [the police] hate us, so?"
Father: "I guess because we're different."
Son: "Just because somebody's different doesn't mean they have to hate 'em. It's stupid."
Father: "It's been stupid for a long time."

At first, I had difficulty uncovering "regular" and admirable Arab characters—it was like trying to find an oasis in the desert. Yet, I discovered more than 50 motion pictures sans Arab villains, five percent of the total number reviewed here. Refreshingly, the movies debunk stale images, humanizing Arabs.

As for those Arabian Nights fantasies of yesteryear, only a few viziers, magicians, or other scalawags lie in ambush. Mostly fabulous Arabs appear in *The Desert Song* (1929), *Ali Baba and the Forty Thieves* (1944), *Son of Sinbad* (1955), and *Aladdin and His Magic Lamp* (1969). The movies present viewers with brave and moral protagonists: Aladdin, Ali Baba, and Sinbad. Emulating the deeds of Robin Hood and his men of Sherwood Forest, Arabs liberate the poor from the rich, and free the oppressed from corrupt rulers.

Worth noting is the presence of glittering Arabs in non-fantasy movies. A heroic Egyptian princess appears in the movie serial, *Chandu the Magician* (1932). A courageous Egyptian innkeeper assists British troops in *Five Graves to Cairo* (1943). *Gambit* (1966) displays a compassionate Arab entrepreneur. In *King Richard and the Crusaders* (1954), Saladin surfaces as a dignified, more humane leader than his counterpart, Richard.

Some independent Israeli filmmakers, notably those whose movies were financed by the Fund for the Promotion of Israeli Quality Films, allow viewers to empathize with Palestinians, presenting three-dimensional portraits. To their credit, producers of *Beyond the Walls* (1984) and *Cup Final* (1992) contest the self-promotional history and Palestinian stereotypes spun out by most other filmmakers. Both movies show the Palestinian and the Israeli protagonist bonding; the two men are projected as soul-mates, innocent victims of the Arab-Israeli conflict.

Notes

1. The 22 Arab states are Algeria, Bahrain, Chad, Comoros, Djibouti, Egypt, Iraq, Jordan, Lebanon, Libya, Mauritania, Morocco, Oman, Palestine, Qatar, Saudi Arabia, Somalia, Sudan, Syria, Tunisia, United Arab Emirates, and Yemen.

2. Jay Stone, *Ottawa Citizen* 16 March 1996.

3. William Greider, "Against the Grain," *Washington Post* 15 July 1979: 4E.

4. Jerry Mander, *Four Arguments for the Elimination of Television* (New York: William Morrow, 1978).

5. See ADC, "The Anti-Discrimination Hate Crimes," (Washington, DC, 1996).

6. For movies featuring African-American actors destroying reel Arabs, see *Best Defense* (1984), *Iron Eagle* (1986), *The Delta Force* (1986), *Wanted: Dead or Alive* (1987), *Firewalker* (1986), *Kazaam* (1996), *The Siege* (1998), and *Rules of Engagement*(2000).

7. Matthew Sweet, "Movie Targets: Arabs Are the Latest People to Suffer the Racial Stereotyping of Hollywood," *The Independent* 30 July 2000.

8. Lawrence Suid, *Sailing on the Silver Screen: Hollywood and the U.S. Navy* (Annapolis, MD: Naval Institute Press, 1996): 151.

9. Greider 1E.

10. Sweet.

11. Edward W. Said, *Orientalism* (New York: Pantheon, 1978): 125.

12. I.C.B. Dear and M.R.D. Foot, eds., *The Oxford Companion to World War II* (Oxford: Oxford University Press, 1995).

13. William Zinsser, "In Search of Lawrence of Arabia," *Esquire* June 1961: 72.

14. "Fencing by Ear," *Missou* Fall 1997: 11.

15. Adolph Zukor, "Most Important Events of the Year," *Wid's Year Book* 1918. For more on Palestinian portraits, see my essay "Screen Images of Palestinians in the 1980s," *Beyond the Stars, Volume 1: Stock Characters in American Film*, ed. Paul Loukides and Linda K. Fuller (Bowling Green, OH: Bowling Green State University Press, 1990).

16. Mareen Dowd, "Cuomos vs. Sopranos," *New York Times* 22 April 2001.

17. *Censored!*, documentary, American Movie Classics, 7 December 1999.

18. Dowd.

Ignorance is a delicate exotic fruit; touch it and the bloom is gone.
—Lady Bracknell, *The Importance of Being Ernest*, Act I

Viewing Islam through Dark Clouds

By
ASLAM SYED

The events of 9/11 have led not only to unprecedented changes in international affairs but also to numerous studies of Islam. In many ways, it seems that Islam was revealed in the early hours of that fateful day. Muslim history, culture, religion, and politics are judged not through history or proper context of their Holy Book but through the dusty clouds that followed the destruction of the twin towers of New York City and the attack on the Pentagon in Washington, D.C. This article critically examines several recent studies that currently buttress the attitudes and actions of powerful components of contemporary U.S. leadership.

Bernard Lewis's book, *What Went Wrong: Western Impact and Middle Eastern Response*, appeared in 2002. He claims that his study had been completed before the 9/11 terrorist attacks yet that it is "related to these attacks, examining not what happened and what followed, but what went before—the larger sequence and larger patterns of events, ideas, and attitudes that preceded and produced them" (p. 1).

For Lewis, what preceded and produced these terrorist attacks were neither the real motives of the planners and perpetrators of these horrible crimes nor the post–cold war search for new enemies but, instead, the Muslim

Aslam Syed received his doctoral degree from Columbia University. He is Professor of History (since 1987) at Quaid-i-Azam University, Islamabad. His academic interests include transcultural historiography, Islam, Sufism, and philosophy of history. He is the author of Muslim Response to the West (1988) and editor of Islam and Democracy in Pakistan (1995). He has been a visiting professor at the University of Pennsylvania, Freie University, Berlin, a senior Fulbright Scholar at Harvard, and Quaid-i-Azam Distinguished Professor at Columbia University. At present, he is DAAD Visiting Professor at Humboldt University in Berlin.

DOI: 10.1177/0002716203255391

awareness that Christendom "constituted the only serious rival to Islam as a world faith and a world power" (p. 3). It was with this awareness, Lewis argues, that Muslims invaded Europe, "captured the ancient Christian city of Constantinople, invaded and colonized the Balkan Peninsula, and threatened the very heart of Europe, twice reaching as far as Vienna." (p. 3). Muslims developed "a world civilization, polyethnic, multiracial, international, one might even say intercontinental" (p. 6). Muslims incorporated ancient knowledge of Greece, ancient Middle East, Persia, India, and China into their intellectual tradition and transmitted it to Europe and elsewhere. In almost every field, we are told, Muslims were the teachers and Europeans their disciples, eagerly learning from them not only the intricacies of sciences and philosophy but also benefiting from their trade, commerce, and technology. Muslims were not just transferring knowledge and various skills; rather,

> To this rich inheritance scholars and scientists in the Islamic world added an immensely important contribution through their observations, experiments, and ideas. In most of the arts and sciences of civilization, medieval Europe was a disciple and in a sense a dependant of the Islamic world, relying on Arabic versions even for many otherwise unknown Greek works. (P. 7)

"And then, suddenly, the relationship changed" (p. 7). According to Lewis, the rapid change in the relative position of the Arab world and Europe was the result of Muslims missing the Renaissance and then, oddly enough, the Reformation. Muslims missed Martin Luther's protest against the Pope, the Thirty Years' War, the Counter Reformation, and the exodus of Jews and Muslims from Spain. They neglected Europe's technological revolution. Even though each of these events was brought about by social, economic, and religious factors that shaped the politics of some parts of Europe, Lewis believes that Muslims were altogether untouched by these historical experiences.

Even more intriguing is the author's reason behind this failure to reap the fruits of European advancements: the lands of Islam dismissed them because "they were still inclined to dismiss the denizens of the lands beyond the Western frontier as benighted barbarians, much inferior even to the more sophisticated Asian infidels to the east" (p. 7).

At this stage of his analysis, Lewis reflects on those moments in history when humans learn paradigmatic lessons: "Usually the lessons of history are most perspicuously and unequivocally taught on the battlefield, *but there may be some delay before the lesson is understood and applied*" (p. 8, emphasis added). This passage may very well reveal the underlying agenda for undertaking this study. That the Muslims did not learn any lesson from their defeat in Spain in 1492 or from the conquest of Astrakhan in 1554 (there are other defeats he does not mention) suggests that such a stubborn community is still waiting for a battlefield where an ultimate lesson will be taught.

Muslims, particularly the Ottomans, whose real or imagined attitudes Lewis uses to paint his portrait of Islam, were not unaware of Western skills in weaponry and warfare. But they were "generally contemptuous of the infidel West" and, therefore, only selectively employed these new innovations. "The Turks in particular adopted such European inventions as handguns and artillery and used them to great effect, without thereby modifying their view of the barbarian infidels from whom they acquired these weapons" (p. 13). This sort of analysis remains elusive throughout his narrative. Apparently, even reminders from Grand Viziers to Sultans that something must be done against the increasing might of the "infidels" had no effect in adopting European technology in defense of European incursions. We do not know whether Lewis is complaining here or seeing what the Sultans did not see.

After a revealing introduction, Lewis tries to substantiate his assertions. These are treated under chapters titled "The Lessons of the Battlefield"; "The Quest for Wealth and Power"; "Social and Cultural Barriers"; "Modernization and Social Equality"; "Secularism and the Civil Society"; "Time, Space, and Modernity"; and "Aspects of Cultural Change." Each chapter assumes that an eternal competition and conflict existed between Muslims and Christians, a competition that is invariably lost by the Muslims. Amazingly, Muslims fail to understand the underlying

---

Out of his historical labyrinth emerge secularism and civil society for Christianity and an intolerant Islam for the Muslims.

---

reasons behind the phenomenal success of the "infidels," thus contradicting Lewis's own theory of change. Compared to this complacency, Europe and, later on, the United States emerge as a single entity where London, Paris, Vienna, Madrid, Amsterdam, Rome, and even Moscow and New York show an amazing receptivity to the new ideas and innovations generated by each other at different times. Thus, the 1804 Serbian uprising against the Ottomans is not seen in its proper historical setting but is attributed to the influence of the French Revolution as if Europeans had no idea of freedom prior to the Paris revolution. Muslims, we are told, did not learn anything from the French Revolution. And despite two centuries of defeat by the Christians, Muslims understood military remedies inadequately and instead launched a "quest for other causes and other cures" (p. 34).

The quest for power and wealth leads to other fantastic theories. Should Muslims live or even travel to the lands of "infidels"? Lewis tells us no, because some Moroccan postulated that even when a Christian government was tolerant and allowed the Muslims to practice their religion, "it is all the more important for them to leave, because under a tolerant government, the danger of apostasy is greater" (p. 36). Lewis argues that "even traveling abroad was suspect; the idea of studying under infidel teachers was inconceivable" (p. 43). I believe Lewis knows the hollowness of this assertion, as historical analyses of Muslims, including some of his own earlier works, do not support this claim. Is Lewis, for example, ignorant of the fact that the Prophet of Islam asked the literate prisoners of war after the Battle of Badar to teach his companions the art of reading and writing to earn their freedom? Is Lewis unaware that the Prophet of Islam told his followers to seek knowledge even if they had to go China? Does Lewis fail to recognize that numerous philosophers, Sufis, and scholars adopted the sayings of Moses and Jesus in their writings, or that Ibn-i-Khaldun mentions his Jewish teacher with pride? I believe he knows all of these details, perhaps better than anyone in this field. Unfortunately, such details reveal a relationship between Muslims and other People of the Book that runs counter to the political agenda that this book intends to advance.

Lewis further contradicts his earlier thesis in turning to an examination of the age of Colonialism, which he also sees as the triumph of Christianity over Islam. He asserts that most Muslim states would never have achieved independence had they not been trained in the Western languages and ideas of freedom, liberty, national sovereignty, and responsible government. Why? Because, Lewis argues, the most effective movements against colonialism were not inspired by Islam but by Westernized elites. Why this sudden openness to the ideas of the infidels? He does not provide an answer.

This underlying thesis again surfaces in his comparison of corruption:

> The difference between Middle Eastern and Western economic approaches can be seen even in their distinctive forms of corruption. . . .In the West, one makes money in the market, and uses it to buy or influence power. In the East, one seizes power, and uses it to make money. (P. 63)

It will indeed be interesting to know how, without money, one seizes power in the East or how those who buy power in the West cease to make money after they seize power.

Lewis further describes three areas in the social and cultural divide between Muslims and Christians that are not based on actual historical discourse but on his interpretation and understanding of Islam. These are the status of women, non-Muslims, and slaves. Selective instances are given to illustrate the point that these three groups "did not benefit from the general Muslim principle of legal and religious equality" (p. 86). To substantiate this point, he uses three Turkish sources. It would have been instructive if he had also looked, for example, at South Asian Muslims, whose slaves married the daughters of their masters and inherited empires and where women became queens.

With respect to the status of Christians, Jews, and other non-Muslims, Lewis fails, for example, to acknowledge the refusal of the ruler of Morocco to send his Jewish subjects to gas chambers when parts of Christian Europe pressured him to do so. Again, a little reading of the Umayyad, Abbasids, Ottomans, and Mughals would reveal how unfounded many of Lewis's claims are. Even Theodor Herzl mentions many Christian and Jewish officers running various departments under the Ottomans (see Lowenthal 1956). More recent examples include a Hindu, Joginder Nath Mandal, serving as the first president of Pakistan's Constituent Assembly and Justice Cornelius, a Christian, serving as the chief justice of Pakistan's Supreme Court. Again, Lewis ignores embarrassing counterexamples that undercut his arguments. Moreover, when evidence is not available to support his point of view, he simply issues a fatwa: "To forbid what God permits is almost as great an offense as to permit what God forbids" (p. 86).

Issues like secularism and civil society are treated in the same way. Out of his historical labyrinth emerge secularism and civil society for Christianity and an intolerant Islam for the Muslims. On one hand, we are told that Christendom was blessed with the Reformation, the French Revolution, and the American Revolution, which apparently led to the development of institutions that make Christian countries more tolerant than Islamic ones. On the other hand, Lewis insists that secularism "is, in a profound sense, Christian." What is even more baffling is the argument that the ouster of the Shah of Iran had the effect of "Christianizing Islam." Reflecting on the post-Shah Iran, Lewis says, "They have already endowed Iran with the functional equivalents of a pontificate, a college of cardinals, a bench of bishops, and, especially, an inquisition, all previously alien to Islam" (p. 109). He goes on to predict a Reformation in Islam too. So the problem of not sharing the historical experience of Europe is solved. Soon, Muslims will have their Reformation, Counter Reformation, French Revolution, and who knows what else. His enthusiasm for Christianity does not stop here; he sees its impact even in non-Iranian Muslims and Jews: "Looking at the contemporary Middle East, both Muslims and Jewish, one might ask whether this is still true, or whether Muslims and Jews may perhaps have caught a Christian disease and might therefore consider a Christian remedy" (p. 116).

According to Lewis, this process is already under way. But there are problems such as the lunar calendar, lack of harmony in the Middle Eastern music, and many other cultural legacies that are barriers to full Westernization or, to use his own terms, the "Christianization of Islam." Muslims have no idea of dining; they know only how to eat. They have no idea of time, no notion of frontier, no idea of military bands and uniforms. They have no team spirit because they lack harmony. They have no timetables; hence, no precision. This all smacks suspiciously of the return of the "white man's burden" to put these people on the right track. The author's missionary zeal, racist remarks, and selective combination of fiction and fact leave no room but to say that this is an unprecedented absurdity in historiography that excels in propagating hatred and hostility. No wonder war hawks seek his advice and some media commentators use his terminology in sharpening their diatribes against the "other."

If this book is any reflection of how Lewis felt about Islam and Muslim history before 9/11, it is not difficult to imagine what his protégés have written about this subject after Black Tuesday. For Daniel Pipes and Martin Kramer, September 11 is a wake-up call. Its images must remain permanently etched in our collective psyche and its culpability extended to all Muslims with a "political ideology." Kramer would even include those non-Muslim American scholars who have been teaching Islam, writing about Islam, or occasionally criticizing the Israeli policies toward the Palestinians. Pipes's preoccupation has been to magnify and exaggerate the dimensions of the so-called political Islam.

Regrettably, their analyses darken our understanding of Islam and the Arab world rather than bring the light of an understanding of its changing complexities.

Pipes approaches his subject like a spy who knows the villain all along, but he reveals his insights to bewildered readers only after he builds his story to a crescendo. In his new preface to a 1983 book, he shows how Islam has hated the United States through the examples of the Iranian Revolution and the Wahabism of Saudi Arabia. He ignores the Arab reaction to Khomeini's political ideology or, for that matter, the Iraq-Iran War. The Iranian Revolution was a popular revolt against the fascist regime of an American puppet, and the Arab reaction to it was to safeguard their own vested interests as well as to appease their American friends. Why does he fail to mention these events? Surely, they do not support arguments for a universal Muslim hatred of Americans. To demonstrate Islamic hatred toward America, he quotes a prayer: "I pray to Allah [for] the destruction of the United States of America" (Pipes 2002, ix). As a self-proclaimed Arabist, he should also know the Muslim prayer said five times daily that affirms the blessings that Allah sends to the House of Abraham and his descendants.[1]

Part II of Pipes's (2002) book is more or less a reproduction of Lewis's argument about Muslim encounters with Europe. Like his mentor, he is elusive about the attitudes of the Jewish people toward Christianity, as that would be embarrassing to the present political agenda of the Christian Right and Zionism. Conscious that it is not easy to come up with a simplistic explanation for the fourteen hundred years of complex Muslim history, he nonetheless repeats a familiar theme: "The Muslim world feels something has gone very wrong, but has been frustrated in its attempt to right matters" (p. x). An idea crafted by Bernard Lewis now becomes a Muslim idea because Pipes has his hands on the Muslim pulse. What is even more questionable is his insistence that he is capable of offering insights into Muslim affairs. He says, "I urge the readers to focus on the first two sections of the book which offer a *still-rare attempt* at a cohesive interpretation of Islam in politics"

(Pipes 2002, x, emphasis added). Such self-proclaimed insights hardly deserve comment, but they do convey the intellectual poverty of such ill-conceived assertions.

Martin Kramer goes even a step further. As the director of the Moshe Dayan Center for Middle Eastern and African Studies at Tel Aviv University, he singles out Bernard Lewis as the only scholar who has written objectively about Islam and even "sympathetically." "Lewis thus stands alone," Kramer asserts, "in his explicit assessment of the crucial role of Jews in the emergence of a detached, even sympathetic understanding of Islam in Europe" (Kramer 1999, 2). In his new capacity as the editor of *Middle Eastern Quarterly*, founded by Daniel Pipes, he was asked by the Washington Institute for Near Eastern Policy to "educate" Americans on the "failure of Middle Eastern Studies" in the United States. It would be relevant to mention here that this institute had on its board and committee people like Richard Perle and Paul Wolfowitz, and it is not difficult to imagine what sort of scholarship this study was assigned to discover. After taking to task almost every scholar from Hitti to Learner who had something positive to say about the Arabs and the Palestinians, his wrath descends on Edward Said's *Orientalism* (1978).

Edward Said (1978) neither invented Orientalism nor suggested an alternate methodology to study the East, particularly the Middle East. Instead, he registered a powerful and well-argued protest against the likes of Lewis, who look at the Muslim world with contempt or as a fossilized phase in history. Said's exposé of such self-styled authorities had mixed results. It neither became an undisputed piece of scholarship nor was considered a polemic, but it is a work that no one can ignore. It has, however, since its publication in 1978, become a nightmare for those who want the American academia to look at the Middle East through an Israeli prism.

The fact that Martin Kramer's booklet is another crude attempt to disparage alternate views of the Middle East manifests this deep-seated bias. He demonstrates it through a generous use of words like *superficial, misguided,* and *wrong* to describe the analyses of those scholars who do not approve of the policies and rhetoric of those who share his sympathies, and he lays blame for these misguided views at the feet of Edward Said's intellectual legacy. Furthermore, he argues that because of the professor of comparative literature at Columbia University, "the institutions of Middle Eastern studies—departments, centers, professional associations, grant committees—have become bastions of conformism, hostile to intellectual diversity" (Kramer 2001, ix). This, according to Kramer, has resulted in the ouster of those scholars who held "other approaches" from the academic and research institutions that he terms "the empires of error." (He does not elaborate on his assertion about these ousters.) What disturbs him even more is that these institutions continue to receive millions of dollars from the Department of Education. It follows that the age of undisputed Orientalism (i.e., prior to 1978) produced the only true understanding of the Middle East. His diagnosis is simple, as is his solution: Title VI funds should be given either to individual scholars or to think tanks instead of academic institutions under the sway of Said's analyses (Kramer 2001, 124).

Underlying an argument about the academic views of different scholars is a distrust of the freedom of expression and free inquiry at universities and colleges where students and teachers discuss, and often debate, these issues. Indeed, Kramer's and Pipes's paradigm became clear to those who teach and do research on the Middle East when a Web site posted their profiles and depicted student demonstrations in support of peace in the Middle East as the outcome of their academic pursuits.[2]

The views expressed by Lewis and his protégés against Muslims and Islam go beyond the decencies of politics and civil discourse. The unfortunate events of 9/11 provide them with an opportunity to say that Muslims are irrational, violent, and require (deserve?) only a classroom of battlefields in which they may finally learn the lessons that have escaped them for centuries. They base their assertions on the emotions generated by the terrorist attacks, the scapegoating that often follows the horrors that people can inflict on one another, and the creation of an "other" that is distorted far beyond its reality. They view fourteen hundred years of Islam through the billowing clouds of the twin towers. Regrettably, their analyses darken our understanding of Islam and the Arab world rather than bring the light of understanding to its changing complexities.

Notes

1. *Darud-i-Ibrahimi*, which constitutes an obligatory part of the *Salat*.
2. See CampusWatch.org.

References

Kramer, Martin, ed. 1999. *The Jewish discovery of Islam: Studies in honor of Bernard Lewis*. Tel Aviv: The Moshe Dayan Center for Middle Eastern and African Studies, Tel Aviv University.

———. 2001. *Ivory towers on sand: The failure of Middle Eastern studies in America*. Washington, DC: The Washington Institute for Near East Policy.

Lewis, Bernard. 2002. *What went wrong: Western impact and Middle Eastern response*. New York: Oxford University Press.

Lowenthal, Marvin, ed. and trans. 1956. *The diaries of Theodor Herzel*, chaps. 9, 20, 21. New York: Dial Press.

Pipes, Daniel. 1990. *The Rushdi affair: The novel, the Ayatollah, and the West*. New York: Carol Publishing Group.

———. 2002. *In the path of God: Islam and political power*. New Brunswick, NJ: Transaction Publishers.

Said, Edward. 1978. *Orientalism*. New York: Random House.

VISIT SAGE ONLINE AT: WWW.SAGEPUB.COM

Find what you are looking for faster!

Our advanced search engine allows you to find what you are looking for quickly and easily. Searches can be conducted by:

- Author/Editor
- Keyword/Discipline
- Product Type
- ISSN/ISBN
- Title

Payment online is secure and confidential!

Rest assured that all Web site transactions are completed on a secured server. Only you and Sage Customer Care have access to ordering information. Using your Visa, MasterCard, Discover, or American Express card, you can complete your order in just minutes.

Placing your order is easier than ever before!

Ordering online is simple using the Sage shopping cart feature. Just click on the "Buy Now!" logo next to the product, and it is automatically added to your shopping cart. When you are ready to check out, a listing of all selected products appears for confirmation before your order is completed.

WE'RE ONLINE!
Visit our Web site at: http://www.sagepub.com

F999008

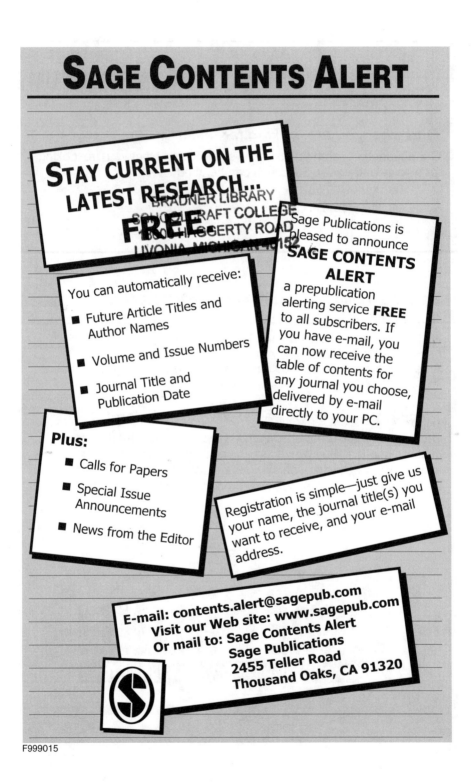

SAGE CONTENTS ALERT

STAY CURRENT ON THE LATEST RESEARCH... FREE

BRADNER LIBRARY
SCHOOLCRAFT COLLEGE
18600 HAGGERTY ROAD
LIVONIA, MICHIGAN 48152

Sage Publications is pleased to announce **SAGE CONTENTS ALERT** a prepublication alerting service **FREE** to all subscribers. If you have e-mail, you can now receive the table of contents for any journal you choose, delivered by e-mail directly to your PC.

You can automatically receive:

■ Future Article Titles and Author Names

■ Volume and Issue Numbers

■ Journal Title and Publication Date

Plus:

■ Calls for Papers

■ Special Issue Announcements

■ News from the Editor

Registration is simple—just give us your name, the journal title(s) you want to receive, and your e-mail address.

E-mail: contents.alert@sagepub.com
Visit our Web site: www.sagepub.com
Or mail to: Sage Contents Alert
Sage Publications
2455 Teller Road
Thousand Oaks, CA 91320

F999015